THE REMINISCENCES OF
Captain Franklin F. Shellenbarger
U.S. Maritime Service (Retired)

INTERVIEWED BY
Paul Stillwell

U.S. Naval Institute • Annapolis, Maryland

Copyright © 2003

Preface

This oral history originated with a suggestion from Captain Douglas Burnett, a Naval Reservist and maritime attorney who came to know the interviewee as an expert witness in legal cases. He indicated that Captain Shellenbarger would be a worthy subject for an oral history because of his blend of both Navy and merchant marine experience. Captain Shellenbarger has been most cooperative throughout the interviews and as the transcript moved through various stages toward completion.

The resulting memoir covers Captain Shellenbarger's seagoing service from the time of his battleship duty in 1938 until he finally retired as a merchant ship master in 1979. During those years he was involved in the Navy's preparation for its role in World War II, worked in the civilian aircraft industry, trained as a merchant marine officer, and then served in cargo ships during the latter stages of the war. Once the war ended, he served in one commercial ship after another as they made hundreds of voyages to the world's ports. A highlight was serving as chief officer and acting master of the only U.S. nuclear-powered merchant ship, the Savannah. Shortly afterward he became a full-fledged master himself and spent the next 15 years commanding ships' crews. As he relates candidly, the first year was the hardest because of a collision at sea and the death of one of his officers. His years on board ships encompassed an amazing range of technology. After boot camp, he was briefly assigned to the old sailing ship Constellation, which had been built in the 19th century, a great contrast to the nuclear-powered Savannah.

George Van, a former naval officer, did the initial transcription of the interview tapes. Both Captain Shellenbarger and I have edited the transcript in the interests of accuracy, smoothness, and clarity. For the sake of continuity, some sections of material have been moved to different interviews from the places in which they originally appeared. Duplicated material has been deleted. In addition, I have inserted footnotes to provide further information for readers who use the volume.

Ms. Ann Hassinger of the Naval Institute's history division has made a significant contribution through her diligence in the overall process of printing, proofreading, and overseeing the binding of the completed volumes.

Finally, the Naval Institute expresses its gratitude to the Marine Society of New York for its financial support to facilitate completion of this memoir. Captain Shellenbarger served as president of the organization from 1994 to 2003. The Marine Society made the contribution in his honor.

Paul Stillwell
Director, History Division
U.S. Naval Institute
March 2003

CAPTAIN FRANKLIN FORREST SHELLENBARGER
UNITED STATES MARITIME SERVICE (RETIRED)

Born: 26 May 1920 in Auglaize County, near Wapakaneta, Ohio

Married 1944, divorced 1951, two children; married since 1953 to the former Mary Ivil

Education

1932-1936	Owego Free Academy, Owego, New York
1936-1937	One-year postgraduate in industrial arts, Owego, New York
1938	Four-month U.S. Navy communication school, San Diego
1941	Three-month course, Elmira Aviation Ground School, Elmira, New York
1942	Four-month course at Maritime Officers Training School, Fort Trumbull, New London, Connecticut

Naval Service

26 January 1938	Enlisted in the U.S. Navy as apprentice seaman at Navy Recruiting Station, Buffalo, New York.
26 January 1938	Transferred to the U.S. Naval Training Station, Newport, Rhode Island.
26 May 1938	Rating changed to seaman second class.
1 June 1938	Transferred to the U.S. Naval Training Station, San Diego, California.
5 June 1938	Received at the U.S. Naval Training Station, San Diego, California.
18 November 1938	Transferred to USS Colorado (BB-45) via USS McDougall (DD-358).
20 November 1938	Received in USS Colorado
16 February 1939	Rating changed to seaman first class.

1 May 1939	Transferred to USS Herbert (DD-160).
29 August 1939	Transferred to the receiving ship Seattle (ex-CA-11) at New York for the USS Helena detail.
18 September 1939	Transferred to USS Helena (CL-50).
16 February 1940	Rating changed to signalman third class.
14 September 1940	Transferred to USS Texas (BB-35) in flag allowance of Commander Battleships Atlantic Fleet.
23 December 1940	Transferred to USS New York (BB-34) in flag allowance of Commander Battleships Atlantic Fleet.
16 February 1941	Rating changed to signalman second class.
8 March 1941	Transferred to USS Arkansas (BB-33) in flag allowance of Commander Battleships Atlantic Fleet.
25 April 1941	Transferred to USS Texas (BB-35) in flag allowance of Commander Battleships Atlantic Fleet.
26 May 1941	Honorably discharged.
26 March 1943	Accepted appointment and executed oath of office as ensign, U.S. Naval Reserve (Merchant Marine) on inactive duty.
Oct 1941-Sep 1942	Aircraft electrician, Glenn Martin Company, Middle River, Maryland
Oct 1941-Jan 1943	Student at Maritime Officers Training School
Jan 1943-Jun 1944	Instructor at Maritime Officers Training School

Merchant Marine Service

Jun 1944-Apr 1945	Third and second officer with American South African Lines
Apr 1945-Sep 1951	Second officer in various ships of American Export Lines
Sep 1951-Aug 1963	Chief officer in various ships of American Export Lines

Aug 1963-Mar 1964	Chief officer, relieving master, and assistant ship superintendent of the nuclear ship Savannah
Mar 1964-June 1979	Master of various ships of American Export-Isbrandtsen Lines
1979-1982	Shoreside during dispute between unions
November 1983	Formation of Captain F. Shellenbarger, Inc.
1994-2003	President of the Marine Society of New York

(The following pages contain a detailed listing of Captain Shellenbarger's service with American Export-Isbrandtsen Lines.)

Deed of Gift

The U.S. Naval Institute is hereby authorized to make available to individuals, libraries, and other repositories of its choosing the tapes and/or transcripts of five oral history interviews concerning the life and naval career of the undersigned. The Naval Institute may also, at its discretion, use the material in electronic/digital format, including posting on the Internet. The interviews were recorded on 28 April 1997, 11 June 1997, 12 June 1997, 18 November 1997, and 19 November 1997, in collaboration with Paul Stillwell for the U.S. Naval Institute.

The undersigned does hereby release and assign to the U.S. Naval Institute the rights and title to these interviews, with the exception that the undersigned retains the right to use the material for his own purposes, as he sees fit. The copyright in both the oral and transcribed versions shall be the sole property of the U.S. Naval Institute. The tape recordings of the interviews are and will remain the property of the U.S. Naval Institute.

Signed and sealed this 17TH day of AUGUST 2001.

Franklin F. Shellenbarger
Captain, U.S. Maritime Service (Retired)

Interview No. 1 with Captain Franklin F. Shellenbarger, U.S. Maritime Service (Retired)

Place: Captain Shellenbarger's home, Point Pleasant, New Jersey

Date: Monday, 28 April 1997

Interviewer: Paul Stillwell

Paul Stillwell: Just to begin at the beginning, Captain, could you tell me when and where you were born and something about your parents and family background?

Captain Shellenbarger: I was born in Ohio, on a farm near a little town called Wapakoneta, the 26th of May, 1920. When I was about three years old, my father left Ohio and settled in New York State in what's known as the Southern Tier, between Elmira and Binghamton. I can remember very well riding in this old Dodge touring car with my baby sister and my father and mother—muddy roads, rain, windows, and things.

I attended a small grade school in Smithboro, New York, a little village of about 350 people. My father had purchased a farm and was going to continue as a farmer, but after only about one year the barn caught fire, and he lost everything. After the mortgage was foreclosed, he began working for other people. He did various odd jobs for a long period of time, mostly as a tenant farmer. He did spend a couple of years working for the Erie Railroad as a carpenter.

When I was about 12 years old, Dad went to work on a farm with the rest of the family in Pennsylvania, and I went to live with my half-sister. My two half-sisters had joined us in New York. I don't want to go into the details of why my father had divorced his first wife. He got the custody of the two girls, my half-sisters.

Paul Stillwell: Why did you go to live with one of them rather than staying with your parents?

Captain Shellenbarger: In those days the Pennsylvania school system did not have a good reputation. I was starting high school at the age of 12, and my father and mother wanted me to stay in the New York school system. So I went to live with my half-sister and her husband. He was a custodian for the county courthouse for Tioga County in Owego, New York. I completed high school in June 1936.

Paul Stillwell: How much of a factor was the Depression on the family's living style?[*]

Captain Shellenbarger: Very much so. It was typical Depression. We were on welfare. I became 16 in May 1936. When I graduated from high school, I was big for my age.

I'm probably one of the few people who have ever been personally fired by the senior Thomas Watson, who was the founder of IBM, which at that time was known as International Time Recorder.[†] It was located in Endicott, New York, which was the nearest large place. I lied about my age. I said I was 17, and I wasn't. After about two weeks, personnel called me in and said, "You'd better go in and see the old man." To put it bluntly, he reamed me up and down and told me I would never work for that corporation in all my life, because I was a liar and a very untrustworthy person.

Paul Stillwell: Was that your only association with him?

Captain Shellenbarger: That was my only association with him, except later that summer I worked as a caddy on the golf links. When I found out that he was golfing with a gentleman named George F. Johnson, founder of the Endicott-Johnson Shoe Company, which is long gone now, I turned down the job as caddy, because I didn't want to attract his attention. It's just one of those little incidents that you remember.

Anyway, my father was on the WPA.[‡] We were receiving relief, so I was eligible for something called the NYA, National Youth Administration.

---

[*] Following the crash of the New York Stock Exchange in late October 1929, the United States was plunged into the Great Depression, from which it did not recover until the nation geared up for World War II at the beginning of the 1940s. The Depression was marked by high unemployment and many business failures.

[†] Thomas J. Watson (1874-1956) was an American industrialist. After working for the National Cash Register Company for 15 years, in 1914 he became president of a company that became the International Business Machines Corporation in 1924. He led the corporation from 1914 to 1956.

[‡] WPA—Works Progress Administration, a Depression-relief agency that sometimes created make-work projects in order to stimulate employment.

Paul Stillwell: Before we get to that, please tell me how you were able to graduate from high school at 16.

Captain Shellenbarger: I had skipped a grade or two when I was in, I think, the fifth or sixth grade. So I moved right on up and stayed, so I was probably the youngest boy in my class.

Paul Stillwell: I take it you were a good student along with that.

Captain Shellenbarger: Well, I guess I must have been. I could have been a hell of a lot better if I'd studied more, but I didn't. [Laughter] I did a tremendous amount of reading.

Paul Stillwell: What sorts of things?

Captain Shellenbarger: I was fascinated with things about ships and the sea. Whenever I went to the library, there were all kinds of things. There used to be a series of books—ridiculous, of course, now—about World War I. I can't remember the name of the series, but I can remember very well some of the incidents that supposedly that took place in World War I in the North Sea with the British. Also, by the time I'd finished high school I'd gone through Gibbons's Decline and Fall of the Roman Empire in about 12 volumes. I think the reason I kept my Latin studies up was because all the footnotes were in Latin. [Laughter]

I can remember because I was doing not too well in some of my other subjects. My history teacher, Madeline Skeels, and Elsie Dutcher, the Latin teacher, couldn't understand why I was doing all right in those studies and doing so poorly in trigonometry and algebra.

Many people aren't aware of it, but the New York State School System those days—I don't know how it is now—was separate from New York City. New York City's a disaster, but the New York State School System had a regents system and a high school system. When you graduated from high school, you got a regents' certificate and a high school certificate, and for the regents you had to have more qualifications completed. So, due to my regents' qualifications, I went back for a postgraduate year in high school from 16 to 17. When I was 17, I applied for the Maritime College in Fort Schuyler.*

Paul Stillwell: How would you explain your fascination with ships and the sea?

Captain Shellenbarger: I don't know. I don't really know, because I was born on a farm. We didn't have movies or television in those days. It's just somehow or other I developed the interest. This village of Smithboro was on the Susquehanna River. A number of us, the boys in that little town, had a rowboat that we used for camping out on an island in the river. We spent a lot of time in the summertime with the rowboat. Somehow or other, the water fascinated me. I don't know why.

Paul Stillwell: You found your destiny.

Captain Shellenbarger: Well, you know, two of the fellows there went into the Navy after I did, and they got caught by the war. Lyle Hill, as I recall, was a signalman. I know he was on the destroyer Helm at Pearl Harbor. I have been seeing Lyle about twice a year. He was a signalman first class at the end of the war. Later, when I was in the Navy, I met another one of those friends who was in this group, a fellow by the name of Jacob Livengood. He became a gunner's mate, and he was on the Quincy when it went down.† He died at a very early age; he was only 62. After he came out of the Navy, he went to work for IBM and put in his 20 years there. We used to joke about the fact that I could never work there.

Paul Stillwell: How much interest did you have in the events of the wider world at that time—Hitler and the Japanese and so forth?‡

---

* Fort Schuyler, at the southern tip of the Bronx in New York City, has long been the site of a maritime college. It is now part of the State University of New York.
† On the night of 8-9 August 1942, between Guadalcanal and nearby Savo Island, a Japanese surface force surprised Allied forces and sank four cruisers, the USS Astoria (CA-34), USS Quincy (CA-39), USS Vincennes (CA-44), and HMAS Canberra.
‡ Adolf Hitler was Chancellor of Germany from 1933 until his death in 1945.

Captain Shellenbarger: I was an avid listener of the radio and world news. Even when I was in school, I was interested in radio. A friend of mine named Sandy Coleman was an amateur radio operator who went back to the days of the spark gap. He had a little station in a garage in the lot next door to where we lived, and I was always fascinated with it. So I always listened to world news on the radio, because he made a short-wave radio for me. When I got in the Navy and had some money, I bought one myself, which leads up to something on the Texas that I'll tell you about.

Paul Stillwell: What was your involvement in the National Youth Administration?

Captain Shellenbarger: That was during my postgraduate year in high school. What I did was take four hours of studies in the morning, and I've forgotten what two of them were because I'd already gotten my high school certificate. And you didn't get any credits for this, but I also had two hours in a course they called industrial arts. I was sort of taken under the wing of the industrial arts instructor, and I spent two to three hours in the afternoon working on stage sets, showing movies.

I even assisted, believe it or not, as an instructor for some of the other industrial arts classes because I was fairly good at using machines, woodworking. Of course, with industrial arts you worked with woodworking, metalworking, and a lot of different kinds of machines. It's not strictly carpentry or anything else.

During this period when I was living with my half-sister and her husband—he'd be my brother-in-law—I helped out with the finances. I can't remember how much they paid, but the NYA paid for these hours that I put in at the school. Also, on weekends this gentleman who was the instructor let me work on some apartment buildings he owned in Owego, New York. (Remember, this is Owego, not Oswego. It's down in the Southern Tier.) I used to work on weekends and evenings with his maintenance man, Charlie Fuller, doing wallpapering and painting. I remember in the summertime we'd do the roofs with some kind of a tar mixture.

I also got to know a man named Albert Hubbard. Back around the time of the Spanish-American War there was a writer who apparently was fairly well known at the time, and his name was Elbert Hubbard.* Some of his writing speaks of his son, Bertie. His son was Albert H. Hubbard, who was my benefactor in many, many ways. And the reason I remember that is because right across the street I did lawns. Charlie Fuller and I worked around Mr. Hubbard's house. Right across the street was a naturalist whose name was J. Aldon Loring; he had been with Theodore Roosevelt in Africa.† Mr. Loring used to show me various curios, and I guess maybe that was one the reasons I decided I wanted to see the world.

Paul Stillwell: Did you have a career goal at that point?

Captain Shellenbarger: Other than just to get out of Owego—get somewhere and do something—I had no career goal because in my imagination it was beyond reach. I remember who steered me to the Navy after they turned me down from the Maritime College.

Paul Stillwell: Well, please tell me about that. We talked about that before the tape recorder was running.

Captain Shellenbarger: When I became 17, I'd completed my postgraduate year. Mr. Hubbard knew that I was interested in the sea. Of course, his house was right on the Susquehanna River, and we watched the boats there. They were all rowboats in those days, believe me; you didn't even see a sailboat out there. But he said due to my grades, I might be eligible for this maritime college he knew about. So we submitted an application to the maritime college in Fort Schuyler. As I recall, they accepted me. And then, of course, it would have been tuition free, because I was a resident of New York State, but they did say that I would have to give them around $800.00 for uniforms and books. Of course, that was an absolute impossibility.

---

* Elbert Hubbard (1856-1915) was an American lecturer, publisher, editor, and essayist. He is probably best known for the essay "A Message to Garcia," written in 1899, which dealt with the search for the Cuban rebel Garcia. He died in the sinking of the passenger liner Lusitania in 1915.
† Theodore Roosevelt, an adventurous individual, served as President of the United States from 1901 to 1909. He was a strong proponent of the Navy.

Paul Stillwell: You told me before we turned on the machine that it might as well have been $80,000.

Captain Shellenbarger: Might just as well.

Paul Stillwell: Was the Naval Academy a possibility at all?

Captain Shellenbarger: No, I don't think so, because I think you had to have a political appointment. The only person I knew even vaguely connected was my half-sister's husband; Paul Bennett was his name. He worked as a custodian, and his father was connected politically. He was what they call a town supervisor or something like that.

During that same period I ran afoul of the law, and the county judge was a fellow by the name of Nathan Turk.

Paul Stillwell: Do tell.

Captain Shellenbarger: As a matter of fact, if it hadn't been for him brushing me with a white paintbrush, I guess I would never have gotten in the Navy.

Paul Stillwell: Was this a little mischief making?

Captain Shellenbarger: It was. I got involved with a gang and did some things I shouldn't have done, and we got caught. [Laughter] I can't recall what it was, but I know we got caught doing a little shoplifting at a five and dime. And so, of course, I was put on probation until I was 21 or something else happened. I learned years later that Judge Turk became the Grand Master of Masons in the state of New York. Today that means something to me, because I'm a 50-year Mason myself. He was really, really nice when the Navy came asking questions.

In those days when you joined the Navy they investigated. You had to be a high school graduate, they checked with the chief of police to see if you had a police record, and they checked with your minister to see if you were reliable. This was at the end of the Depression.

Paul Stillwell: They could be very selective.

Captain Shellenbarger: They could be very selective, and they were.

Paul Stillwell: What did he do for you to facilitate getting into the Navy?

Captain Shellenbarger: I had to get the recommendation from the local chief of police, and he apparently put the word in that due to my youth and everything, there was no record.

Paul Stillwell: Did you a favor.

Captain Shellenbarger: He did me a favor, a tremendous favor.

Paul Stillwell: When did you enlist?

Captain Shellenbarger: When I signed up originally, in July 1937, they completed the paperwork at the recruiting station in Elmira, New York. You couldn't be sworn in there for some reason, I presume because they didn't have the facilities or whatever. They said that I would go on a waiting list. Then I got word that I had been accepted and was to proceed to Buffalo in January 1938. I can't remember the exact date.

Paul Stillwell: So you were still 17 at that point?

Captain Shellenbarger: Yes. Because I was 17, it was a minority enlistment, which expires the day before you're 21. And, of course, the day before I was 21 was May 25, 1941, and I'd already been on Neutrality Patrol up there, been on the Texas.

Paul Stillwell: We'll get to that.

Captain Shellenbarger: But, anyway, this was why I was turned down for the maritime college. Due to my interest, I discussed it with Mr. Hubbard, and he said, "Well, why don't you try for the Navy?" As I say, my father was absent, so Mr. Hubbard sort of took an interest in me, and he did me a lot of favors.

Paul Stillwell: Did you need to get parental consent because you were not yet 18?

Captain Shellenbarger: Oh, yes. Of course, my father and my mother were happy to see me get anything where I was going to earn some money.

Paul Stillwell: Well, the other thing was that it would give you a degree of stability as well.

Captain Shellenbarger: Yes. They were very concerned that I'd been involved in the incidents that I did.

Paul Stillwell: What happened then from Buffalo onward?

Captain Shellenbarger: Well, in January in 1938 I was given transportation from Elmira to Buffalo. I stayed overnight in Buffalo at a hotel. The next morning I joined up with a group from different parts of the state and maybe some from Pennsylvania and Ohio; I don't remember. We were given a final physical in Buffalo, then sworn in and put on a train and sent to Newport, Rhode Island, for boot camp.[*]

The platoon chief—I think that's what they called them in those days—was a chief quartermaster by the name of Swenson. He used to carry some kind of a cutlass thing around his belt as the platoon commander. It was a typical boot camp operation. We did a lot of marching, a lot of studying, a lot of drills. And during that time we took a lot of tests, and I guess maybe I did all right because I was selected for group A communications school.

---

[*] "Boot" is a slang term for a newly enlisted sailor or Marine. Recruit training is known as boot camp.

Paul Stillwell: What sort of barracks did you have?

Captain Shellenbarger: They were big barracks; that's all I can remember.

Paul Stillwell: Open bays?

Captain Shellenbarger: Open bays. Huge things.

Paul Stillwell: Hammocks?

Captain Shellenbarger: No, they weren't hammocks. They were bunk beds, two high. And I can't remember the name of the island.[*] I went back there years and years later. I had to go into Davisville for something or other on a Liberty ship to load supplies for the Pacific.[†] I was second officer right then. I got a day or so off, and I went over to Newport and went around that area. I wanted to look, and, of course, by that time the place was so blown up I couldn't find my way around. But, anyway, when I graduated from boot camp, I had to wait to go to the group A comm school in San Diego.

Paul Stillwell: Any impressions about the town of Newport? Did you get liberty there?

Captain Shellenbarger: While we were in boot camp, there was no liberty. That was it.

Paul Stillwell: Did you have any trouble adjusting to the discipline?

Captain Shellenbarger: No, not that I recall. I had no problem with it.

Paul Stillwell: Any homesickness problems?

---

[*] The Newport Naval Training Station was on Coasters Harbor Island in Narragansett Bay's East Passage.
[†] Davisville, Rhode Island, was the site of an Advanced Base Depot and Naval Construction Battalion Center.

Captain Shellenbarger: No. Never had any homesickness, because I'd been living away from home for some time.

Paul Stillwell: Right. And this was what you really wanted.

Captain Shellenbarger: It was what I wanted, and I really enjoyed it, in spite of my being a little bit rebellious at times. I had a couple of arguments with the chief, whom I had to call "Sir."

Paul Stillwell: Why were you rebellious?

Captain Shellenbarger: I don't know. There was something that he had us doing one time that bothered me. It seems to me we were hauling a 3-inch cannon around somewhere. It was supposed to have been field artillery. It wasn't on the island. We'd gone over the bridge, and we were hauling this gun around. You know, they were hauled by men. They had ropes with toggles in them, and you had to haul these guns around. I can't remember, but we'd set the thing up and we'd fire blanks. I know that he came up while we were hauling this gun, and he whacked me on the legs a couple of times. Of course, I was wearing puttees, you know, the leggings. But he whacked me on the leg with his cutlass.

Paul Stillwell: What was the content of the training? What subjects?

Captain Shellenbarger: Practically all I can recall is we were each issued a Bluejackets' Manual.* I don't have mine here; it's at the Marine Society.†

Paul Stillwell: That's been the Bible for years.

---

* The Bluejackets' Manual, which has been published by the U.S. Naval Institute in various editions over the years, has long been considered the "bible" for Navy enlisted men. It is a basic textbook and reference volume on a wide variety of naval subjects. Formerly these topics were addressed in chapters designated by letters from A to N.

† At the time of the interview, Captain Shellenbarger was serving as president of the Marine Society of the City of New York. He discusses the Marine Society at some length in the final interview of this oral history.

Captain Shellenbarger: It's been the Bible. We went through that thing, and I can remember we even had some slides and picture shows showing damage to ships during World War I. And we were really thoroughly indoctrinated as to what the projectiles were like, how they were built. We got intensive training with the firearms. We fired on the rifle range with the .30-06s, the .45s, the old Colt. We did a lot of marching, but we also had a lot of classes. We were expected to learn the things that were in the <u>Bluejackets' Manual</u>. I found mine when my mother died some years ago. I didn't realize that I'd sent it home. It had become so dog-eared that somewhere in my naval career I had put canvas over it and shellacked it.

Paul Stillwell: That looks impressive, I'll bet.

Captain Shellenbarger: It's in our library in the Marine Society in New York City now. And the strange part about is that my mother had put a picture of me in the book. It was apparently taken at Newport, because I'm wearing the leggings and my hat and everything. My mother had slipped it in there. My mother and my father both died in California, and I fell heir to a lot of this stuff. Out of five children, five of us and the two half-sisters, seven altogether, only two of us are still alive, myself and one of my younger brothers.

My next younger brother just died in November, and his estate now is being handled by a trust. I just got a bunch of stuff here two weeks ago from the trustee because he called me up and said, "Is there anything there? I'm cleaning out the house." Of course, I told him I wanted any pictures that were there. Of course, my father and mother both lived with this brother and died there and they're both buried in Lancaster, California, along with my brother and his wife and his stepson. They're all buried in Lancaster. Hopefully, we'll get out there next year.

Paul Stillwell: Did you have to wash your uniforms as part of that training?

Captain Shellenbarger: Oh, yes, and the proverbial salt-water soap, the big brown bar that you chopped off pieces. You washed in a bucket. You washed your clothes, and then you had to roll them and tie them off with clothes stops.* Everything had to be stenciled just so in a precise place. And it all had to fit in a seabag. One seabag—that was it.

Paul Stillwell: Well, one by-product of all this training and togetherness is building a sense of teamwork and camaraderie.

Captain Shellenbarger: Definitely, yes. And there probably were a lot of rough times. I can remember being rousted out at 11:00 o'clock at night and doing drills in the drill hall because of something or other that our platoon hadn't measured up to during the day. I guess there was a lot of competition between the platoons, because I can remember the chief saying, "I don't want you guys dirtying my record." I learned a tremendous amount from him, and at that time it did me a hell of a lot of good. There's no question about it, and I'd like to see everybody do their tour of duty. [Laughter]

Paul Stillwell: Well, another rationale for getting you up at 11:00 o'clock at night is that you might have to do that on board ship for general quarters.

Captain Shellenbarger: That's right. One of the things that impressed me was the fact that in case of battle there might be times when you'd be in a part of the ship that would have to be flooded. They'd say, "When those watertight doors are closed, they're closed till the end of the battle." I think that later on made a major decision in my life. Instead of being a radioman, I wanted to be on the bridge. [Laughter] And it did affect me, because when I finished San Diego, the radio school, at the end of the comm school you had a certificate as a third class radioman, third class signalman, third class quartermaster. And when I was transferred, of course, they parceled us out.

Paul Stillwell: Well, why don't you tell me about the training in San Diego?

---

* A clothes stop is a small cotton lanyard used for fastening parts of a uniform to a line after washing or for securing uniform items that are rolled up.

Captain Shellenbarger: Well, the training in San Diego was sitting for hours in front of a typewriter, headphones, and a brass key.

Paul Stillwell: Did you have an aptitude for learning and picking up the Morse code?

Captain Shellenbarger: No, I didn't, so I didn't graduate with my class. I did fine with flags and quartermaster work, but somehow or other I was slow with the code. I became a radio amateur, and I have no problem with it today, but at that time it was a problem.

Paul Stillwell: Well, different people have different talents.

Captain Shellenbarger: Yes. So I didn't graduate with my class. I graduated with the next class. They just dropped me back a class, and I spent many more hours. [Laughter] Even today I've got a picture of myself in radio class. I couldn't recognize myself except that I remembered very well I always picked up a headset that only had one earpiece because the things hurt my ears. I think I've still got a copy of it.

Paul Stillwell: What do you recall about the living conditions and training facilities in San Diego?

Captain Shellenbarger: They were quite good comparatively. We did get liberty in San Diego. I spent a lot of hours in Balboa Park and the zoo. I can't remember why, but I remember a couple of times I went to the airport, which was down near the bay. And right across from the drill field we could see North Island and the planes and everything.* As a matter of fact, I even took a picture of one of the airplanes that crashed right off the beach at the training station. I went back there in 1960 on vacation, and, of course, I just couldn't believe how it had changed.

Paul Stillwell: You probably saw some of the old aircraft carriers there too.

---

* North Island Naval Air Station is on the end of the Coronado peninsula, across the harbor from San Diego.

Captain Shellenbarger: Oh, yes. Saw the Lexington, Saratoga. As a matter of fact, one of the pictures in the album showed the Wasp, when it had just been launched. This was when I was on the DD-160. Somebody looked at my honorable discharge, and on the back they list the ships you've been on. I can't remember who it was now, because it happened a good long time ago, but he looked at it and said, "Gee, you were on so many ships in three and a half years. You must have been a real foul ball to get bounced around like that." [Laughter] And I sometimes wonder. But I did. A lot of it was circumstances. When I left the communications school—

Paul Stillwell: Were you rated at that point?

Captain Shellenbarger: No, I was what they called a striker.*

Paul Stillwell: For all three of those ratings?

Captain Shellenbarger: No. You had the choice actually. I was a seaman first class, and I had the sparks, the striker rating, which didn't mean any extra money.† It was still $54.00 a month. I think they called it communications school, and they gave you the others. You studied, you had to learn flags, had to learn semaphore. I can't remember what else we learned. But it was primarily to be a radioman. So when I graduated from there with the extra month, I was assigned to the USS Colorado, BB-45.

Paul Stillwell: She was probably then at San Pedro.

Captain Shellenbarger: She was at San Pedro. It would have to be the fall of '38, because I had four months in Newport. Then I spent a month additional in Newport living in a hammock when I was on the Constellation.‡

---

* A striker is a non-rated man who is in training for potential advancement to petty officer in a particular rating.
† The rating badge for a radioman shows a series of electric sparks.
‡ USS Constellation was commissioned in 1855 as a 22-gun sloop of war and subsequently served in the Civil War and had other duties including being a training ship at Newport. She had several periods in and out of commission. In August 1940 she was recommissioned to serve as a symbol of the Navy's past.

Stillwell: Well, please tell me about that.

Captain Shellenbarger: It happened because we were waiting for a ship; supposedly this detachment would be going on a ship for the class in San Diego. Seems to me it was the Vega. It was an old Hog Islander.* You looked at them at sea, and you couldn't tell which direction they were going till you saw which way the wake was. But all we did was maintenance on the Constellation. I never tarred so much rigging in my life, and it was just something to keep us busy while we were waiting. Then something happened. The ship broke down, and they said that this group that was going to the communications school couldn't wait for this supply ship. So they sent us by train across to San Diego.

Paul Stillwell: What was it like living in a ship that old?

Captain Shellenbarger: Horrible. [Laughter] But I suppose now that I know more about history, I guess it was interesting. But, of course, we had to line up and be marched to the mess hall and stuff like that. It was still boot camp routine.

Paul Stillwell: Did the Constellation have any sort of a modern dining facility on board or cooking facilities?

Captain Shellenbarger: No, there was nothing on board. We had to march to the regular mess hall for the boot camp, except because we had graduated we weren't restricted to the training station. I can't recall whether we had liberty then. I don't recall going back into Newport, Rhode Island, for any reason, mostly because at the end of the day I was tired out and ready for bed.

Paul Stillwell: Well, my memory from being on board the Constellation is that the overhead is very low.†

---

* "Hog Islander" is a nickname for a type of cargo ship built in the World War I era.
† In recent years the Constellation has been preserved as a tourist attraction in Baltimore's inner harbor.

Captain Shellenbarger: Oh, yes, very, very low. You were forever ducking your head. If you didn't, you'd bang your brains out. And I understand, of course, from what I've read in those days that the average person was shorter. They were smaller, you know. It's hard for me to realize, but it's true, because I've been aboard the <u>Victory</u> in England and have a model of the <u>Cutty Sark</u>.* I built a model of the <u>Cutty Sark</u> years later and, of course, when my wife and I visited Greenwich I had to go aboard the <u>Cutty Sark</u>. It's dry-docked there, you know.

Paul Stillwell: Did they have stanchions in the berth deck for you to rig your hammocks?

Captain Shellenbarger: No, they weren't stanchions. They were hooks on the overhead.

Paul Stillwell: I see. There were beams on the overhead that had the hooks on them?

Captain Shellenbarger: Yes. They were tremendous big things. They had these hooks on the bottoms of them, and that's where we slept.

Paul Stillwell: Were you strictly on the rigging? Did you do any hull maintenance?

Captain Shellenbarger: I don't recall that we did any hull maintenance at all. All I can remember is we did a little bit of deck work. That was the first time I'd ever seen oakum and used it to pay and pitch deck seams. Because we did that a little bit, and there was a man who must have been a carpenter. He was trying to teach us how to do a neat job of it and how we had to sharpen a chisel afterwards. After you'd payed with the pitch, you'd scrape it. Years later I was on a merchant ship with a teak deck.

Paul Stillwell: What was the purpose of the <u>Constellation</u> at that point?

---

* HMS <u>Victory</u>, the flagship of British Admiral Lord Horatio Nelson in the Battle of Trafalgar, is preserved as a memorial at Portsmouth, England. The <u>Cutty Sark</u> was a 963-ton British three-masted square-rigger completed in 1869 for the tea trade between Britain and China. She made her last voyage in 1935 and has since been a floating museum.

Captain Shellenbarger: I don't really know what it was. I know that later on during the war I heard that for a while that King had used it as a flagship.*

Paul Stillwell: And so did his relief, Admiral Ingersoll.†

Captain Shellenbarger: Oh, yes?

Paul Stillwell: Did they have any radio equipment on board?

Captain Shellenbarger: Not that I know of, not aboard. Frankly, I don't think anybody would have lived aboard. It was just the name, and then everything was ashore because they had a lot of stuff ashore connected with the Constellation.

Paul Stillwell: But you did live aboard it?

Captain Shellenbarger: We actually lived aboard it. There must have been about 30 of us that I can remember.

Paul Stillwell: What were the heads like?

Captain Shellenbarger: The heads we went ashore. There was no latrine aboard.

Paul Stillwell: Did officers live on board too?

Captain Shellenbarger: Not that I recall. I'm sure there were a couple of chiefs there. As I recall, one was a chief boatswain's mate because he was our boss for the working details each day.

---

* Admiral Ernest J. King, USN, served as Commander in Chief Atlantic Fleet from 1 February 1941 until he was transferred 20 December 1941 to Washington, D.C., to serve as Commander in Chief U.S. Fleet (CominCh).
† Admiral Royal E. Ingersoll, USN, served as Commander in Chief Atlantic Fleet from 1 January 1942 to 15 November 1944. He was promoted to four-star rank in July 1942.

Paul Stillwell: Did you have any apprehension going up in the rigging?

Captain Shellenbarger: Not a bit. Not in those days. Even later on I did rigging on the Helena, built in the Brooklyn Navy Yard.

Paul Stillwell: So it sounds like strictly a place to put you for a while.

Captain Shellenbarger: It was a place just for us to wait for this ship, which, as I recall, was the Vega. They said, "No, now that class is going to be starting, you guys are going to have to get over there," and they sent us by train. We had to change trains in Chicago. Seems to me we changed in New York, too, but I don't recall.

Paul Stillwell: Well, that was a digression from getting you on board the Colorado.* She was certainly a lot different from the Constellation.

Captain Shellenbarger: Oh, yes. Now, in the Colorado we lived in hammocks. Yes.

Paul Stillwell: Did you have division messes in that ship?

Captain Shellenbarger: Yes. They had division messes, and when you first came aboard—no matter what you were—you still had to put in three months as a mess cook.†

Paul Stillwell: What division were you assigned to?

Captain Shellenbarger: I know how it was on the Helena. I can't remember too well on the Colorado, but I'm almost sure it must have been the same. They had C Division,

---

* USS Colorado (BB-45) was commissioned 30 August 1923. She had a standard displacement of 32,600 tons, was 624 feet long and 97 feet in the beam. Her top speed was 21 knots. She was armed with eight 16-inch guns, ten 5-inch broadside guns, and eight 5-inch antiaircraft guns.
† A mess cook does the extra chores involved with feeding the crew but not the cooking itself. Mess cooks serve the food, wash mess trays, and clean up the mess deck.

which was divided into R for the radio, N for the quartermasters, and L for the signalmen. And I did my mess cooking.

Radio central in the Colorado was in the double bottoms. When general quarters sounded, you went down a trunk, and when you got everybody down there, boom, 16-inch-thick armor plate was the top hatch to that trunk. I never saw the topside of it, but there allegedly was a Marine up there with a .45. If you tried to come through the hatch before general quarters, you'd get shot. [Laughter]

I never got up there that far, because you remember in those days there was no air-conditioning, no fans. For general quarters everything was shut down, and general quarters sometimes lasted two or three hours. At the end of two or three hours, I don't know if you can imagine what it's like with about 35 or 40 men in radio central all smoking, farting. The place was blue. You couldn't breathe, and I can't remember how long I was there, but it wasn't long. I went to the division officer and asked if I could get transferred out.

One of the problems was that I had been interested in radios—listening to the short wave, tuning radios, doing this, doing that. And all my time on the Colorado I never touched a knob on a radio. They sat you in front of a typewriter and, of course, to continue our training we had classes, you know, sending to each other with test equipment. You'd have keys and buzzers and stuff like that, but you could listen; you copied Fox schedules.[*] Of course, there were about ten guys there all training at the same time, and they were all copying the same thing. You sat there with your earphones plugged into a jack and a key and a typewriter. That was it. You never tuned in a radio. That was done by a first class that did that up at the head of the shack.

Paul Stillwell: How good by then were you at copying? Had you improved?

Captain Shellenbarger: I had improved. They used to send it at 12 words a minute, and I guess I was doing about 95% of it. It wasn't outstanding. That's for sure. And so when I

---

[*] "Fox" was the word for the letter F in the phonetic alphabet of the day. The Fox schedule referred to the messages sent on the fleet broadcast.

went to the division officer and asked if I could get transferred out, he said, "You don't like it down here, do you?"

And I said, "Frankly, I don't."

He said, "Well, what do you want to do, go to the quartermasters or signals?"

I said, "Well, wherever they've got a vacancy up there."

And he said, "Well, it's no problem. It's only administrative. We're in the same division. You're on the same ship. All I've got to do is get an okay from the exec." So they cleared it with him. As a matter of fact, he came around the next day. He knew I had a signalman third class certificate already, so he said, "They can use you on the signal bridge." So I went on the signal bridge.

Paul Stillwell: You must have felt like you'd been liberated.

Captain Shellenbarger: I did. I did. And I picked it up fast. I was very good at semaphore and could do 20 words a minute with semaphore, and I loved it.

Paul Stillwell: Well, for most people it's a matter of finding your niche, and you did.

Captain Shellenbarger: I did. I could probably get more accurate dates, because I've got records for these things. I can't remember. The fleet came around to the East Coast to do maneuvers in the Caribbean.

Paul Stillwell: That was in early 1939. The plan was for the fleet to visit New York City during the World's Fair, but the visit was called off because of the international situation.

Captain Shellenbarger: Yes, it had to be the spring of '39. That's right, because I wasn't on the Colorado that long. What happened was that when we came through the Panama Canal and had the maneuvers in the Caribbean, they wanted the Colorado to do a test firing. It was at the island of Culebra, which they used for target practice and where they simulated attacks.

Somebody decided they wanted some long-range target practice. They wanted to see if the 16-inch/45s on the Colorado could shoot a longer range; I don't really understand it. Normally for a long-range target you would use four bags of powder. I know because a friend of mine was a gunner's mate on there, and he said, "No, at least this firing, they're going to use five bags." Everybody was a little bit concerned about it, but in those days you didn't worry about it. These were orders, and they put five bags in.

We had four turrets and had only two guns to a turret on Colorado. They cracked the liner on five guns, so when the rest of the fleet went back to the West Coast, the Colorado went into the Norfolk Navy Yard at Portsmouth. They had to get these guns removed and either replace the liners or new guns—I don't know which they did. But, anyway, we were in there for what must have been five or six weeks.

Paul Stillwell: That's a long time to change gun barrels.

Captain Shellenbarger: Well, you've got to take the top of the turret out, get the breech of those things out. I can remember the operation. It was a massive operation, and when you're in the shipyard there's no signaling to do. We had work details—painting and chipping.

I guess we'd been there about three weeks with this little piddly thing over there across the dock, the USS Herbert, DD-160. A message came over, "Is there any seaman first class on the Colorado who would be willing to exchange duty with me?" To this day I don't remember the guy's name.

Somehow or other, the word got to me and I said, "Gee, I live on the East Coast." This ship was assigned to the East Coast. I said, "Maybe that would be a good deal. I'm getting tired of chipping paint on here." Remember, I was still a first class seaman. It had to be approved by the SOPA, who there was the captain of the Colorado, and he said he saw no reason to disapprove of it.[*] Boom, about a week later I was aboard the USS Herbert, DD-160.

Paul Stillwell: Well, we'll get there. I've got a few more questions about the Colorado.

---

[*] SOPA—senior officer present afloat.

Captain Shellenbarger: Okay, about the Colorado.

Paul Stillwell: Did you feel a sense of claustrophobia down inside that radio central?

Captain Shellenbarger: I sure as hell did. Especially when that 16-inch armored hatch was closed behind us. I definitely felt a sense of claustrophobia there, plus the bad air, and I just was not happy with it.

And on the Colorado, when I was on the bridge—of course, this is another little incident you might be interested in. My first battle station was something: make sure that the ensign was flying. I guess you'd call it indoctrination. You know, new guy in the gang. The chief said to me, "Okay, you're going to go back there, and your battle station is on the after searchlight platform. And during battle you're to see that the flag doesn't come down, even if you have to climb up that cage mast and hang onto it with your teeth." Because I remember that's what he told me. [Laughter]

Of course, everybody was watching. You're going to have battle practice. You've got a tug out there towing a target. Eight guns out there. The ship was going to do a broadside. Nobody told me what was going to happen, and I was thinking, "Gee, it'll be quite a big bang and everything." I thought no more about it, and they didn't tell me the steps I should have taken—tied my pant legs around the ankles, tied my blouse wrists with clothes stops. You can guess what happened. Do you have any idea what the concussion is when you fire a broadside on a battleship?

Paul Stillwell: I've been there for one gun, not eight.

Captain Shellenbarger: All right. When those eight fired, it wasn't long range. This was short-range battle practice.

Paul Stillwell: Right off the beam.

Captain Shellenbarger: The guns were right off, and lowered. They weren't elevated for long range. What happened was a cloud of smoke, burnt gunpowder, seawater. The blast split my pants leg and took my jumper off. There I was, up there in my skivvies. [Laughter] And, of course, I looked up at the bridge after the first firing. Everybody up there was going "Ha-ha-ha-ha-ha." They knew what was going to happen. So I got my indoctrination, and was told, "Actually, you handled it well."

Of course, my worry was the fact that it had blown my uniform off. You went to battle stations in those days in your blues, and you paid for your replacements. You know, it didn't make any difference.

Paul Stillwell: Well, what happened the next time they fired a broadside?

Captain Shellenbarger: Of course, I was still at general quarters. We always used to watch for the signal flags Fox-Cast-Dog, F-C-D, because that meant the end of the general quarters. When it was over, of course, I had to get in uniform right away. I had to go right down and get my uniform and clean up. The chief was down there and he said—I've forgotten what he was calling me—somewhere I got my nickname, Shelley. Navy practice, I don't know if it still is, was always to address you by your last name. Is it still true?

Paul Stillwell: No. Now they call you Petty Officer So-and-so.

Captain Shellenbarger: Oh.

Paul Stillwell: A little more dignified.

Captain Shellenbarger: A little more dignified. Because I can remember somewhere along the line one of the chiefs said, "No way I'm going to say Shellenbarger every time I want to talk to you." He said, "You're Shelley, and that's what you're going to be known by." And all my life since then that's been my nickname. But, anyway, he said, "You handled yourself really well back there. We've had guys go back there. You know, they come screaming off the platform, but you stayed there. You were of value. You did a nice job." So it was a compliment, and I felt a lot better about it. But I didn't feel happy about it when the next inspection came around and I had to have so many jumpers and so many trousers there. I had to go to small stores and get them replaced.

Paul Stillwell: Well, how did you prevent that problem in subsequent incidents?

Captain Shellenbarger: You tied clothes stops around your legs. You put them like that to keep the blast from getting up your legs and then getting inside your jumper.

Paul Stillwell: So you put them around your wrists also.

Captain Shellenbarger: Put them around your wrists. Same thing. And, of course, they said, "Before the blast, be sure you take your hat off too." However, they never said anything about putting something in your ears. I guess in those days nobody worried about those things.

Paul Stillwell: And a lot of people's hearing suffered as a result.

Captain Shellenbarger: Probably suffered as a result.

Paul Stillwell: Did you wear white hats or flat hats for that?

Captain Shellenbarger: No, white hats. The only time you ever wore the flat hats were when you went ashore in the dress uniform, and I don't know what ever happened to them.* I can remember having a flat hat, and the ribbons used to have the USS Colorado on it. I even had one that said USS Herbert. I don't think I had one from the Helena. That was in 1939, and I think they stopped putting the names of the ships on them. They just said "U.S. Navy" on the ribbon on the flat hats.

---

* These flat hats looked like the ones Donald Duck wears in Disney cartoons.

Paul Stillwell: What do you recall about the mess cooking?

Captain Shellenbarger: I don't recall too much about it, other than the fact that it was mostly just going to the galley and bringing these things with pots stacked in them. I'd bring them down and put them on the table, then have to clean them up afterward and return them.

Paul Stillwell: Did you get tips on payday?

Captain Shellenbarger: Tips?

Paul Stillwell: Some ships did.

Captain Shellenbarger: I never heard of them.

Paul Stillwell: What do you remember about being on the bridge during tactical maneuvers or battle line formation?

Captain Shellenbarger: See, on the <u>Colorado</u> I was not a supervisor of the watch. The supervisor of the watch would get the signal from the signal officer, and he'd just sing out what flags to snap into it and run them up to the yardarm. That's all. And then we'd get the "Execute," and down they'd come. The thing to do was get them back in the flag bag real fast, because you might be using that flag the next time around.

As I recall, on the flag bag it seems to me there were two sets of flags on each side because we had enough. And then we used the repeaters, of course.[*] The thing I liked best was the old 24-inch signal searchlights, the carbon arc lights. They had the big brass shutters with that crank handle on them. On later ships, they had the ones that were automatic, where you just hit a key. The solenoid would open the shutters on the light.

---

[*] If all the flags of a given letter or number had been used, repeaters were substituted for that flag later in the signal.

Franklin F. Shellenbarger, Interview #1 (4/28/97) – Page 27

Paul Stillwell: Were you pretty good at receiving and sending the code on flashing light?

Captain Shellenbarger: Yes, I was pretty good at that. And, of course, when we were in harbor we used to use the yardarm blinkers.* And, there again, height didn't bother me in those days because the electricians on the ship did not change the bulbs on the blinker lights. Signalmen did.

Paul Stillwell: Interesting.

Captain Shellenbarger: Just like in the old sailing ship days, you had the footropes. You had the rail on the yardarm and when you went out there you had to unscrew the top. And inside—I can remember to this day—there were eight bulbs in there, special bulbs. Of course, everything was DC electricity anyway so that when you hit the key down below, the lights would [hand-clapping sound].† You know, there was no lag of the light, so that you could read the yardarm blinker. They'd go on and off real fast.

We could send 14-15 words per minute with those yardarm blinkers. And there was a tremendous amount of blinker traffic in San Pedro Harbor when the battleships were all at anchor there. You'd have to watch for somebody calling your call sign. They'd use the tactical signal, so you'd watch for a B45 from some other ship, which quite often would be the your division flagship. I think it was the West Virginia.‡

Paul Stillwell: Did you have a safety belt when you went out on the yardarm?

Captain Shellenbarger: Yes.

Paul Stillwell: What do you remember about boat rides back and forth to the fleet landing?

---
* Rather than being one-directional, as the regular signal lights were, the blinker lights located on the yardarms of a mast could be seen from all directions.
† DC—direct current.
‡ In 1939 the West Virginia (BB-48) was flagship of both Battleship Division Four and the entire Battle Force. The other ships in the division were her two sisters, Colorado (BB-45) and Maryland (BB-46).

Captain Shellenbarger: It could be rough. [Laughter] Long Beach was where we had the landing and sometimes with a Santa Ana blowing there you'd be ashore, and you had to get back for your watch.* You could wait for your ship's launch, which was usually a 50-footer, an open launch. They also had water taxis, which you had to pay for. Because I know whenever possible we rode the ship's launches. And when you'd go alongside, sometimes you really had to jump to hit the gangway. Of course, the officers were on one side and the enlisted on the other, and they had to jump, only the officers had to jump out of a motorboat. [Laughter] We had more freedom.

Paul Stillwell: And if you weren't sober, I'll bet that was quite a challenge.

Captain Shellenbarger: It was. It was quite a tough challenge. I've heard stories that they had to take people aboard in slings, but I never saw it happen.

Paul Stillwell: I've heard those stories as well. Used the airplane crane and a cargo net or something.

Captain Shellenbarger: Yes. When I was on the Colorado there was one incident. They had the old Curtiss SOC biplanes on there.† Being a radio striker, I stood by for a friend who was in the aviation unit, a radioman. They sounded flight quarters on a Sunday afternoon for a guard mail trip to San Diego. When I went up to the plane, the pilot took one look at me, and he said, "Who the hell are you?"

I said, "Oh, I'm the radio operator. I'm on duty. I'm supposed to be standing by for—[the guy's name]."

He said, "The hell you are. You know what you have to do?" He said, "You've got to be able to handle the hook from the crane. You've got a lot of duties besides

---

* Santa Ana is the name for a strong hot dry wind from the north, northeast, or east in southern California—in other words, a wind not coming in from the sea.
† The Curtiss-built SOC Seagull was a biplane that first entered fleet squadrons in 1935, primarily in a floatplane version to perform observation and scouting missions for battleships and cruisers. It served through World War II. The SOC-1 version was 31 feet long, had a wingspan of 36 feet, gross weight of 5,437 pounds, and maximum speed of 165 miles an hour. It was armed with two .30-caliber machine guns.

handling the radio."* So they got somebody else. I didn't get restricted to the ship for two weeks, but my buddy did. He was unauthorized.

Paul Stillwell: What do you recall about liberty in Long Beach?

Captain Shellenbarger: I don't remember too much. They had the Pike, where we'd go and play games and flirt and various things.† I don't recall that I ever made any connections there. We used to ride into Los Angeles on the old Big Red, the interurban trains.

Paul Stillwell: Did you get up to Hollywood at all?

Captain Shellenbarger: Never got to Hollywood, no.

Paul Stillwell: What were the attractions in Los Angeles?

Captain Shellenbarger: Just looking around, sightseeing, and what have you. At that time I didn't know anyone there, so we were just going up and looking around to say we'd been there—more than anything else. The big attraction, of course, was the Pike in Long Beach. Actually, there was nothing in San Pedro. Today there's a water world or whatever there.

Paul Stillwell: I interviewed one man who said that you met three kinds of women there: the professionals, the semi-professionals, and the gifted amateurs.‡ [Laughter]

Captain Shellenbarger: How true! [Laughter] In those days I was such an amateur that I really didn't even know how to perform. I didn't learn that until later on in Norfolk.

---

* After the floatplane landed on the water at the end of a mission, it was lifted back aboard ship by means of a crane that hooked onto an attachment on top of the airplane.
† The Pike was a large amusement park near the fleet landing.
‡ This was from William Huckenpoehler, who served in the USS Arizona (BB-39) shortly before World War II. See Battleship Arizona: An Illustrated History (Annapolis: Naval Institute Press, 1991), page 177.

Paul Stillwell: Was that in the Colorado as well?

Captain Shellenbarger: Yes, I spent a lot of time in Norfolk in those days, when—believe it or not—the Naval Operating Base had one pier. And don't ask me why, but it was pier seven. That was one pier. That was it. That was the Naval Operating Base.

Paul Stillwell: So ships anchored out in Hampton Roads?

Captain Shellenbarger: Yes, most of the ships anchored out. Very seldom ever got anything alongside. The ones that did come alongside were mostly stores ships or what have you. They did nest some destroyers in there at times. But when I was on the Herbert, running in and out of there, we used to anchor all the time. Because we'd have to swing out our whaleboat with the old radial davits and put the boat booms out. And, of course, the Herbert still had the old cat and bill anchors.* There was only one destroyer, the Truxtun, that had the newer patent anchors on the bow. It had been in a collision some time. They'd put a new bow on it and, of course, at the same time they put new anchors on it.

Paul Stillwell: Did you have any liberty in the Caribbean while you were in the Colorado?

Captain Shellenbarger: Yes, they assigned us liberty ports. Must have been after the maneuvers in '39. We went into a port called Mayaguez in Puerto Rico. And then they must have had another maneuver of some sort, because I remember we went into a place called Gonaives in Haiti. What a miserable place. And from what I understand they haven't changed too much in the years.

The main street had a ditch on each side, and that was their wash water, the toilet, and everything else. And because this was a liberty port and there was going to be a bunch of sailors coming ashore, I don't know where they'd gotten it, but they had a lot of miserable beer in washtubs and ice, and that was our liberty.

---

* The old-fashioned anchors had to be hoisted up and stored on deck or a billboard recessed into the hull, rather than in a hawsepipe. They had to be brought up and secured on deck.

Well, being an actual history, of course, they had these little tents, you know, set up with a line up to the tents, and you know what they were.

Paul Stillwell: What sort of precautions or warnings did they give you about venereal disease?

Captain Shellenbarger: They didn't have condoms. They issued us some kind of a tube of something or other you were supposed to use.

Paul Stillwell: That was for afterward, following sex, wasn't it?

Captain Shellenbarger: For afterward, yes. Because there were the regular weekly short-arm inspections.*

While we were in Gonaives, I can remember talking to somebody ashore, asking about the Marines because the Marines had left Haiti not too long before that.† Yes, this had to be the spring of 1939, because in 1939 I only spent a relatively short time on the Herbert.

Paul Stillwell: Well please tell me about that ship.

Captain Shellenbarger: The Herbert was a typical four-piper.‡ I went on there, and this was where I got a tremendous shock. As a seaman first class, I'd been a signalman with a radioman's certificate and a quartermaster's certificate. Now I found myself in the bridge gang of a four-piper in reduced commission. She was used to train midshipmen, both reserve and regular, out of Harvard, Yale, and the Naval Academy, because I can remember going into Annapolis and picking up middies.

---

* "Short-arm inspection" is the nickname for a medical examination of a man's penis.
† On 15 August 1934 the last elements of the First Marine Brigade withdrew from Haiti, ending an occupation of 19 years.
‡ USS Herbert (DD-160), a Wickes-class destroyer, was commissioned 21 November 1919. Displacement was 1,090 tons, length 314 feet, beam of 32 feet, and draft of 9 feet. Top speed was 35 knots. She was armed with four 4-inch guns, three 3-inch guns, and 12 21-inch torpedo tubes.

We'd go out for two weeks, do all kind of drills. We were supposed to be helping instruct them. I don't know whether we did or not, but I remember now that at that time they had a rail line from Annapolis to Baltimore, because I can remember riding it, and it was relatively cheap and fast. Beautiful way to go to Baltimore.

We went into Boston. I'm trying to think of when I must have left the <u>Colorado</u>, and I'd have to check back. Something doesn't jibe. But the thing I remember is that we went into Boston for one of these middie cruises to pick up the unit from Harvard. And we got in there on Bunker Hill Day. And, of course, the Bunker Hill Monument is in Charlestown.[*] So because we were a naval vessel in the Boston Navy Yard, Charlestown, we had to put a detachment ashore and march that day.[†] Somehow or other, that upset me; I don't know why.

But, anyway, I learned so much on the <u>Herbert</u> that it did me just 1,000% good. I went out on that ship with a first class quartermaster; I'll never forget this guy's name, Alonzo C. Dunham. I think he ended the war as a jaygee, or he might even have ended up as a lieutenant commander, mustang.[‡] The second class signalman was the mail orderly. Every time we were in port, he was at the fleet post office. And me—I was the third guy on the bridge, standing a quartermaster's watch.

I learned how to use a stadimeter and alidade, bearing circle.[§] I never learned so fast in my life because if I didn't, Dunham would probably have taken me back in the corner and beat the hell out of me, because that's the sort of a guy he was. He'd come down into the little compartment where we lived. The deck department was up forward of the boilers, engine department was aft. Of course, since I was the junior man and Dunham was the first class, you know who did all the work.

Paul Stillwell: Yes. Probably you learned a lot about plotting and piloting too.

---

[*] The monument, in the form of an obelisk, commemorates the Revolutionary War Battle of Bunker Hill, fought on 17 June 1775.
[†] Charlestown, formerly an independent city between the mouths of the Charles and Mystic rivers, became a part of Boston in 1874. It was long the site of the Boston Navy Yard, later renamed Boston Naval Shipyard in 1945. The Navy closed the shipyard in 1974.
[‡] Jaygee—lieutenant (junior grade). "Mustang" is Navy slang for a former enlisted man who has risen through the ranks to become an officer.
[§] The stadimeter is a mechanical device for measuring the range to another ship when the height of her mast is known. An alidade is a rotating circular device mounted atop a compass to measure bearings to various objects.

Captain Shellenbarger: Oh, I learned so much about plotting, piloting. When I was off watch, he'd come through because his quarters were up forward. If I was reading something like, say, a detective story instead of a Coast Pilot or a Bowditch, he would knock it out of my hands, and it went over the side.* Back in the after port corner of that compartment where the deck gang lived was the gyro cage. Believe me, I learned gyro there, too, because that was my job. An old Mark 6 with the rollers on the thing. I don't know if you ever saw one.

Paul Stillwell: No.

Captain Shellenbarger: Anyway, they had two rollers on them instead of later on it was just a magnetic thing. But I learned a lot in a hell of a hurry there. And rigging, cross pointing.

Our skipper on that ship was Lieutenant Commander Sherman.† He was fine in so many ways, and, here again, here was an academy graduate. When he'd come up to the captain's chair, he'd put his foot up on the stanchion. And Dunham said, "I'm sick and tired of painting that damn stanchion where his foot is." And somewhere in my scrapbook is a picture of Dunham sitting in the captain's chair with his foot on this, because we put cross pointing and Turk's heads on this stanchion for him to put his foot against. The first time the skipper saw it, he burst out laughing. He was a great guy.

The exec was a two-striper, M. R. Stone.‡ He was supposed to be studying Japanese, I think. The separation between enlisted and officers was greater with him. Not with the skipper because he had been a submarine skipper, where everyone lived together. Remember these were the R and O boats.§

I can remember so well we did go in to the dock once, pier seven in Norfolk. Being the junior man, I was the guy who was always standing the quartermaster watches,

---

* Nathaniel Bowditch (1773-1838) was an American mathematician and astronomer. He wrote The American Practical Navigator in 1802. The U.S. Navy bought the rights to it, and in revised editions it has been used since then as a guide to the principles of navigation.
† Lieutenant Commander Earl V. Sherman, USN.
‡ Lieutenant Martin R. Stone, USN.
§ The early U.S. submarines were designated by letter-number combinations rather than names. O-1 through O-16 were commissioned in 1918. R-1 through R-27 were commissioned in 1918-19.

every port. I seldom ever got a chance to go ashore. Once in a while, Dunham would feel sorry for me and relieve me and let me go ashore. And he used the vernacular, "To get my ashes hauled."

Paul Stillwell: That's still a little euphemistic.

Captain Shellenbarger: [Laughter] But, anyway, the skipper came down and his cabin—are you familiar with the four-pipers? You probably aren't.

Paul Stillwell: That's before my time.

Captain Shellenbarger: All right. The four-pipers, right underneath the bridge, which was faired out, was the skipper's cabin. One day he came out of his cabin, which was right on the main deck, of course. He came back and said to me, "Would you please go across the dock to the skipper of that submarine over there and extend my compliments and invite him over for dinner. He can have dinner with me."

I looked across the dock, and I said, "I don't see any submarine." And that was the only time I ever saw him blow his top. All I could see was the conning tower sticking up there, and I thought it was an oil drum. That's my recollection, because I went over there, and I didn't go inside the thing. I guess I was scared to or something. I just hollered down the hatch and asked for somebody. And the guy stuck his head there, and I said, "Captain Sherman, the captain of the destroyer over there, apparently knows your captain, and he said he wants him to come over for dinner." I don't know who I was talking to. I don't recall that I ever knew.

And he said, "Okay, I'll take care of it." And the guy did come over because I was the quartermaster, and I was on the gangway when he came aboard. I took him up to the captain's cabin.

I got very familiar with that bridge, because in those days the rudder mechanism was all taken care of by the quartermasters. The mail orderly was ashore with some of the signalmen, so I worked with Dunham on a lot of things. One of the things was that they had the—how do I remember?—nine and a half turns of phosphor bronze wire on the wheel in the bridge came down through the overhead in the captain's cabin because we had to take the panels down. Went down the starboard side, through fairleads under the railing, back into the steering engine in the steering engine room. We had to grease these cables, and we had to go back into the steering engine room. I don't know how so much happened in such a short time but, boy, I learned a lot on the Herbert.

Paul Stillwell: Did you learn celestial navigation also?

Captain Shellenbarger: I learned how to take azimuths. I learned a little bit about how to get altitudes of the sun—you know, meridian altitude at noontime. And, of course, when I went to Fort Trumbull to get my license, boy, that was valuable because I had all the elementary knowledge.*

Paul Stillwell: Did you work out the star sights?

Captain Shellenbarger: I didn't work any star sights. No, not there.

Paul Stillwell: You made brief reference to the exec and the gulf between him and enlisted men. How would you describe that?

Captain Shellenbarger: Nothing more than what was normal in those days. Because we were in reduced commission, I think we were a lot closer than the crew of an average destroyer. I can't remember. It seems to me we only had about 65 officers and men on there, because we had to allow for taking these midshipmen out all the time. And I can remember one time we went alongside—the first time I ever saw the Texas. It wasn't for fueling, because I don't think we did fueling at sea then.

Paul Stillwell: Very little.

---

* Fort Trumbull in New London, Connecticut, was the name of the school for merchant marine officers that Shellenbarger attended in World War II.

Captain Shellenbarger: I think it was exchange movies or guard mail or something like that. And, boy, I can remember what Sherman he called me, because he never called me Shelley. He called me Giz. Don't ask me why. Maybe it was after I busted the stadimeter, the rectangular thing you used to get your distance and hold station, because I had to learn how to do that, too, you know. That's one of the quartermaster's jobs. I didn't put it in its box in its proper place, and the thing fell on the deck and instead of a rectangle it became a parallelogram. The skipper was standing there, and that's the first time he ever called me. He said, "Giz, you know you're going to have to stay in the Navy 20 years to pay for that?" [Laughter] I believed him. I believed him for about two weeks.

Paul Stillwell: But what you're saying is that he was generally friendlier than the exec.

Captain Shellenbarger: Yes, he was.

Paul Stillwell: How much interaction did you have with the midshipmen?

Captain Shellenbarger: Not too much. Not much, no. I can remember somebody saying, "Well, you know, this midshipman is Henry Ford II."[*] He looked like just another midshipman to me. The difference was that they wore caps with black, black or blue, some kind of a stripe around the top.

Paul Stillwell: Dark blue.

Captain Shellenbarger: Dark blue, yes. That's the only thing I can remember about them really, other than the fact that they were there to learn. That was it.

Paul Stillwell: Did they seem eager and willing to learn?

---

[*] Henry Ford II, who served as a Naval Reserve officer in World War II, was later president and chairman of the board of the Ford Motor Company.

Captain Shellenbarger: Yes. I think they were. They were all very enthusiastic, even those that got seasick. That's one thing that I've been very fortunate. I was never seasick.

Paul Stillwell: Do you remember how well the ship rode? Did it roll a lot?

Captain Shellenbarger: It rolled a hell of a lot. It really rolled. That's why the skipper raised hell with me because he said, "You should have known better than to leave the stadimeter sitting out even for ten seconds." And it hit the deck. And I remember we used to adjust compasses. We took care of the chronometers.

As a matter of fact, in fairly recent years somebody was talking about shipping a chronometer. Of course, today they're all quartz. But putting the little wedges underneath the balance wheel to stop the motion of the thing for shipping. These are things that Dunham taught me so much about. He had been skipper of what they called a sound boat and, of course, the old Hydrographic Office was part of the Navy. And he had helped survey the coast along Colombia and Venezuela down there a couple of years. He must have been in the Navy 14 or 15 years then. And there was another thing. The first time I ever went in New York Harbor was on the Herbert, and we anchored down at Stapleton. Whenever we anchored anyplace with Dunham, you didn't take the normal cross bearings and plot them on the chart. You took horizontal sextant angles, because that's the way the survey boats did.

Paul Stillwell: That's interesting.

Captain Shellenbarger: And you plotted your horizontal sextant angles, because that's the way the survey boats did it. You know, it's funny. You talk about it, and these things come back.

Paul Stillwell: What do you recall about the camaraderie in that ship? I mean, it was a much smaller ship and crew than the Colorado.

Captain Shellenbarger: Yes. In the crew there, everybody got along fine. There was more separation between, say, the deck people and those they called the snipes, the engine gang, because they had the quarters aft. But I think that the engine gang stayed pretty much to themselves. And yet they were all friendly with no problem like that, because, still being junior man, I was the guy that had to wind all the clocks and set them and take care of the things, which meant that I had to go into both boiler rooms, and they had airlocks because they were pressurized. Had to go in the engineers' compartment back aft to set their clocks, wind them, which as I recall was only weekly, and I think they were all seven-day. But a good bunch. I enjoyed it actually.

There were times that I felt that I was being picked on by my boss, by Dunham, but, of course, to this day I'm so thankful that he taught me so much.

Paul Stillwell: Well, it was really fortuitous that you went to the ship when you did, because you learned a lot more than you would have in the Colorado in that period.

Captain Shellenbarger: Oh, yes. Definitely. Definitely.

Paul Stillwell: What were the messing arrangements like in the Herbert?

Captain Shellenbarger: In the Herbert messing was—you had the galley, which was— that's funny, I can't remember where the galley was.

Paul Stillwell: You're not expected to remember everything. [Laughter]

Captain Shellenbarger: All I can remember is the spud locker was between the two forward stacks or the two after stacks. It seems to me that there was another house back there, because I can't remember whether the torpedo tubes were down on the main deck level or on top of the house. In later destroyers they were up on top of the deckhouse, and I know the head was in the after house. You had to go all the way over the deck, regardless of the weather. You had to be careful you didn't catch your feet in the padeyes going down the deck to the head, which, of course, was back in the stern. And you had to be careful about following seas, because sometimes a following sea would come right in, and you'd be up to your waist or your neck in water.

Paul Stillwell: But you had to go outside the skin of the ship to go forward and aft.

Captain Shellenbarger: Oh, yes. You had to. Yes. Because you had the two boiler rooms, and you had the engine room.

Paul Stillwell: There was no longitudinal passageway inside.

Captain Shellenbarger: Nothing. You had no longitudinal inside. As I recall, there were only two chiefs on the ship, and even the chiefs had to go up onto the foredeck right behind the chain locker and go down through like a booby hatch into their quarters. It was miserable, because I can remember Dunham saying one time that he'd never want to be a chief and have to live in that hole up there. He would much prefer to be down where he was. I think there was a first class machinist down there—only two firsts, and they were in this little separate compartment. And the only thing was that their bunks, I think, were fixed, where our bunks in the regular crew compartment folded up.

Paul Stillwell: Triced up, I think they called it.

Captain Shellenbarger: Yes. I can't remember whether it was two or three, but I remember there was a row of portholes in there by the lower bunk. It was always better to be in the upper bunk, because the lower portholes leaked.

Underneath the bunks on each side of this compartment was like a settee, and you had lids in them, and that was your clothing compartment. We kept them in there. And that's what you sat on for the mess tables and the mess tables—it's funny I can't remember that. Seems to me the mess tables, when they weren't in use, flipped up with some kind of a pin, toggle pin, to hold them in a vertical position. There couldn't have been more than one mess table in there, because you sat on the tops of these clothing lockers.

Paul Stillwell: Did you have a cafeteria-style serving line?

Captain Shellenbarger: No, there was a mess cook who brought the food in from the galley—somewhere.

Paul Stillwell: Well, the first time I went to sea was in a destroyer escort that was built during World War II, and I remember sitting on those locker tops just as you described.

Captain Shellenbarger: Yes, they were like that. Strange.

Paul Stillwell: Well, anything else? What do you remember about the gunnery in that ship?

Captain Shellenbarger: They had 4-inch guns, and I remember they were fired a few times, but I don't recall that I ever had anything to do with the guns or the torpedoes. We had torpedo tubes.

I was kept busy and occasionally even stood radio watches. We only carried one or two radio operators. I don't know why. Allegedly I had a third class radioman's certificate, so a couple of times I found myself standing radio watches in addition to bridge watches. Because, like I say, we were in reduced commission and when you went anywhere, handled stores or anything, everybody, even the third class petty officers handled stores just like everybody else.

You did a lot more things, but probably you learned more because of it. It was very interesting.

In August 1939, I remember we were in the Brooklyn Navy Yard, and word came—I don't know whether it came directly from the Bureau of Navigation or just from the fleet.[*] Whatever it was, the message came for the Herbert, "Transfer one seaman first class to the Helena detail."

---

[*] Prior to World War II, many personnel assignments were made by the Bureau of Navigation. On 13 May 1942, it became the Bureau of Naval Personnel (BuPers), a title that better described its function.

Paul Stillwell: Didn't specify what he was striking for?

Captain Shellenbarger: No. Nothing whatsoever. And, of course, here I'd been in the bridge gang there learning a lot, and by that time I was really enjoying it. Got a hell of a lot more responsibility, and it was much better in many ways compared to what I'd done on the Colorado, and I went to the exec. He said, "Well, I can't do anything about it. Let's talk to the skipper."

We went in to the skipper, Lieutenant Commander Sherman. He looked at me, and he said, "I know how you feel. You want to stay here. I've got something to tell you. I'm being transferred the same day you are, and I have no choice." He said, "You have no choice either. You're going to go to the Helena detail." At that time the Helena was not in commission, so I went aboard the old Seattle. That was the receiving ship.*

Paul Stillwell: Why did you get picked, of all the seamen first class?

Captain Shellenbarger: There were no other seaman firsts on the ship.

Paul Stillwell: Well, then that did leave him no choice.

Captain Shellenbarger: You see, he said there was no choice. He said I was the only seaman first class. They had a couple of seaman second class. There were very few unrated men on the ship.

I've got the feeling that he told me he was going to the Reuben James, 245, and later that ship was sunk up in the North Atlantic during Neutrality Patrol.† I've often

---

* Originally commissioned as the armored cruiser Washington in 1906, the ship's name was changed to Seattle in 1916, and in 1920 she was assigned the hull number CA-11. From 1923 to 1927 she served as flagship of Commander in Chief U.S. Fleet. In August 1927 she became the receiving ship, essentially a floating barracks, for the port of New York and remained in that capacity until 1941. She stayed in New York throughout World War II until being placed out of service in 1946.

† On 31 October 1941, the U-552 torpedoed and sank the destroyer Reuben James (DD-245) with the loss of 115 lives. She was escorting a convoy from Halifax, Nova Scotia, to the British Isles and was lost about 600 miles west of Ireland. She was the first U.S. warship lost to enemy action in World War II.

wondered if Commander Sherman was on there when it went down.*

Paul Stillwell: Well, you mentioned the Seattle. That's a neat story. Tell me about her.

Captain Shellenbarger: Well, when we were on the Seattle, I guess they called it the Helena detail. There must have been 300-400 people from the fleet that had been assigned to the Helena; this was in September 1939. I can't recall when, but shortly after that they called the fleet reservists to active duty, because I know we got an awful lot of reservists on the Helena when we did commission her.†

The Sacramento had just come back from the Asian station, and they were looking for somebody who could serve as coal passers.‡ There was no such thing as a coal passer in the fleet in those days, but there were firemen who had to be coal passers. So I know they went around on the Seattle looking for people to go on the Sacramento to be coal passers.

Paul Stillwell: Well, the Seattle still burned coal at that point, didn't she?

Captain Shellenbarger: It just had shore power. It was just a receiving ship. It was a dead ship, really. It wasn't, you know, a steaming vessel, and I can't remember some of the other ships that are in there.

Paul Stillwell: Yes, but they probably burned coal for auxiliary steam, didn't they?

Captain Shellenbarger: I don't remember.

---

* Lieutenant Commander Heywood L. Edwards, USN, the commanding officer of the Reuben James at the time of her sinking, died in the action. He had relieved Sherman as skipper. Sherman retired as a rear admiral in 1947 and eventually died in 1977.
† USS Helena (CL-50), a St. Louis-class light cruiser, was commissioned 18 September 1939. She had a standard displacement of 10,000 tons, was 608 feet long, and 62 feet in the beam. Her top speed was 33 knots. She was armed with fifteen 6-inch main battery guns and eight 5-inch dual-purpose guns.
‡ The gunboat Sacramento (PG-19) had been commissioned in 1914. In January 1939 she left the Philippine Islands, bound for New York. She subsequently served as a Naval Reserve training ship on the Great Lakes in 1939-40 before heading for Pearl Harbor, where she was in December 1941 when the Japanese attacked.

Paul Stillwell: I interviewed a fellow who said that he was involved in that briefly in the Seattle.*

Captain Shellenbarger: Yes, it's possible because it was known as the receiving ship Seattle. The Kearsarge was in there also, the old crane ship.† I remember seeing the Dahlgren, high-pressure job.

Paul Stillwell: Were these all at the Brooklyn Navy Yard?

Captain Shellenbarger: They were all at the Brooklyn Navy Yard then when the Helena was fitting out.

Paul Stillwell: Was she launched by the time you got to her detail?

Captain Shellenbarger: Yes, it had been launched.‡ It was in dry dock most of the time, though. I remember because, there again, I was one of the guys that had to go up and help rig the yardarms with the signal halyards. And the reason I remember that so well is because you're out on that footrope, and you look down and there's no water. It's a dry dock. And on the ways was the North Carolina being built.§ Somewhere I had a picture of it that I took, which I shouldn't have. I took a lot of pictures I shouldn't have.

Because the Helena was built in a navy yard, the commissioning crew had to do a hell of a lot of work on the ship. A lot of details like man ropes, railings, and do this, do that. There were things that the navy yard didn't do, and that was one of the things. Then, of course, we were commissioned and went on our shakedown cruise. We went on there in

---

* This appears in the oral history of Rear Admiral Jackson K. Parker, USN (Ret.), who was an enlisted man before being commissioned.
† USS Kearsarge (BB-5) was commissioned as a battleship on 20 February 1900. She was decommissioned 10 May 1920 for conversion to a crane ship. She was designated Kearsarge (AB-1) on 5 August 1920. On 6 November 1941 she lost her name for use in a new aircraft carrier and became known simply as Craneship Number 1. She was eventually sold for scrap in 1955.
‡ The ship was launched on 27 August 1939.
§ USS North Carolina (BB-55) was the U.S. Navy's first fast battleship, capable of 27-knot speed. She was commissioned 9 April 1941.

September, and our shakedown cruise started because, I think that picture shows us in Buenos Aires right after the first of the year. I think that we were down in Montevideo.

Paul Stillwell: Who was the first skipper?

Captain Shellenbarger: His name was Demott, Captain Max B. Demott. I was in communication with a guy who was a forest ranger. He was in the signal gang, Bill Degnan. And the first class on there, of course, he was older than I was. He ended the war as a mustang: Lieutenant Commander C. R. Watson. Nice guy, really nice guy.

After commissioning, we made a shakedown cruise to South America. We were starting to work with the British then, because on our way down we stopped off at the island of Fernando de Noronha, close to Brazil, to investigate some vessel that was suspicious. I don't recall what we did, but I know that we launched aircraft. Of course, this was all part of the shakedown cruise. You mentioned the name Jack Chew.[*] He was one of the division officers on there. Of course, he was on when it went down in Kula Gulf later, and he saved a lot of lives apparently, and he was quite responsible.[†] I've got a book written by one of the Helena association people.[‡] That is at the office in New York. I don't have a copy here.

But the thing that I remember so well about the Helena was those two damned things that we had to lift up. See, it was similar to the Brooklyn class. The St. Louis and the Helena were the last two, so they modified them. They didn't have the 5-inch/25 antiaircraft batteries. They put the 5-inch/38s, the twin mounts in there, and when those things were elevated up—I don't know whether they went to 90, I think 85 degrees, you could stand on the signal bridge and literally look down the barrel of an antiaircraft gun. So when they fired those things, the muzzle blast on the bridge was unbelievable. Unbelievable. We fired the first broadside there, and all the glass was knocked out of the

---

[*] Lieutenant John L. Chew, USN, was in the first crew. The oral history of Chew, who retired as a vice admiral, is in the Naval Institute collection.
[†] On 6 July 1943, the Helena was sunk by a Japanese torpedo at Kula Gulf in the Solomon Islands. For a first-person account see John L. Chew, "Some Shall Escape," U.S. Naval Institute Proceedings, August 1945, pages 887-903.
[‡] Ray J. Casten, Our Ship the Helena (Self-published, 1991).

bridge. It was terrible, and I'm sure it was Demott was the first skipper. The exec seemed to do most of the piloting, take the ship in and out of port and everything.

Paul Stillwell: What were your duties in the Helena?

Captain Shellenbarger: On the Helena I made signalman third, and I was a watch supervisor. And, of course, at that time during the shakedown cruise we weren't in company with other ships, so there wasn't a heck of a lot to do other than just keep good lookout, work with quartermasters, and stay out of the skipper's way, because the sea cabin was back in the after starboard corner of the chartroom. And as you stood watches there—as I say, there wasn't much signaling to do. I do remember one time we were doing speed trials. After delivery we went to Rockland, Maine, and I didn't learn till years and years later the reason they did the speed trials up in Rockland, Maine. You're probably aware of it.

Paul Stillwell: They have a measured mile up there.

Captain Shellenbarger: A measured mile, but do you know why? It's because the water is cold. You get much more efficiency out of your engines from steam turbines, your condensate, your boilers, so you can do better speed up there than you can in warm water.

Paul Stillwell: So those are really artificial conditions up there. [Laughter]

Captain Shellenbarger: So that's the reason for it. But this was off Guantanamo, and the St. Louis was the sister ship.* She was the other modified ship with the things, and we were doing a speed trial down there. I don't know what we were doing, but it had to be better than 37 knots.

Paul Stillwell: That's amazing.

---

* Guantanamo Bay, on the south coast of Cuba, near the eastern end of the island, for many years provided a fleet anchorage and training area for U.S. Navy ships.

Captain Shellenbarger: We were both doing it in opposite directions at that speed, and I was on a blinker light. And it was just some routine message that I was sending from the Helena to the St. Louis. And here I was, going like that, and I don't think I ever finished the message.

Paul Stillwell: Because you zipped by so quickly.

Captain Shellenbarger: So fast, yes.

Paul Stillwell: That would be a great moment to experience.

Captain Shellenbarger: Unbelievable. Yes, it was something to see. And those were the first ships that I ever saw that had a rooster tail behind them.[*] And, of course, being in the merchant marine during the war, I didn't see that much of destroyers zip-zipping around. We were too busy doing other things to watch it, but the next time that I saw a real rooster tail was one of the Sea-Land ships coming out of Kobe, Japan. I was headed in and saw one of the Sea-Land ships that the Navy later took over.

Paul Stillwell: The SL-7s?

Captain Shellenbarger: SL-7s.[†] A friend of mine, Bob Fay, is skipper of the one in Bayonne now.

Paul Stillwell: They do about 33, don't they?

---

[*] "Rooster tail" refers to the plume of water thrown up astern of a ship moving at high speed.
[†] The eight cargo ships of the SL-7 class were built in the early 1970s in European shipyards for the SeaLand Corporation. Equipped with steam turbines, they are capable of 33 knots—the fastest cargo ships ever constructed for the U.S. merchant service. In the early 1980s the U.S. Navy acquired them and converted them to fast sealift ships for operation by the Military Sealift Command. All eight took part in the Desert Storm/Desert Shield operation in 1990-91.

Captain Shellenbarger: They'll do about 33. And I saw this thing coming out of Kobe, a containership with this rooster tail behind it. [Laughter]

Paul Stillwell: Well, when you were going one way and the St. Louis the other, you had a relative speed close to 75 knots.

Captain Shellenbarger: That's right.

Paul Stillwell: That's amazing.

Captain Shellenbarger: Eighty miles an hour. Oh. If you can just visualize that,

Paul Stillwell: I can. I wish I'd been there.

Captain Shellenbarger: Oh, I tell you, it was something.

Paul Stillwell: Well, the Helena was almost 20 years younger than the two you'd been in. What were the habitability conditions?

Captain Shellenbarger: Oh, well, they had bunks. They had nice lockers. And, there again, I remember very distinctly it was CR, CS, and CN divisions, because we were down between number two and three turrets, the barbettes for two and three turrets down there. We were down there with the fire controlmen. I don't know whether they had a separate division, but I know that the pharmacist's mates were down there. The reason I remember that so well is in that album that I sent to the Naval Institute there are pictures of us aboard the Graf Spee.* And looking through them years later I suddenly looked at the top. Besides a couple of grinning characters there, I saw a bedspring antenna. That ship had

---

* In December 1939 a squadron of three cruisers—Ajax, Achilles, and Exeter—damaged the German cruiser Admiral Graf Spee in a gun battle off Uruguay's River Plate. The German ship went into the port of Montevideo to repair damage. The German skipper, Captain Hans Langsdorff, believed a superior force awaited him if he returned to sea, so he removed the crew and ordered the Admiral Graf Spee scuttled on 17 December. He then committed suicide.

radar. I don't know how efficient it was or any of that, but there was a bedspring radar. I know we pried loose more nameplates and stuff on that thing. We loaded up.

Paul Stillwell: What were the circumstances of going aboard Graf Spee?

Captain Shellenbarger: I don't know why. Somebody decided. We came in, we anchored there.

Paul Stillwell: This was only a few weeks after she had sunk.

Captain Shellenbarger: Only a few weeks after she'd sunk. That's right. As a matter of fact, they claimed it was very dangerous because the after magazine blew up. It had to be the after one, because somewhere in that album there's a picture of the Graf Spee smoking. They were taken down there, because naturally it was such a recent event that people were aboard peddling all kinds of souvenirs and things. And then, of course, when we got to Buenos Aires, we met a lot of the sailors from the Graf Spee. We'd drink beer with them, party with them, and everything like that and, of course, they're just sailors like we are.

Paul Stillwell: What did they say?

Captain Shellenbarger: The ones we talked to were very, very happy they were in Argentina, and I understand a lot of them stayed there. I understand that they were offered the opportunity of being repatriated to Germany, and I heard that the majority of them said, "To hell with that. We like this place." And the ones that I talked to, we got along fine. That one picture I think I showed you, it was autographed by a couple of sailors that we had partied with. And the Argentineans treated us great. We had all kinds of parties and what have you.

Paul Stillwell: What language did you speak with these sailors in?

Captain Shellenbarger: English. They speak English. My experience is that practically everybody in the world speaks some English. Like you go to France. I've been in and out of French ports many times, and even in Montreal the pilot speaks good English, but when it comes time to talk to the tugs, he uses French.

Paul Stillwell: Was their feeling one of relief? Were they just glad to get out of the war?

Captain Shellenbarger: Yes.

Paul Stillwell: Did they say anything about Nazism?

Captain Shellenbarger: No. None of them that we were with. It might have been on their minds, but they certainly didn't discuss that. When we went on liberty, we'd been told by the exec that we would be seeing a lot of the German sailors from the Graf Spee. As a matter of fact, they told us at morning quarters, "Please, do not discuss politics." Because they were afraid of brawls or something, but we got along fine with them.

Paul Stillwell: Did they talk about the battle in which she got shot up?

Captain Shellenbarger: I don't recall. They might have talked to some people about it, but I certainly never talked to them about it. It was only in later years that I read accounts of it. I remember because one of the smaller British cruisers, the Achilles, I used to see all the time in India because that was transferred to the Indian Navy.[*] Of course, I don't know what happened to the Ajax. Of course, the Exeter was the one that got kind of badly mauled by the 11-inch guns on the Graf Spee.

Paul Stillwell: Well, what can you just say about liberty in general in those South American ports, Montevideo and Buenos Aires?

---

[*] The light cruiser Achilles, which spent part of World War II in the New Zealand Navy, was transferred to the Indian Navy in 1948 and became RIN Delhi. HMS Ajax served throughout World War II and was later sold for scrapping in 1949.

Captain Shellenbarger: Very enjoyable. Very enjoyable.

Paul Stillwell: What made it so?

Captain Shellenbarger: I don't know. We were in a new group together. You had your buddies already from the shipyard time in the fitting-out period. While we were on the Seattle and worked together on the Helena, like in any big ship, you've got your own little clique, your gang. You go ashore together, liberty gang, and the people in Buenos Aires, Montevideo, and we stopped in Santos, Brazil, on the way back. Brazil, Argentina, and Uruguay greeted us with open arms. And I don't know how to describe it, but in Brazil, believe it or not, we got in during the Mardi Gras.

Paul Stillwell: What was so good about it?

Captain Shellenbarger: Five days: wine, women, and song. They had streetcars, and somebody told me they'd imported them from the States. You stepped on things like running boards into the seats, and you'd pop on and off the streetcars. And they never charged us any fare. When you'd hop onto the streetcar, all of a sudden you'd get this feel of real cold on your back through your jumper. You were wearing whites, and there'd be a couple of girls back there with some kind of a spray device with perfume in it. And it must have had some kind of like ether or something that evaporates, because it was cold when it hit you. And then there'd be this giggling, "Ha-ha." It was something. And, of course, it's probably more so today than it was then, but it's still like it is in Rio, during the Mardi Gras time. This was Santos, Brazil, and it was something. We really enjoyed ourselves.

Paul Stillwell: Sounds like a great cruise altogether.

Captain Shellenbarger: Oh, it was.

Paul Stillwell: Well, please tell me a little more.

Captain Shellenbarger: Of course, on the way down we had the crossing-the-line ceremony, and there are pictures also in that album of the crossing-the-line ceremony.

Paul Stillwell: What specifically do you remember about the initiation?

Captain Shellenbarger: Other than the fact that I was a pollywog, that was about it.[*]

Paul Stillwell: Got beat up probably.

Captain Shellenbarger: Got beat up and dunked in salt water, and it seems to me there was some diesel oil mixed in there and all kinds of garbage and stuff, which you had to go through and come back up and meet King Neptune, and be formally declared that you were a shellback.

Paul Stillwell: What do you recall about being on board the Graf Spee herself?

Captain Shellenbarger: Well, I don't remember that much about it. The only reason was that I happened to be on watch when they sent the whaleboat over, because you didn't have walkie-talkies or anything like that. Whenever you sent a boat you had to send a signalman in the boat so you could communicate. And, of course, when you had a boat out, the bridge watch on the ship had to keep an eye on the boat all the time in case there was some reason that the signalman over there started waving his flags. Or if it was night, which seldom ever happened, you also had to carry with you the blinker gun. I don't know whether they still have them, but they had that shoulder stock and a round black tube. I know they still had them in World War II.

Paul Stillwell: The Aldis lamp?

---

[*] In the Navy's traditional equator-crossing ceremonies, the novice pollywogs are initiated by the shellbacks who have crossed the line previously.

Captain Shellenbarger: It wasn't an Aldis lamp. It was the blinker gun. You had to aim them, because an Aldis lamp you can see from the side angles a little bit more. This thing was you had to aim it directly at the guy that was receiving you, and the light would come on. As I recall, that worked on the same principle as the Aldis lamp was the mirror would rock in and out of focus.

Paul Stillwell: How far from the Graf Spee was the Helena anchored?

Captain Shellenbarger: Oh, it wasn't a hell of a long way away.

Paul Stillwell: Mile or two?

Captain Shellenbarger: I'd say less than a mile. The harbor isn't that big.

Paul Stillwell: I see, so no problem keeping the boat in sight?

Captain Shellenbarger: Oh, no, no. No problem. No.

Paul Stillwell: What do you remember about the condition of the Graf Spee?

Captain Shellenbarger: The thing that I recall more than anything else was the fire damage. After the explosion there must have been a tremendous fire, but apparently in one magazine the charges didn't go off, and that's what caused the big problem, the fact that it didn't blow apart like it should have.

Paul Stillwell: Were there safety concerns in going on board?

Captain Shellenbarger: I think that was part of the reason why there was only the one trip over. And then, like I think I mentioned before, the ship's photographer was a pharmacist's mate. They didn't have a photographer rating or anything like that, and he went along. He was the guy that took pictures, and he's the one that I got the set of pictures from that was in that album.

Paul Stillwell: And you used what, screwdrivers or something to pry off these nameplates?

Captain Shellenbarger: Sure, you had a toolkit in the boat. "Pass me up that hammer. Pass me up the screwdriver." And, of course, being a signalman, I went up on the bridge, and the flag letters were in the German script, so I got several of those, and I don't know whatever happened to them over the years.

Paul Stillwell: Then the flags had survived the fire?

Captain Shellenbarger: No. They were pretty well charred.

Paul Stillwell: Well, you said when the tape recorder wasn't running that you took off so much loot that it decreased the freeboard on your boat.

Captain Shellenbarger: I can't remember what all there was, but there was an awful lot of stuff in there. I can't remember how many were in the boat, but it couldn't have been too many people.

Paul Stillwell: What happened to the loot?

Captain Shellenbarger: It went back to the ship, and I don't know whatever happened to it. I don't know. I've kept two little pieces, that's all, two little nameplates.

Paul Stillwell: Did any of the Helena's officers go aboard to get intelligence information?

Captain Shellenbarger: There was a lieutenant (j.g.) with us, and I presume he had instructions. I know the photographer was there, and he spent more time with the lieutenant taking pictures. Whether they were doing intelligence, I don't know. I have unfortunately a very low opinion of naval intelligence through some later incidents that happened with me.

Paul Stillwell: Well, we can get to those.

Captain Shellenbarger: If you are really interested in hearing all this stuff, it's going to take days. [Laughter]

Paul Stillwell: Well, I've done that before.

Captain Shellenbarger: You know, we're talking about things that are souvenirs. My wife says I've got sticky fingers.

Paul Stillwell: Where's that from?

Captain Shellenbarger: The Helena.

Paul Stillwell: It says "Secondary Conning Station, B-0201B."

Captain Shellenbarger: That's where I slept when I wasn't in my regular bunk.

Paul Stillwell: Now you keep that on your key chain.

Captain Shellenbarger: I keep that on my key chain: secondary conning station.

Paul Stillwell: Well, evidently there was no security. Nobody was guarding the Graf Spee, for whatever reason.

Captain Shellenbarger: No, apparently not.

Paul Stillwell: She must have eventually been salvaged and scrapped.

Captain Shellenbarger: I think so. Yes. Who did it, I don't know, but from what we heard by the grapevine was that our going over there was a sort of a minor diplomatic incident, and yet we heard nothing about it afterwards. Of course, it might have been top level. Somebody said something. Somebody might have got a reprimand or maybe awarded. Maybe they learned something. Who knows? It's possible, because I'm sure that there were things on the ship that somebody must have looked at. I know that some of them went inside the conning tower and around. I never went inside anything; there was an outside ladder, and I just went up to the bridge wing. Being a signalman, all I was interested in was to take a look and see what they had in the way of signal gear.

Paul Stillwell: Well, Captain Langsdorff of the Graf Spee was noted as a humanitarian and greatly concerned about his crew.

Captain Shellenbarger: They were put ashore before the explosion.

Paul Stillwell: Well, it might explain why he didn't take her out into deep water and scuttle her.

Captain Shellenbarger: Well, if they'd gotten out into deep water, I'm sure the British would have been waiting for them.

Paul Stillwell: Well, and then he probably would have lost more crew members.

Captain Shellenbarger: Lost a lot more, yes. That was the 17th of December when it was scuttled, so it was within two or three weeks later that we were there.

Paul Stillwell: Were there safety concerns in going on board?

Captain Shellenbarger: I think that was part of the reason why there was only the one trip over.

Paul Stillwell: You mentioned Guantanamo in passing. What else happened there besides running along with the St. Louis?

Captain Shellenbarger: You know, it's funny, I can't remember that. I'm sure that that had to be on our way back that we stopped off there, because we got liberty. And the only thing I can remember about it is going ashore and having a baseball game in the heat, and in those days your beer was with 3.2 beer.

Paul Stillwell: I take it that you did not get to Havana.

Captain Shellenbarger: This is something I didn't mention. I was in Havana on the Herbert.

Paul Stillwell: Do tell.

Captain Shellenbarger: As a matter of fact, in the album there's a picture of the Herbert going in past Morro Castle, and this was on one of our middie cruises. We had two or three days of liberty, and we were greeted with open arms. We tied up at a commercial dock, one of the commercial lines that had regular runs to Havana, and the dock was free because their ships were elsewhere, and it's the same outfit that ran the Morro Castle.*

Paul Stillwell: Ward Line, I think.

Captain Shellenbarger: Ward Line, yes. And later on they called it AGWI Lines. There again, when we went ashore for liberty, we rode on a train out into their sugar fields. We went to what I think was a rum distillery, and it was a tour that had been put on by the officials for the crew and the middies and everybody. I don't remember too much more about it but walking along the seashore and the waterfront. In those days—this was

---

* On 8 September 1934 the burning passenger liner Morro Castle went aground at Asbury Park, New Jersey. In all 134 people died on board the ship; arson was suspected as the cause of the fire.

1939—the city was clean, and it was well run. Nothing of any great incident there, other than the fact that I was there. Another time we went into Santiago with one of our cruises with the Herbert.

Paul Stillwell: You sure did a lot of steaming during your brief time on board.

Captain Shellenbarger: Yes, we did a lot of steaming. We went into Santiago, and, there again, I had some pictures. I think it's still in that album, because my wife saw it, and I remember that the natives in Santiago didn't like to have their picture taken, and we took them. All I can remember is I snapped the picture. The girl lifted her skirt up over her face [laughter], and she was wearing nothing below the waist. And I've got the picture in the album. As a matter of fact there's one of the pictures in there is, as I recall, was one of our outings in Buenos Aires coming back from the barbecues. A bunch of us were coming back on the bus, and we had a hell of job talking because we'd consumed a lot of beer. And we had a hell of a job convincing the bus driver that we had to stop and go take a leak. Here was this line of sailors, and I stood there with my stupid camera taking pictures. [Laughter] Oh, I tell you.

Paul Stillwell: Well, I think one of the appeals of Havana back then is casino gambling, which wasn't available in the United States.

Captain Shellenbarger: It probably was, but, of course, that was no concern of ours.

Paul Stillwell: Not on $54.00 a month.

Captain Shellenbarger: Well, no it wasn't. No, by the time you paid for your clothing and your other—what in the hell did they call it? On a merchant ship we called it a slop chest.

Paul Stillwell: Small stores?

Captain Shellenbarger: Small stores. Yes, small stores. And, of course, on the Helena and the battleship we always had a gedunk stand that charged.* We didn't pay cash, as I recall. No, because that was deducted from your pay.

Paul Stillwell: Did you have chits?

Captain Shellenbarger: We had chits. That's right. Yes, I recall that, because on some of the British gas ships I've worked in more recent years, the skipper said if you wanted wine or beer or anything like that he gave us chits, because that's the way they handled it on those ships.

Paul Stillwell: What about after you got back from the cruise? What happened then?

Captain Shellenbarger: Well, the Helena was transferred to the West Coast in 1940. I was approached, and they said that, "You will have to extend your enlistment or reenlist. Otherwise we will transfer you to an East Coast vessel." I had a lot of thought about it. Should I stay with the ship or not? And there again it's a flip of the coin. You don't know what your life's going to be. So I said, "Well, I guess I'll stay here on the East Coast." That's when I was transferred to the Texas.† And, of course, by that time I was rated, so I went right into the signal gang.

Paul Stillwell: Were you part of the ship's company or the flag allowance?

Captain Shellenbarger: Ship's company. And then, I don't know why, but all of a sudden—it certainly wasn't at my request—I was transferred to the flag. And I don't know whether my records would ever show anything about why or anything, but maybe they just had a vacancy, and the ship's company had an excess of signalman thirds so I was

---

* Gedunk is a Navy slang term for candy, ice cream, and sodas—snack-type food.
† USS Texas (BB-35) was commissioned 12 March 1914. She had a standard displacement of 27,000 tons, was 573 feet long, and 95 feet in the beam. Her top speed was 21 knots. Her main battery comprised ten 14-inch guns, and her secondary battery included 21 5-inch guns. She served in both World Wars and was eventually decommissioned in 1948.

transferred to the flag. And it was while I was with the flag that I immediately was upgraded to a second class signalman.*

Paul Stillwell: You moved up quickly.

Captain Shellenbarger: I moved up fairly fast, yes. Well, of course, this is the beginning of the war when there was a lot of moving up. There were times before that when people had to reenlist in order to make third class.

Paul Stillwell: And in two years you'd made second class.

Captain Shellenbarger: Yes, that's right, so then I was on Admiral Le Breton's enlisted staff in the New York.† I can't remember the chief of staff's name, four-striper. I remember the flag secretary was Malcolm Sylvester.‡ Lieutenant Taylor was the flag lieutenant.§

I remember them so well because on the Texas you had the ship's company's bridge and signal bridge. Then you had the flag bridge. And you had a signalman on watch on the flag bridge, so I was the flag signalman on watch. When the flag secretary or the flag looey would give me a message to be sent, I would have to relay it to the ship's company, because we didn't have any facilities. We didn't have any signal gear up there on the flag bridge. What we did was one hell of a lot of plotting. And, of course, there again was where my quartermaster training on the Herbert came in, because once they found out that I could plot and knew how to use parallel rulers and dividers, they kept me busy.

And what would happen was the Texas or the New York would have four of the new destroyers—the Gleaves class, they called them. Kearny was one of them, 432. They were one of the newer classes and had new sonars. We would cruise around, and we would locate German submarines. They would send by flashing light to us through the

---

* The advancement to second class was on 16 February 1941.
† Rear Admiral David M. Le Breton, USN, Commander Battleship Division Five.
‡ Lieutenant Commander Malcolm D. Sylvester, USN.
§ Lieutenant Ennis W. Taylor, USN.

ship's company signal bridge, come to the flag bridge. We would get the positions of the submarines. I've forgotten what the designation they used, but it was a German sub here. And then—purely by coincidence, you know—we would report to the CNO, "Submarine's located." I was plotting all these latitudes and longitudes of the submarines, and we sent those messages to Annapolis, NAA, in plain language.* Purely by coincidence the British were listening. [Laughter]

Paul Stillwell: Purely by coincidence.

Captain Shellenbarger: But, mind you, while we were up there on Neutrality Patrol we had recognition signals with the British which changed every two hours.† We saw some camouflaged battleship over on the horizon, and he started sending signals. You immediately came up with an answering signal—immediately—because, remember, we were also now wearing camouflage paint. I don't know if you've seen the pictures of the early camouflage paint. The bottom of the hull was painted the dark blue, and then they called it a haze gray on the top part of the hull and the superstructure, which made them hard to see against a horizon.

Paul Stillwell: Well, and also the Atlantic ships, some of them had that kind of a mottled effect with the paint.

Captain Shellenbarger: Yes, but that's what we were wearing at that time, because I know we were challenged a number of times by ships. We'd stumble across a convoy or something like that. Needless to say, when they saw strange vessels, they wanted to know who the hell they were right away fast.

Paul Stillwell: And that gave you a great deal of incentive to identify yourselves so you didn't get blasted.

---

* Annapolis, Maryland, was the site of a Navy radio transmitting and receiving facility.
† In the period from 1939 to 1941—when the United States was not yet an active combatant in World War II—the American republics maintained what was euphemistically called a Neutrality Patrol of a zone in the western Atlantic. Ostensibly neutral, it in fact aided Britain in its war against Germany.

Captain Shellenbarger: You'd better believe it. That's right. And, of course, I can't remember where we were, but I know that we were still at sea when we got word that the Bismarck had left where it had been for a long time.* And I can remember Commander Sylvester was the one, because they discussed these reports in the flag plot up there. And, of course, as a member of the staff you'd hear these things. They were discussing and they'd say, "Well, we'd better get out of here," because we were up around Denmark Straits then.

Paul Stillwell: Were you in the New York at that time?

Captain Shellenbarger: We were in the Texas, because it was just shortly before my getting discharged, so this was in May 1941, and we left in a hurry. And there's a reason I remember it so well, because the destroyers had no problem making speed, but here was a World War I battleship with up-and-down engines, triple-expansion reciprocating engines, and the low-pressure cylinder on that thing was enormous.

Paul Stillwell: I was in that engine room two months ago down in Houston.†

Captain Shellenbarger: Oh. It's unbelievable because we made at least 21 knots. I couldn't believe it, and the vibration was unbelievable, but, boy, we were hurrying. We were headed for Newport. That's where we were based. We got there and, of course, for the preceding couple weeks Commander Sylvester and Lieutenant Taylor would back me in a corner saying, "Come on. Reship. Reship."‡

I said, "No, I'm leaving the Navy."

They really put a lot of pressure on me, and they told me, "Hey, look, you're on the admiral's staff. We will guarantee, reship, you'll be first class within a month, because we

---

* In May 1941, the German battleship Bismarck, accompanied by the cruiser Prinz Eugen, entered the Atlantic to operate as a surface raider. In a gun duel on 24 May against the British, she sank HMS Hood and damaged HMS Prince of Wales. The Bismarck herself was damaged on the 26th by British torpedo planes and sunk on the 27th by gunfire from the British battleships Rodney and King George V.
† The battleship Texas (BB-35) has been a memorial on display in the San Jacinto State Park, near Houston, Texas, since April 1948.
‡ "Reship" or "Ship over" means to reenlist for an additional term of service.

have the ratings assigned now." They knew, because they were the ones that assigned the ratings for the ship. They said, "The staff always came first." If you were on the staff, you got promoted as soon as there was a vacancy. So they said, "We'll guarantee within a month you'll be first class, and within six months you'll be chief." We knew what was going to happen, but, of course, we thought it was going to happen in the Atlantic, because, after all, it was really getting tough up there.

Paul Stillwell: Why were you so reluctant?

Captain Shellenbarger: I had set my heart on getting back with a girlfriend I had been corresponding with. We still visit her. She was my first girlfriend in high school.

Paul Stillwell: Where did she live?

Captain Shellenbarger: She lived in Owego in Tioga County. Her father was superintendent of schools there. I wanted to get out because of her.

Paul Stillwell: Well, our life changes for a variety of reasons.

Captain Shellenbarger: That's right.

Paul Stillwell: Well, we've really made a big jump from 1940 to mid-1941. What goes in between there? Please tell me about Le Breton, for example.

Captain Shellenbarger: Needless to say, I didn't have that much to do with him, but he seemed to be very competent, and he certainly knew his job.

Paul Stillwell: What kind of personality?

Captain Shellenbarger: Very pleasant. Very pleasant. When he'd come on the flag bridge, it wasn't a question of "Attention, everybody." With King it would have been an entirely different story. Now, one of those ships, and I know it was the Texas, because I remember King's remark about the deck, but with Le Breton, he was a very pleasant person. You know, he'd pass the time of day. And due to my interest in radio, I had always carried with me a small short-wave radio receiver. Some of my ham friends would remember the name, but there was something made by a company called National called the Echophone, or maybe National bought it later, but it was a little gray box about this wide, this deep, this high. And I carried that around with me from ship to ship until they banned radios and cameras.

Paul Stillwell: So this was about eight inches square, six inches high?

Captain Shellenbarger: Something like that, and it would receive short wave. When they passed the word, I was on the Texas, and I was in the flag then. This must have been early '41 when they banned them.

Paul Stillwell: Did you carry this in your seabag?

Captain Shellenbarger: Yes, either that or lashed alongside of it, but it had been up in the flag plot, and I remember Lieutenant Taylor came by and he said, "You know they are banned now. This has become the property of the U.S. Navy. It belongs to the admiral's staff." And it stayed there.

Paul Stillwell: I assume you were not compensated for it.

Captain Shellenbarger: Of course not. I was thinking, "I'm lucky I'm not in the brig." [Laughter]

Paul Stillwell: Well, I don't know why there'd be a problem on receiving something; I can see why they wouldn't want you sending.

Captain Shellenbarger: No, no. This was something that came up during the war and I, being a ham radio operator now, I can realize it. I realize that there was a risk even then. A lot of those earlier sets were what they called super-regenerative, and at a certain point on the dial they produced a squeal that could be picked up by directional compass.

Paul Stillwell: Well, that could be equally a problem if it belonged to the Navy as it would be if it belonged to you.

Captain Shellenbarger: I know that, but it stayed up there, and it stayed in use because we listened to shortwave for the fleet. So needless to say, it stayed on the ship when I left. [Laughter] But it was really funny about it. And then later on during the war they put receivers aboard Liberty ships and had all kinds of shielding on them to prevent this.* And, of course, it didn't matter to them, because they were superhets, and they didn't have regenerative squeals anyway.

Paul Stillwell: Well, did you feel a sense of excitement? I mean, you were really closely exposed to the war in these duties.

Captain Shellenbarger: Yes, Neutrality Patrol. I don't think I ever felt any sense of danger of any kind because we weren't at war. We realized that we were doing things that we shouldn't have been doing and that somebody was going to take a shot at us sooner or later. I think that was common knowledge throughout the ships.

Paul Stillwell: Well, which is what happened to the Kearny and the Reuben James.†

---

* The Liberty ship was a mass-produced cargo ship designed by the U.S. Maritime Commission for use by the Allies in World War II. All told, American shipyards built 2,770 Liberties. The standard Liberty was 442 feet long, 57 feet in the beam, and had a light displacement of 3,337 tons. It had a cargo capacity of 10,920 deadweight tons. For details see John Gorley Bunker, Liberty Ships: the Ugly Ducklings of World War II (Annapolis: Naval Institute Press, 1972).
† On 17 October 1941, after depth-charging the suspected location of a German U-boat in the North Atlantic, the destroyer Kearny (DD-432) was torpedoed by a U-boat but survived.

Captain Shellenbarger: And that's what happened to the Kearny and Reuben James. That's right. So we were expecting it in many ways, but, needless to say, we were all young, and we hadn't experienced any of the things that we saw later on during the war.

Paul Stillwell: Well, there must have been at least an implied danger if you were changing recognition signals every two hours.

Captain Shellenbarger: Oh, yes. Definitely. We knew what would happen if we made a boo-boo, and the British had very excellent signalmen. They didn't hesitate to tell us we made a mistake.

Paul Stillwell: Well, in what sort of thing?

Captain Shellenbarger: If we made a mistake in the recognition—I can't remember exactly what they were. Most of them were letter, number, letter changes, and if we made a mistake, we'd get some remark complaining usually, "You bloody Yanks, can't you read the flags?" You know, something like that would come back.

Paul Stillwell: Were there ever cases in which you would send a message by flashing light directly to a British ship to tell them about the Germans?

Captain Shellenbarger: No. No.

Paul Stillwell: Okay. You would not go that far?

Captain Shellenbarger: No, no. We were sending these messages in plain language to NAA, to Annapolis.

Paul Stillwell: Presumably the Germans could pick those up too.

Franklin F. Shellenbarger, Interview #1 (4/28/97) -- Page 66

Captain Shellenbarger: Oh, I'm sure they did, and I'm sure that's one the reasons why they popped the Kearny and the Reuben James, because they knew what we were doing. I mean, how could you help but know it? They listened to them just like anybody else.

Paul Stillwell: Well, you remember in 1939 the German liner Columbus?

Captain Shellenbarger: Yes, the Columbus.

Paul Stillwell: She was trying to get back to Germany, and she was shadowed. I think the crew scuttled her, but they knew the Americans were tipping off the British.

Captain Shellenbarger: Yes. Well, with FDR there was a lot of close relationship with the British, which has always amazed me why Admiral Ernest King was such an Anglophobe, and he was—absolutely.* He cost the lives of many a merchant seaman because he wouldn't accept their recommendations for convoys and escort vessels. And I was fortunate, but this was later on, after I got out of the Navy.

Paul Stillwell: You've mentioned a number of incidents from the Texas with Le Breton. What do you remember from Texas with King on board?†

Captain Shellenbarger: The one thing that I remember about him was the uniform, which he wasn't there personally, of course, but these were his orders as mentioned in his biography.‡ And he mentioned the fact that somebody, he laughed about it and said, "How do you like the Cossack uniform?" Well, those of us who seen the Germans knew that the Germans had a uniform which was white blouse and blue trousers. And our idea was that here was King, trying to make us look like Germans. And, of course, the other fact is that

---

* Franklin D. Roosevelt (FDR) was President of the United States from March 1933 to April 1945.
† On 17 December 1940 as a rear admiral, King became Commander Patrol Force, embarked in the Texas. On 1 February 1941 he was upgraded to four stars as Commander in Chief of the newly designated Atlantic Fleet. In April 1941 he moved his flag from the Texas to the more modern heavy cruiser Augusta (CA-31).
‡ Thomas B. Buell, Master of Sea Power: A Biography of Admiral Ernest J. King (Boston: Little, Brown, 1980).

the only blues we had were heavy serge, and then here we are down in the Caribbean with them. That was one of the things that we experienced with King.

And then, of course, for the admiral's inspection on the Texas it wasn't just ship's company; the rear admiral and the staff were also inspected, and I was on watch on the bridge. When he came up there, I was so shocked that I was speechless, and King talked about the "chicken shit on the deck." Those were his words exactly. I don't even recall where it was at, other than the fact that he came on the bridge. I can't remember too well why, because this was down on the ship's signal bridge, because we didn't have that red mastic on the flag bridge.

Paul Stillwell: Is that like a non-skid material?

Captain Shellenbarger: It's like a non-skid material. As I recall, they put it on hot and then it sort of hardened.

Paul Stillwell: Sort of like terrazzo?

Captain Shellenbarger: Something like that, yes. And what had happened, when they were stripping the ship they'd taken up all the teak decks, and they'd chipped all this paint that had been accumulating since World War I. And a lot of this paint had gotten into the deck, and rather than remove the deck it had stayed there, and so the red deck was mottled with paint chips, and we hadn't done anything about it. And he came on and he was going around looking here and checking for things. It was a white-glove inspection, and he turned around to me, "Who's the watch supervisor?"

"I am, sir."

He says, "What's this chicken shit on deck?"

And I told him. I said, "It's paint chips."

"Hmm!" That was it. That was the only conversation I ever had with him. Of course, the feelings had been very strongly about the uniforms. We'd heard that the medical officers had really raised hell about it because it was wearing heavy serge in the

Caribbean and heat. You don't have any air-conditioning on these ships. We had the blue trousers from our uniforms.

Paul Stillwell: The ones with the 13 buttons?

Captain Shellenbarger: The 13-button job.

Paul Stillwell: And you had a white jumper with that?

Captain Shellenbarger: And we had our white jumper with it.

Paul Stillwell: Now, was King was on board the Texas in the tropics?

Captain Shellenbarger: He was there. He was down there. At that time I think he had become Commander in Chief of the Atlantic Fleet.

Paul Stillwell: Yes, he was in early '41, yes.

Captain Shellenbarger: That's right. He'd been just recently named Commander in Chief of the Atlantic Fleet, and Le Breton was in command of the battleships in the Atlantic. There were only three battleships there, because the Wyoming was a target ship. King wasn't on the Texas when I was there. This was strictly Le Breton, and with Le Breton we went from the Texas to the New York to the "Arky" and back to the Texas. This incident about the deck was when he came to the Texas for an admiral's inspection

Paul Stillwell: Well, you've described a number of things from the Texas. What do you remember separately about the New York and the Arkansas?

Captain Shellenbarger: We had pretty good quarters on the New York, same as the Texas.* That wasn't too bad. Of course, the Texas, being fitted for a flag it had accommodations for the enlisted flag personnel, and I can't remember how many there were. There couldn't have been more than seven or eight officers and maybe, you know, there was a flag yeoman. There couldn't have been more than 20, 25 of us enlisted men, and I know that the Texas had quarters for us, and so did the New York, but the Texas had a flag bridge where the New York didn't.

Paul Stillwell: The Texas had previously been the U.S. Fleet flagship, so that's why she would have had better accommodations.

Captain Shellenbarger: Accommodations, yes, because I know that when we went on the Arkansas, there they dumped us down in one of the old original coal bunkers, which had high overheads.† On that one we had to sleep in cots. Didn't have bunks or anything. But I don't think we ever spent more than three weeks or four weeks on the "Arky."

Paul Stillwell: What would be the occasion for moving from one ship to another?

Captain Shellenbarger: Primarily because the other ship, I guess, had some other assignment or something or other. I don't know the reason why, and this was something the enlisted man doesn't know. He goes where he's told to go. That's what it amounts to.

Paul Stillwell: When would you say chronologically that incident happened with Admiral King inspecting the flag bridge of the Texas?

---

* USS New York (BB-34) was commissioned 15 April 1914. She had a standard displacement of 27,000 tons, was 573 feet long, and 95 feet in the beam. Her top speed was 21 knots. She was armed with ten 14-inch guns, 16 5-inch guns, and eight 3-inch guns. She was eventually decommissioned in 1946 after service in World War II.
† USS Arkansas (BB-33) was commissioned 17 September 1912. Following modernization in 1925-26 she had a standard displacement of 26,100 tons, was 562 feet long and 106 feet in the beam. Her top speed was 21 knots. She was armed with 12 12-inch guns and 16 5-inch guns. She was the oldest U.S. battleship in active service during World War II, eventually being decommissioned in 1946.

Captain Shellenbarger: It had to be in the spring of '41. Had to be because by that time he was, you know, Commander of the Atlantic Fleet.

Paul Stillwell: And you left not too long after that.

Captain Shellenbarger: I left not too long after that, so it was in a very short period of time.

Paul Stillwell: Did all these three ships have similar duties when you were on board?

Captain Shellenbarger: On the Arkansas I know we didn't make any patrols. With the Texas I think we made two or three patrols. They never lasted more than two or three weeks. On the New York we made one up in the North Atlantic, and the "Arky" I can't remember because we didn't go up there. And the thing that I liked about the "Arky" was you didn't have the vibration. The "Arky" had turbines, the old Parsons turbines.

Paul Stillwell: Even though she was an older ship.

Captain Shellenbarger: She was an older ship, yes. Of course, I didn't realize till years later all the difference it makes with the way the ship rides and feels.

Paul Stillwell: Did you ever go down into the engine room of the Texas when she was under way?

Captain Shellenbarger: I think I was down once or twice.

Paul Stillwell: Was it noisy?

Captain Shellenbarger: Quite noisy, yes.

Paul Stillwell: That's probably sort of like the gunnery experience you described that the Navy really didn't concern itself with hearing protection at that time.

Captain Shellenbarger: No, no. I know they didn't, and all this time I never saw anybody with ear protectors. I know we never had ear protectors.

Paul Stillwell: It was probably viewed as not being very manly if you did something like that.

Captain Shellenbarger: I don't doubt that. Probably what would happen then. I don't doubt it.

Paul Stillwell: Did you have better chow being part of the flag?

Captain Shellenbarger: No. No. We ate the same thing as the ship's company. Beans for breakfast on Wednesday and Saturday.

Paul Stillwell: Corn bread too?

Captain Shellenbarger: Corn bread too.

Paul Stillwell: Where were those ships homeported while you were on board? The New York, I think, was out of Norfolk.

Captain Shellenbarger: I think it was, yes. The Texas was out of Newport. That's where I was discharged, and when I signed off there they gave me transportation from Newport back to Buffalo.

Paul Stillwell: And I think Newport was where the Augusta was for a while when King had her, and the Constellation, which you've described, was there as a relief flagship.

Captain Shellenbarger: Yes, I know that I read somewhere that he used the Constellation as a flagship. Well, so I assumed that they just used the name, and they were actually based ashore, because I know there were no eating facilities or toilet facilities aboard the Constellation. I've often wondered what they ever did with it, and I understand that the thing fell apart finally down in Baltimore. Not even afloat. Is it afloat anymore?

Paul Stillwell: Well, she was recently towed into dry dock for repairs, and, of course, the more they do to her the less she is like the one built in the 1800s.

Captain Shellenbarger: Well, look at the job they just did on the Constitution and how much money that cost.[*] They practically rebuilt the ship. I'm the president of the Marine Society of New York, also a member of the Boston Marine Society, and I go to their annual dinner every year. Have been for the last five or six years. And invariably on the dais my wife and myself were seated next to the captain of the Constitution, and the one that we got quite friendly with through the four years in a row was a fellow name of Dave Cashman.[†] We used to joke about it because I told him what a dead-end career, once you became captain of the Constitution you know you're on your way out. [Laughter] And he would say, "Well, look at all the opportunities I have to do a little networking up here."

In his case I think he did because I think he ended up on the governor's staff because you have to attend all these social functions. And I said, "It's an ideal position to be in. As long as you've got to go, you might as well—" He always looks us up when we come up each time, and we're due up there the 13th of May. Dave used to come in regular naval uniform. There was another one who wore a dress uniform of the Revolution, I guess.

Paul Stillwell: Tyrone Martin?[‡]

---

[*] USS Constitution, a wood-hull frigate launched in 1797, gained fame in the War of 1812 as "Old Ironsides." To this day she is maintained at Boston as a commissioned ship of the U.S. Navy.
[†] Commander David M. Cashman, USN, commanded the frigate Constitution, 1987-91.
[‡] Commander Tyrone G. Martin, USN, commanded the frigate Constitution, 1974-78. He is also the author of A Most Fortunate Ship: A Narrative History of Old Ironsides (Annapolis: Naval Institute Press, 1997.)

Captain Shellenbarger: I think that's it. I don't know whether we got a picture of it or not, but it's interesting, to say the least. I've often hoped to get the time to go over and see the Constitution, having spent those weeks aboard the Constellation. You see, the Boston Marine Society's based right there, right in the old navy yard. The Boston Marine Society is in the old Shawmut Bank Building. Tip O'Neill, being an honorary member of the Boston Marine Society, when they made a National Park out of the old Charlestown Navy Yard, somebody said, "Well, what are we going to do with this old bank building?"* It became the headquarters of the Boston Marine Society. No rent. All they do is pay for the electricity and telephone.

Paul Stillwell: It's intriguing to think that you were in the Navy from 1938 to 1941, and you served in one of the newest ships in the fleet in the Helena, the Texas from World War I, the Herbert from not much after World War I, the Seattle from practically the turn of the century, and the Constellation from the 19th century.

Captain Shellenbarger: [Laughter] Yes, that is when you stop and look at it that way.

Paul Stillwell: That is a variety of experience.

Captain Shellenbarger: It is. A variety is right.

Paul Stillwell: Well, what other highlights do you have to wrap up your naval service?

Captain Shellenbarger: As far as my naval service is concerned, I think that just about covers it. Oh, probably if I stopped and really went back through it, I probably might remember little incidents here and there, but it's like I suddenly remembered about the Herbert, you know, going into Havana and things like that. But right off of the top of my head I can't think of anything particularly about my naval career.

---

* Thomas P. "Tip" O'Neill (Democrat-Massachusetts), was Speaker of the U.S. House of Representatives, 1977-87.

Paul Stillwell: Did you ever afterward have any regrets that you had not taken their offer and stayed in the Navy at that point?

Captain Shellenbarger: No, I don't think so. I don't think I ever had any regrets to that effect. After I got out of the Navy, came home, still with this affair. I went to work for Glenn Martin, following up my secondary love of electronics, which wasn't electronics in those days; it was electricity and radio. And I went to work for Glenn Martin, Middle River, Maryland.

Paul Stillwell: Doing what?

Captain Shellenbarger: I actually worked on Norden bombsights.[*] I got a security clearance because of my Navy time, my honorable discharge, which I had to produce for— I don't know who the hell they were, the Secret Service, whoever it was gave me the clearance for it anyway. I must have been a year there, because after the war started I went back to the naval recruiting station.

They said, "Well, there's no urgency right now. Stay where you're at. You're in an essential war industry." Which I was. I was building B-26s by that time, the twin-engine Martin Marauder. And I had been in final assembly, and then my supervisor had been transferred to final checkout. We were at the airport, and that's where we got involved in the bombsight, because when the ships came off the assembly line they were flown first by Martin's test pilot. His crew chief acted as copilot.

And then I made a number of flights, or there might be a hydraulics man or whatever. I was in what they called the electrical division, and I'd have to be working on generators, bomb systems, lighting systems. Later on, they put the twin .50-caliber machineguns up in the turret on the top. They had some kind of device, copper rails around the Bakelite inserts that would stop the firing of the guns when you came across your tail.

---

[*] The Norden bombsight was a precision optical device developed in the early 1930s by Carl L. Norden, a civilian consultant employed by the Navy, together with Lieutenant Frederick L. Entwistle. Its gyro-stabilized automatic pilot kept the bomber straight and level during bomb runs. It was used in both Navy and Army bombers in the 1930s and 1940s.

Paul Stillwell: Cut-out cams.

Captain Shellenbarger: Cut-outs. Right. And there was a lot of stuff like that, and then later on they made a modification just before I left that they put twin .50s right in the tail. We used to have to check out the bomb releases and stuff like that, and so we'd have to make test flights before they were turned over to the Army, which was the Army Air Forces then, for their test flights.

We got a book like this, check out items whether it was electrical, hydraulics, various things that had to be checked out. Plus the fact that I had to check out instruments. And, of course, then if an instrument was bad, you just pulled it out and put a new one in. They didn't take any Norden bombsights up there, but I guess you're aware how those bombsights work.

Paul Stillwell: Not specifically.

Captain Shellenbarger: Once you're set up to drop either a salvo, which is all your bombs, or a stick, which is maybe 20 100-pounders, your instructions tell you whether to drop them 100 yards apart, 300 yards apart, or whatever. So you had this device that they called a salvo meter. It wasn't a salvo meter because a salvo was a big red button, and you dropped everything at once. But when you dropped everything at once you had to make sure your bottom ones dropped first so that they would be clear for the ones in the top of the rack to come down. So this was, you know, part of the job there. And they had this device which fitted into the bracket when we flew where the Norden bombsight went, because what happened once the bombardier said he was lined up and they were all set up with their coordinates to where they're going to bomb, the bombsight was an autopilot, and it flew the plane. Then all you did was flip the switch, and the bombsight kept track of where you were going, and it released the bombs in the rotation you wanted. So that's the way the thing worked.

Paul Stillwell: Where were the bombsights being manufactured?

Captain Shellenbarger: I haven't the vaguest idea, because all I knew was that they were in a huge vault. We had this dummy thing that we used to simulate it. It was sufficient to test out all the adjacent gear, but they didn't put the bombsight in it until it was actually delivered to the Army Air Forces. And then they had this huge vault that they'd bring them out with an armed guard and take them out to the plane. The plane would take off, and then we didn't see it anymore.

Paul Stillwell: Where was the vault?

Captain Shellenbarger: It was in Middle River.[*]

Paul Stillwell: I'm surprised that they didn't turn over the plane without the bombsight and let the Army install it.

Captain Shellenbarger: I don't know. They said that the guys were going out to the plane with the bombsight because, I don't know, maybe they were flying them till they used the fuel up, and I don't know where they were flying to, but they were gone as far as we were concerned.

Paul Stillwell: Did your girlfriend move down from New York to Baltimore to be with you?

Captain Shellenbarger: Of course, I was working a lot of overtime, but when I got a day off I went to see her in Oneonta, where she was in school. I would drive up there, be there maybe four or five hours, turn right around a drive back.

Paul Stillwell: Tough romance.

Captain Shellenbarger: [Laughter] Oh, it was tough, because she met a dentist while she was at school, and all of a sudden I was dumped. [Laughter] Maybe that's why I decided

---

[*] Middle River, Maryland, a suburb of Baltimore, was the site of the Glenn L. Martin Company.

to go back to sea. No, that wasn't it. The draft board was saying, "Well, you're in an essential war industry, but you have to register every three or four months." So I went back to the Navy recruiting office in Baltimore. I met a chief there, and, here again, one guy influences your whole life.

He said, "You've been out too long now. You'll have to go back in the Navy as a second class signalman. Why don't you go across the hall and sign up with the Maritime Service?"

Paul Stillwell: Well, you had been a second class signalman, so you weren't going to lose anything.

Captain Shellenbarger: I wasn't going to lose anything, but he said if I'd been out less than 90 days they'd have taken me back in as first class. And he told me, "Just go across the hall and sign up the Maritime Service. They'll send you to school. You'll get a commission in the Naval Reserve. You'll come out of there as an ensign."

I said, "You know, that sounds better than being a second class signalman."

He said, "Not only that, but you'll get a license as a third mate."

I said, "What the hell's a third mate?"

He said, "Well, you'll be an officer in the merchant marine."

Well, I finished the school in Fort Trumbull, and I had my commission as ensign, I had my license as third mate. Out of 400 I think I was number 25 in scholastic standing. And my navigation instructor, who was also my platoon or section commander, said, "This school is being turned over to the War Shipping Administration instead of the Coast Guard." Because when I was there it was Coast Guard operated. He said, "We need instructors, and we would like to have you stay as a navigation instructor."

And, of course, being patriotic, I said, "Wherever you need me," and I became a navigation instructor. Probably why I'm here today. I wasn't out there getting shot at.

Paul Stillwell: That's right. My guess is that you got paid a lot more by Glenn Martin than you did as a second class signalman by the Navy.

Captain Shellenbarger: Oh, yes. [Laughter]

Paul Stillwell: Do you remember what the figures are?

Captain Shellenbarger: No, I don't remember really. All I know is that I lived in a boarding house on Hamilton Avenue. There were 12 of us, ten men and two women, living in this boarding house at 3100 Hamilton Avenue. The lady who ran the place was Daisy Hahn, and I can remember so well that Sunday afternoon of December 7 her banging on the door saying, "We're at war with the Japs."[*] And I had only turned in, I guess, about three hours before that because we worked overtime. I was third shift: started at 11:00 at night and worked till 7:00 in the morning. I usually worked till about 9:00, and if there was any flying that morning that they wanted to work overtime on a plane.

We didn't get flight pay. We just got straight overtime for the flying in those planes. And, of course, to this day I've often wondered how many of them were in flying condition. They came right off the final assembly line, and then a lot of times when we flew them it was the first time the things had ever flown. I know that on one of them the landing gear collapsed on us at it was taking off down there. Everybody got out of it, but the thing went up in a ball of flames. The gear collapsed, and the Martin Marauder used a four-bladed propeller, and I can remember so well looking at those propellers. They looked like swastikas.

Paul Stillwell: Well, you figure every once in a while there's going to be a lemon among those airplanes.

Captain Shellenbarger: Yes, and you hope it isn't the one you're flying on.

---

[*] In late November 1941, the Imperial Japanese Navy dispatched from the Kurile Islands in the North Pacific a task force built around six aircraft carriers. A force of some 350 fighters, dive-bombers, and torpedo planes attacked U.S. military installations on the island of Oahu, Hawaii, on Sunday, 7 December 1941. The principal focus of attack was the collection of American warships at the naval base at Pearl Harbor. The U.S. Congress declared war on Japan the following day.

Paul Stillwell: Well, this has been a fascinating interview, Captain, and I look forward to getting together with you in the future to hear more of your story.

Captain Shellenbarger: Well, if you think it's interesting.

Paul Stillwell: It certainly is to me. Thank you.

Interview No. 2 with Captain Franklin F. Shellenbarger, U.S. Maritime Service (Retired)
Place: U.S. Naval Institute, Annapolis, Maryland
Date: Wednesday, 11 June 1997
Interviewer: Paul Stillwell

Paul Stillwell: Well, Captain, I appreciate your coming to Annapolis on an early summer day so we can renew this series of interviews. We had talked last time about your naval service in several ships in a relatively short time and then going to work for the Glenn Martin Aircraft Company. Do you have any things to fill in from that first period?

Captain Shellenbarger: No, not that I recall. I've gone back through a number of things. I don't think there were any items that I neglected in the first interview. I'm surprised I remember as much as I do.

Paul Stillwell: What sort of plans did you have at that stage in your life, and how did the war affect those plans?

Captain Shellenbarger: Well, as I indicated before, the reason I left the Navy was the intention of getting a job ashore in a wartime industry and continue my relationship with my girlfriend, whom I had gone high school with. I thought that things were going fine; when I was working at Glenn Martin, she was going to school. Her whole family were schoolteachers. Ended up they were all superintendents or principals of schools and lived a remarkably long life. We joke about it now, because I still see her. I think I mentioned that I visited her and her husband.

But, to put it bluntly, she dumped me—it must have been sometime in either late '42 or '43—for someone that she was going to school with. That was Dr. Lee, a dentist. They've had a very happy marriage, which I'm really happy about, for 50 years now. I visit them at high school reunions; that's where we got reacquainted some years ago. She, unfortunately, had a stroke five years ago, and she's in a wheelchair now. We visited last August, and we'll see them again the end of this month because we stop over in this small town where I graduated from high school, Owego, New York. We went to the Owego Free Academy.

Paul Stillwell: How long did your job last with Martin?

Captain Shellenbarger: It lasted until September 1942, and that rather surprised me when I went back looking at records. It was what they called an essential wartime industry. As I told you before, I was working on bombsights. I was working for this particular supervisor, fellow name of Earl Billbrough. He was the one who had taken me from final assembly out to the airport, and I guess I must have been doing a pretty good job, because he wanted me to stay. I found the work intensely interesting but, of course, I felt that with my three and a half years at sea this wasn't exactly the place for me.

I'd already signed up with the Maritime Service previously, and I was waiting for a call from them. They called me and said that the next class was convening at Fort Trumbull in New London, Connecticut. They were setting up the school as a maritime officers' training school, and in the beginning it was operated by the Coast Guard.

Paul Stillwell: That would explain New London.

Captain Shellenbarger: See, that would be it. As a matter of fact, when I went in there we had a number of Coast Guard officers, and we had U.S. Naval Reserve officers who were Merchant Marine Reserve as instructors. I think it was this transition period that things weren't running too smoothly. I went up in September '42, and I graduated in January '43 with my commission as an ensign in the Naval Reserve. At that time they'd completed the transition from Coast Guard to WSA or Maritime Service School. It was called United States Maritime Service Officers' School, which was a division of the WSA, War Shipping Administration.

I remember a couple of my friends that were Naval Reserve officers had been called from there. They became skippers of LSTs and vessels of that class, where most of the merchant marine people ended up.* I do know a couple of exceptions—one became a DE skipper—but that's where most of them ended up.†

Paul Stillwell: Why don't you tell me something about the curriculum and the training please? They were taking a bombsight man and making a merchant marine officer out of him.

Captain Shellenbarger: [Laughter] Well, this was where my Navy training served, the fact that I'd qualified in group A school as a signalman, as a quartermaster, as well as a radioman. As I indicated before, when I went on the Herbert I learned everything in a hell of a hurry, because the first class quartermaster, Alonzo Dunham, made sure I did.

Paul Stillwell: What was the format at Fort Trumbull? A lot of classroom work? Did you have hands-on training?

Captain Shellenbarger: There was some hands-on training, but primarily it was classroom work. My section leader, Bill Hurder, was head of the navigation department when I was in training. Afterward he personally asked me to stay on as a navigation instructor, because apparently I did very well, primarily because of the training I'd had in the Navy. Because even though I was a so-called signalman, when I was on the Herbert I was everything because you stood the quartermaster watch on the bridge. You had to know how to do azimuths. You had to take bearings. You had to maintain position in formation with the stadimeter and range finder. I wonder if they still have those hand-held range finders they used to have. But they worked.

Paul Stillwell: I don't know.

Captain Shellenbarger: They mounted in a U-shaped bracket. Now today it's radar.

---

* LST—tank landing ship, an amphibious warfare ship capable of putting her bow directly onto a beach, opening bow doors, and lowering a bow ramp to permit vehicles to exit.
† DE—destroyer escort, a type of ship used primarily for antisubmarine warfare during World War II.

Paul Stillwell: Who were your cohorts in the course? Were they mostly people straight out of civilian life?

Captain Shellenbarger: I would say most of them were seamen who had had at least three years' deck time on merchant vessels. Some of them had had this time previously. They had gone ashore and had come back to the sea, because there was a great demand for seamen, of course. You know, with a couple of thousand Liberty ships you had to have men for them.

Paul Stillwell: How demanding was the course of study?

Captain Shellenbarger: For me I didn't consider it that demanding, but for many of the students it was. In particular, I know that I had at least four hours' classroom instructing during the day. As a matter of fact, I've still got pictures of some of the models and things we used for Rules of the Road. And, of course, there was a lot of blackboard time, a lot of workbook. Remember, in those days we were teaching longitude by time sight, Ageton, and it seems to me that we did teach some 214 but not too much that I recall.

But there were four hours in the classroom each day, and then, of course, because it was semi-military we'd have a certain amount of PT.* And usually in the evening after everybody had had the meals and everything, I would have to tutor, usually from about 8:00 P.M. to 11:00 P.M. I would be tutoring students who were falling behind on their grades, not because of lack of wanting to succeed, but primarily because of their school systems where they'd been trained.

We were having people in there who hadn't completed high school, and I remember one fellow in particular who was so upset working with logarithms; he said, "Oh, all I know is decimals."

I said, "Come on. Look. You know dollars and cents. Don't tell me you don't know decimals." You know, that kind of thing. So it was quite a bit of that.

And, of course, Saturdays we used to have parades. I don't know why, but we had parades. And then the underwater sound lab next door came over and decided to use our

---

* PT—physical training.

parade ground for testing out the Hedgehogs, so that put an end to the Saturday parades, which everybody was happy about.* [Laughter]

Paul Stillwell: I'm sure they were. Well, I presume you got trained just in the deck aspects, not the engineering.

Captain Shellenbarger: Not in the engineering, no. Deck aspects: seamanship, navigation, signaling. Of course being a former Navy signalman that was no problem.

Paul Stillwell: What about ship handling? Any of that?

Captain Shellenbarger: Not so much ship handling. You got very little ship handling. During the period I was there, I would say we took our sections and we rowed out on Long Island Sound to a couple of training vessels that they had, and I think they were called the American Seaman and the American Mariner. I don't know what they were. They were Liberty hulls, and I don't know whether they designed them and built them that way or not, but they had quarters aboard for students. The school was using them as training vessels, primarily, I think, for training unlicensed personnel. But they brought them up there to New London so that some of our people could go out and get a little bit of bridge time but relatively little. They learned on the job.

Paul Stillwell: Did you get anything on cargo handling and stowage?

Captain Shellenbarger: They had courses in cargo handling, which I was not involved in when I was training. When I was a student, we got a certain amount of it but not a great deal. No.

Paul Stillwell: How regimented was the atmosphere?

---

* Hedgehog, developed in World War II, was a British-designed spigot mortar that fired its weapons out ahead of the attacking ship. It was the first ASW weapon that could be fired while the surface ship remained in sonar contact with the target. Its name came from the collection of spigots in the launcher; they stuck up like porcupine quills.

Captain Shellenbarger: As a former Navy man I considered it very unregimented, but these merchant seamen squawked. For them it was different, but it had to be that way when you had a large group like that.

Paul Stillwell: Did you get any liberty in New London?

Captain Shellenbarger: I spent a little time in New London. I had a friend of mine who'd been torpedoed. He was with Alcoa.* His father had been a skipper, and he'd gone to sea with his father. This was one the things I was trying to remember and all of a sudden it clicked. His name was Bill Martino, and he was sort of a buddy of mine. The only time we got off was on Sunday afternoon, and he and I used to ride a bicycle over to Mystic. They were just starting to build Mystic Seaport at the time.† There wasn't much there, but it was a nice ride up and down the little hills, and it was good exercise.

Paul Stillwell: Did you have any contact with the Navy submariners there in New London?

Captain Shellenbarger: None whatsoever. No, none whatsoever. We'd see the submarines occasionally in the river, but that was all. I did make a couple of friends. While I was in New London, I joined the Masonic Lodge and, of course, there were quite a few of them from the sub base at the lodge, Union Lodge 31, of which I'm now a 55-year member.

Paul Stillwell: What kind of payroll were you on then? Was the War Shipping Administration financing this effort?

Captain Shellenbarger: The War Shipping Administration, yes. The commanding officer when I first went there was Commander Bosworth, U.S. Naval Reserve, and he was on

---

* Alcoa—Aluminum Company of America.
† Mystic Seaport is a tourist attraction that focuses on the sailing-ship era in the nation's history.

active duty as commanding officer. I talked to him several times, not too much, of course. He'd been chief engineer on Astor's yacht, John Jacob Astor's yacht, the Nourmahal. He was the one I went to when I wanted to get in the Navy. Between him and Bill Hurder, they convinced me to stay there, and then within six months they froze us in our jobs. It took a lot of finagling to get out of there. [Laughter]

Paul Stillwell: Did you have a concern as you read the statistics about all the sinkings of merchant ships in the Atlantic?

Captain Shellenbarger: We didn't get any of those statistics. We didn't hear anything. Nothing. Nobody knew anything about this until after the war.

Paul Stillwell: Nothing in the newspapers?

Captain Shellenbarger: Nothing in the newspapers. An occasional sinking here. There was one that happened within sight of the beach where, you know, the public knew about it, but it wasn't on the radio. It wasn't broadcast nationwide. The only thing I heard was when I'd get an occasional letter from one of my guys that had been in one of my early sections. He would send me a letter saying primarily, "Hey look, I'm going to get my chief mate's license and you've only got a third mate's license."

That's why I wanted to get out of there, because I wanted to raise my license. I didn't want to end up the war as an ensign and a third mate with no time on his license. That went back to even years before when I tried to get into the nautical college in Fort Schuyler. I figured, "Well, I want to go to sea, and if I'm going to go to sea and can't be a radioman, I might as well try and eventually someday be a captain. Who knows?" [Laughter]

Paul Stillwell: Well, it sounds good for morale purposes that you didn't know how bad it was out in the Atlantic.

Captain Shellenbarger: I would say definitely yes. Definitely, for morale purposes. I think that was one of the principal reasons for their keeping it quiet, because they certainly didn't lack for applicants to the school. Of course, a lot of these people who came in were already wearing torpedo pins, because a lot of them had already been torpedoed. Especially in the classes when I was there at the end of my time. I left in June '44, so it was practically a year and a half I was there.

Paul Stillwell: Did you have the option of getting a Naval Reserve commission when you came out of the training?

Captain Shellenbarger: We did have Navy training in our classes and someone—I'm trying to remember who—gave us a lot of indoctrination. I had to laugh because they were teaching us to be ensigns, but they were working right out of The Bluejackets' Manual. I had a lot of talk with the naval instructor; he was a lieutenant jaygee, Merchant Marine Reserve, of course, a fellow by the name of Jack Cooney. And I told him, "I went through this in boot camp in 1938."

He said, "Well, we've got to teach it." And, of course, it was necessary because with the third mate's license we got a commission as ensign.

Paul Stillwell: I take it you didn't want to go on active duty as an ensign.

Captain Shellenbarger: Yes, I did. I wanted to go on active duty as an ensign, but Commander Ford and Bill Hurder said, "Hold off, hold off." And then when I did, later on they said, "Oh, you're frozen in your job. The government has frozen everybody here. You can't leave."

So I went to another friend of mine, a brother Mason. He was the head of the seamanship department, a fellow name of Bill Porter, who I had become friendly with. And he was a commander from the Maritime Service. He had been a former port captain with Esso in Aruba. And not only myself, but one of the fellows who had been an instructor in the seamanship department who had a master's license, a fellow by the name Tom Bown. He said, "Well, Tom is getting released. He is going to Panama City, Florida, to pick up a new ship, John R. McQuigg. And don't ask me who John R. McQuigg was, because with 2,600 Liberty ships who knows who all these people were?* Some of the names ring a bell. Later on I was on the Reverdy Johnson, named for one of the signers of the Declaration of Independence.

But he said, "Tom Bown is going there, and he's looking for somebody as a second mate."

I said, "I don't have a second mate's license."

He said, "Don't worry about it. Everybody's getting a waiver going one grade higher because there's such a shortage." So actually I did have to sign on on the John McQuigg as third mate. That's when we went to Florida in June 1944.

Paul Stillwell: Do you have anything to relate about the period when you were an instructor?

Captain Shellenbarger: Well, I put a lot of hours in. That's all I can say briefly.

Paul Stillwell: Mostly in classroom lectures?

Captain Shellenbarger: Classroom lectures, giving tests, correcting papers, and the tutoring. Bill Martino was another navigation instructor, so we had pretty much the same hours. I think I had the first two hours in the morning, because our classes started at 8:00 to 10:00 and then the next class was 10:00 to 12:00, and then I had from 1300 to 1500. They were different sections, so you taught navigation to one section in the morning and then another section in the afternoon. Sections were, as I recall, about 28 to 30 men. Then there would be an extra hour or so teaching Rules of the Road to some other section. But I don't really recall anything, other than the fact that it was work. Put in a lot of hours, but I'd say I enjoyed it.

Paul Stillwell: Even though you would have rather been somewhere else.

---

* John R. McQuigg served in the U.S. Army in the Spanish-American War and World War I. Following World War I he was a brigadier general in the Ohio National Guard. He served as mayor of East Cleveland from 1907 to 1913 and was the first Ohio-born Commander of the American Legion.

Captain Shellenbarger: Even though I'd rather been somewhere else and, of course, looking back today I think well, gee, how fortunate I was to be there instead of out there getting shot at, but that's the way the ball bounces.

Paul Stillwell: Well, and you had taken the option of going there, even though you had a safe place back at Glenn Martin.

Captain Shellenbarger: Well, that's true, I suppose. Of course, I know the thing at Glenn Martin wouldn't have lasted, not with my three and a half years at sea. I know that Martin had to send letters to the draft board so they'd keep my classification of whatever it was to keep me there.

Paul Stillwell: How highly motivated were the students you observed when you were an instructor?

Captain Shellenbarger: I would say very highly motivated. They all wanted to get back out there, and naturally this was an opportunity for them to get out of the forecastle and get an officer's license, which many of them—I would say most of them—desperately wanted. The merchant marine was expanding so fast, and this was one chance in a million for them to do it. They figured, "Well, if I survive the war, I've got it made." That's what it amounted to. And I suppose basically that was my feeling, too, somewhere in the back of my mind.

Of course, there's no question that we were all very much gung ho, which I've got to say today I don't see. I mean, we were all flag wavers, believe me. And when I got aboard ship and saw some of the unlicensed people aboard ship you really had to be. You were seeing guys in their 50s and 60s. Some of them that were color blind; they couldn't make the officer's grade because of it. Later I was on one ship as chief mate, and the purser came around one and said, "Shelley, do you realize what the average age of our crew is?"

I said, "I haven't the vaguest idea. I know I'm one of the youngest."

He said, "The average in this crew is 53." Now, to get an average of 53 I know there were guys in their late 60s. But as long as they were able to do the job, that was all that mattered.

Paul Stillwell: Well, the Navy expanded greatly in the same time, and it took a number of former enlisted men and gave them commissions, so this was a parallel situation.

Captain Shellenbarger: I would say yes. And, of course, when I got aboard ship, by that time all the ships had gun crews. One of the things that was a sore point for us for all the years that we fought to get veteran status, we've got all these things, I've got copies of them myself, things from Harry Truman, FDR, MacArthur saying what a great job the merchant marine did, because we fought right alongside everybody else.[*] It was long ago proved that the merchant marine did not get a lot of extra benefits, in spite of the wartime bonuses in wartime areas, because to start with they had practically no insurance. The minute they were taken prisoner, their pay stopped. The minute your ship was sunk, your pay stopped. And you bought your own clothes.

And a rather bitter thing for me—and I still hold a grudge against it—was the American Red Cross. After that first trip on the McQuigg we got hit by a hurricane; it was in September 1944, and we sustained a lot of damage. Lost two boats, all of our life rafts, half our deck cargo. Went into Halifax, got it resecured, continued on our way. Then we got hit by a submarine wolf pack up north of Ireland.

The ship alongside of us blew up, the Empire Heritage, which we'd been following in column for days. I can remember it was a Norwegian whaler that had been taken over by the British. And, of course, all those ships they took over and renamed they called them Empire ships. This was the Empire Heritage, and it had this big square hole in the stern where they had ramps to pull the whales up. But because they had oil tanks they had loaded her with gasoline and other things in her tanks, using it as, you know, for commercial purposes. And don't ask me how he did it, but somehow in the middle of the night the Heritage was alongside our starboard beam, and I didn't realize till many years

---

[*] Harry S. Truman was President of the United States when World War II ended; Franklin D. Roosevelt was President during much of the war; General of the Army Douglas MacArthur served in the Pacific Theater throughout the war.

later why. Here's the Irish coast and a flashing light over there, the Malin Head lighthouse, bump-bump-bump, silhouetting all the ships. I didn't realize till later that Ireland was neutral.

Paul Stillwell: I didn't either.

Captain Shellenbarger: They were neutral, and that's why they had all their lights and everything was on.

Paul Stillwell: Southern Ireland, I presume.

Captain Shellenbarger: Yes. Because after all Northern Ireland was part of the British Empire. So, anyway, they got inside of us, and the Empire Heritage bought it.* It blew up right alongside of us and did more damage to us. This was one of the things that I saw, considering the fact I went in so late I saw relatively little action. There were air raids and stuff like that, but to have a ship blow up alongside of you, that's why I got one of my ribbons.

Paul Stillwell: Please tell me about that.

Captain Shellenbarger: Well, that's because we were under enemy attack. The merchant marine gave you a ribbon if you were ever under enemy attack. If your ship was sunk, they put a silver star on it, and I've seen people with five silver stars. How they survived five sinkings—it's incredible. With one or two, that you could recognize, but I remember this one fellow. As a matter of fact, I questioned it. I asked somebody else about it. He said, "Oh, no. That was for true."

---

* The tanker Empire Heritage was the former whale factory ship Tafelberg. She was sunk 8 September 1944, with the loss of 113 men, by a German submarine, U-482, which also sank the rescue ship Pinto the same night. These ships were part of convoy HX305, which sailed from New York on 25 August; the convoy survivors arrived at Liverpool on 10 September.

Paul Stillwell: Well, what did that do you psychologically when you saw the Empire Heritage go up?

Captain Shellenbarger: I don't know, really. All I can say is I can remember that we looked back, and we could see the guys with the lights on their life jackets.

Paul Stillwell: Did you see flames on the water from burning fuel?

Captain Shellenbarger: Very little flames that I can recall, but I do remember one of the radio operators saying that this convoy had been greeted by rescue ships that they put astern of the convoy to pick up survivors. Of course, at the beginning of the war they didn't have anything like that, but by that time—September or October 1944—the convoys would get these rescue ships as they approached the coast. And so Sparks said that they probably would get picked up. But we never learned anything more about it, because everything was so hush-hush. Then I think we went into Liverpool and tied up in Birkenhead, just outside of the Mersey.

Paul Stillwell: Were you more uneasy after an experience like that?

Captain Shellenbarger: I don't think so. Certainly not us, not that I observed. I know that we had a couple of guys in the steward's department who failed to join when we left, but maybe they decided that was a reason. You don't know. Sometimes they'd fail to join because they went ashore and got drunk and lost track of time.

Paul Stillwell: I wonder if it's comparable to driving by an accident on the highway. You say, "Sorry it happened, but I've got things to do."

Captain Shellenbarger: "It wasn't me." I would say there probably is a lot to that. You recognize when a ship blows up with ammunition, because obviously it had a lot of ammunition in it, because we got peppered with all kinds of pieces of metal and things. But we'd already lost our starboard boats in the hurricane, and when we went into Halifax they just threw some extra life rafts on board, so I guess that's it. That is, you say, "Well, that wasn't me." And, of course, if you're like us, you know, loaded with maybe 4,000 tons of dynamite, when they hit you, why, that's it.

Paul Stillwell: Were you in a Liberty ship?

Captain Shellenbarger: Yes, Liberty ship. This was the John R. McQuigg.

Paul Stillwell: Could you describe the ship and its accommodations?

Captain Shellenbarger: Of course, I signed on as third mate and been promoted to acting second mate. And by 1944 there was progress in building the ships; for one thing we had a gyro.* A lot of the early ships didn't have gyros because they didn't make enough of them. That was a tremendous godsend to us, believe me. But bridge equipment was the standard hydraulic telemotor operating the steering gear. You had a completely shielded bridge. The wheelhouse had just a single telegraph. We had an old up-and-down engine down below.† And it had an extension to what they called the flying bridge.

The bridge itself had what they called plastic armor around it. I don't know how effective it was because I just can't remember. I never saw any of this debris that hit. Later on, during an air attack they were strafing ships, but we were fortunate they didn't strafe us, so I really don't know how effective it would be. The ship had only one gyro repeater, and then you had a dummy pelorus over on the other bridge wing.

Paul Stillwell: What was the purpose of a dummy—to make somebody else think you were better off then you were?

---

* A gyrocompass is based on one or more gyroscopes torqued to true north in order to provide true compass readings. Typically, gyro repeaters are in various locations throughout a ship so that compass bearings may be taken at places other than the master gyroscope itself.
† This is a reference to the type of reciprocating, triple-expansion steam engine that Shellenbarger encountered earlier on board the Texas.

Captain Shellenbarger: No. Actually you could take bearings by them. What you would do you'd tell your helmsman to steady up on a certain course, say, like 315, and you would set the movable card on the dummy at 315. So then he'd call out, "Mark, mark, mark" when he was right on. Then you would make the reading, and you'd get the same effect as if you were reading from a gyro repeater, so they were effective for taking bearings. You needed them for station keeping in convoy, like to keep track of things. And, of course, there again, my Navy time really paid off with these things, because this was what I'd been doing, especially on the Herbert.

Paul Stillwell: What sort of watch schedule did you have, one in three?

Captain Shellenbarger: We mates stood four-hour watches. The chief mate—today they call him chief officer—stood the 4:00 to 8:00. The third officer stood the 8:00 to 12:00, and the second officer stood the 12:00 to 4:00, midwatch: 12:00 to 4:00 in the afternoon, 12:00 to 4:00 in the morning. And it was not like the Navy; merchant marine never dog watches.* Four-mate ships came along after the war, but we had just three back then. So when you went aboard as second officer you knew you were going to stand the 12:00 to 4:00. That was it.

Paul Stillwell: And that puts the chief mate on the 4:00 to 8:00 so he can do star sights morning and evening.

Captain Shellenbarger: Yes, but there's a problem if you get, as I did, a chief mate who last went to sea in 1925. But then the nautical almanacs started the day at noon, and, having been a postmaster for 25 years, he wasn't a hell of a lot of good at star sights.

Paul Stillwell: I can imagine.

---

* Dogging a watch means splitting it in half. Instead of a watch lasting from 4:00 P.M. to 8:00 P.M., there were two watches, 4:00 to 6:00 and 6:00 to 8:00, so watch standers would have an opportunity to get an evening meal.

Captain Shellenbarger: The second mate, being the nominal navigator, stayed up until the stars, and then he took star sights and did the navigation.*

Paul Stillwell: Was that you?

Captain Shellenbarger: That was me. [Laughter]

Paul Stillwell: That training came in handy.

Captain Shellenbarger: Yes, it did.

Paul Stillwell: How fatiguing was that routine for you?

Captain Shellenbarger: When you're in your early 20s, it doesn't faze you. You'd drink gallons of coffee, and I have to confess some days I smoked a lot of cigarettes. You had to go inside, make sure you didn't smoke outside, though.

Paul Stillwell: Well, you said you had some bitterness toward the Red Cross because of that one incident. How did that come about?

Captain Shellenbarger: That happened when I was ashore. We stayed in Birkenhead while they made some temporary repairs, primarily to our lifeboats. They came around and patched a few little holes here and there, but I think more to keep light from shining out than to keep the seas from coming in.

My room was on the starboard side, and the first assistant engineer's room was on the port side; we were aft on the boat deck. And during that hurricane in September 1944 one of the seas came over when we were in the trough. We had a coal-burning galley, and most of the coal came into my room and the first engineer's room, so they had to do a lot of work inside. Needless to say, our gear and clothes were in pretty sad shape. When we

---

* In celestial navigation, individuals take sights of the angle above the horizon for various heavenly bodies. These angles are then used with a nautical almanac to compute lines of position on a chart. Where the lines of position intersect is the ship's position at the time of the sights.

got into Birkenhead—and I've still got the seaman's passport that we used to carry—there were still the British rations. They gave me a duffel coat, a pair of trousers, a turtleneck sweater, and a pair of shoes. And while I was ashore there, I think I went for a mail trip, to pick up mail at the consulate, because that's where we'd get our mail in those days. Sometimes the armed guard officer would pick it up for the ship's crew.

In spite of what they say, the merchant crews and armed guards got along together.* In my personal experience I don't know of any instance where there was any conflict or anything like that. They were in many cases farm boys right off the farm, just like a lot of our guys were. And they've had gunnery training. While they were up there training and things, the guys in the merchant crew were down below in the magazines passing up the ammunition. When we got 20-millimeters, the guys who were handling the magazines and bringing ammunition over to the guns were the merchant men.† I know because I served as a loader on a 20-millimeter, and they also trained us how to use them in case the guy got knocked off or something.

Paul Stillwell: When did you serve as a loader? As an officer you did that?

Captain Shellenbarger: Oh, sure. Because we all had positions to do and, of course, because you're up there, and the 20-millimeter is on the bridge wing, you're available. Also, you see, and the skipper's inside. And if he needs something and there's nothing really doing at general quarters, he might say, "Hey, Shelley, get in here and do this and check that." And you'd tell the guy on the gun, "Hey, I'm going inside," and no need to holler.

Of course, he says, "You'll hear them coming anyway." You know, that kind of stuff. We got along great.

Paul Stillwell: Because the merchant ship didn't have the luxury of nearly as many people as the Navy ship.

---

* The armed guard was a small contingent of U.S. Navy personnel on board each U.S.-flag merchant ship to provide visual communications and gun crews.
† In the early 1940s the Navy's Bureau of Ordnance obtained licenses for U.S. manufacture of two foreign-designed light antiaircraft guns, the Swiss 20-millimeter Oerlikon and the Swedish 40-millimeter Bofors.

Captain Shellenbarger: No, no. And, of course, later on, well, with McQuigg, it was far enough advanced in the war that we had a 3-inch gun forward and the magazine forward, the same thing. We had a 5-inch/25 on the stern. Later on I understand some of them had the 5-inch/38s even.

Paul Stillwell: The 5-inch/25 was an old gun by that point.

Captain Shellenbarger: By that time, oh, yes. Sure. And, of course, even when I was on the Helena the first seven of the Brooklyn class had 5-inch/25s when they came out. And the Helena and the St. Louis had the 5-inch/38s.

Paul Stillwell: How many men on board total, both armed guard and the ship's crew?

Captain Shellenbarger: I can't recall exactly how many were in the armed guard. As I recall, it used to be about 15, 16, something like that. There might have been more or less. I can't really remember. The merchant crew, I would say in those days on a Liberty ship would average between 40 and 42, so we're talking about between 50 and 60 men.

Paul Stillwell: Well, how did the Red Cross not live up to expectations? You said you got these uniforms.

Captain Shellenbarger: Oh, I was ashore to get these things. I'd just been issued them and been treated with all respect. The British treat their merchant navy entirely different than the merchant marine in the United States. Our public doesn't know they exist, and I'd say to a large extent even during the war. The majority of them are in factories ashore. They're not around the port area, so they didn't know this. But the British, being an island nation, they recognize this and they call their merchant marine the merchant navy.

Our agent had taken me over, and after I'd gotten my issue of clothes from the ration board, I had it in an old duffel bag. The agent gave me directions how to get back to the ship, and I knew I could do that all right. Then I happened to see this canteen for

American servicemen, operated by the Red Cross, so I thought, "Well, I'll go over and get a cup of coffee." And, boy, it was a very unpleasant experience. There were these three women in Red Cross uniforms, and one of them said, "You? You're not a serviceman. You don't get anything from us."

I said, "I'm an American. I've got a seaman's passport. The ship's been under attack. I just got a ration from the British. They treated me like a halfway decent human being." And, oh, nothing doing. I'm sure all the Red Cross isn't like that, but that sort of left a bitter taste in my mouth which has never left.

Paul Stillwell: Just took one bad experience.

Captain Shellenbarger: Takes one bad experience and so bad that I have refused to contribute to the United Way because the United Way has contributed to the Red Cross. I make my contributions to the Salvation Army because right down the road in Liverpool was the Salvation Army, and they treated me like I had wings of gold.

Paul Stillwell: What are your impressions of Liverpool? That's become famous because of the Beatles since then.

Captain Shellenbarger: [Laughter] Well, needless to say, they weren't there then. To me it was just another darkened, desolate, dingy port because of the war. It didn't look any different than when we got to Manchester because we went on up from Birkenhead. After we got our repairs we went on up to Manchester to finish discharging. Our cargo in the bottom of the ship was 3,000 tons of bulk sulfur, and that was going up to the port of Manchester, which was a little port called Eccles. The thing that fascinated me about that trip was the fact that here's the ship, and we went underneath a canal that was on a bridge. You could see barges going along on this bridge.

Paul Stillwell: How much evidence did you see of bombing or other German damage in these British cities?

Captain Shellenbarger: A lot. There was a lot of damage, and I felt a lot of sympathy to them, because I knew that they'd been taking an awful beating that we had not. Terrific. And yet, surprisingly, you'd go into a pub, and the people you talked to just sort of took it in stride. There weren't a lot of long faces around by any means. Typical of all these pubs during the war, there'd be the sing-a-longs and the music. I'd say that they greeted us with open arms. I certainly felt that way.

Paul Stillwell: Well, to put it in perspective, one point to consider is that the situation you encountered was much different than, say, in 1940 when there was a concern about an invasion. By now the Allies had invaded the continent, and the war was going the other way.

Captain Shellenbarger: Yes, yes. I'm trying to recall and trying to place things in perspective now. We came back from that trip, and Tom Bown got off. We always came back in ballast; there was nothing moving back.* Liberty ships had a shaft tunnel in four and five hatches, and it sort of made a partial bulkhead up maybe, say, 16 feet from the bottom of the hatch. Whenever possible they'd send us into Swansea, a place down near Wales. There's a lot of coal mining in Wales, and there's something that comes out of the mine called schist. It's like a slate, but it's quite heavy apparently and it loads in. They would load it into our holds and, of course, it's loaded on either side of the shaft tunnel. That would give you weight to get your propeller down so when you came back across the Atlantic, oh, I'd say most of the time the propeller was about three-quarters submerged, which was quite satisfactory.

Paul Stillwell: Why would you do that, as opposed to taking water in ballast tanks?

Captain Shellenbarger: You didn't have any ballast tanks.

Paul Stillwell: Ah. So that term "in ballast" doesn't always refer to water ballast.

---

* Traveling in ballast means that the ship was not carrying cargo.

Captain Shellenbarger: [Laughter] No, not in those ships. You had the small deep tanks, but primarily you kept those full of fresh water. That was your reserve feed for your boilers and water for your crew. And your after peaks and fore peaks were also ballast tanks but, there again, they were fresh water tanks because this was also a tip-off. Later on, the ship went into Boston and went into the shipyard, and they started putting steam coils into the forepeak and after peak. Well, you knew right away where you were going. They never told you, of course, where you were going, but anytime they put steam lines into your water tanks to keep them freezing, you knew where you were going.

Paul Stillwell: So if you hadn't taken on this ballast in Wales, would your propeller be mostly out of the water?

Captain Shellenbarger: Roughly half out of the water. And you'd make no speed to speak of, and the ship wouldn't handle worth a damn, and so you took that. But if you didn't have schist—now, when I came back from the Pacific on this same ship, they didn't have anything out in Eniwetok and Guam, so then we took water ballast back there. We just took the fire hoses and filled them full of water, and before we did that, we forgot to take out the sweat boards. The sweat boards are to protect the cargo from being against the sides of the ship, and they fit in little brackets like and they just drop in. But, of course, as soon as the water got in there, they floated.

Paul Stillwell: So were you filling up the holds?

Captain Shellenbarger: You filled up four and five, up to the height of the shaft tunnel to give you the weight of the water back there. Because when you didn't have any stone or schist or whatever it was for ballast, you'd use water ballast. So that was routine on a Liberty ship. You'd use one or the other.

Paul Stillwell: Was there something over the top of this water?

Captain Shellenbarger: It was free surface.

Paul Stillwell: So did you have a concern about stability from this?

Captain Shellenbarger: No, not really because in most cases we were able to get bunkers, and our double bottoms were filled with fuel, and so we didn't have any real problem. I know a couple of times you'd look down and think of the free surface.* Later on, on other ships, there might be a concern, but on the Liberty ships you didn't have to worry about that. As a matter of fact, when they were empty they were so stiff that you could hardly stand up in a heavy sea. You know, they'd go [noise of ship going back and forth].

Paul Stillwell: A very stiff roll.

Captain Shellenbarger: Oh, terrific. Terrible.

Paul Stillwell: Well, where did you go? Did you come back to the States after you went to England?

Captain Shellenbarger: We came back to the States from this trip, and this was when we came back and we got orders to go to Davisville, Rhode Island.

Paul Stillwell: I'm guessing you felt an enormous sense of satisfaction at having done that, as opposed to being back at the school at Fort Trumbull.

Captain Shellenbarger: Oh, yes, and most important was the fact that I was getting sea time on my license. That was something that had started to become a vital concern to me. So, anyway, we went up to Davisville, Rhode Island, which was a port of embarkation for the Seabees.† We went in there and loaded all kinds of stuff for the Pacific, and in our case we didn't know what we were loading. We just put this stuff aboard: boxes and cases of

---

* Free surface effect comes about when a ship's tank or other compartment is partially filled with liquid so that the liquid is free to move from side to side of the ship. Because the liquid goes to the low side of the compartment, a large amount of free surface can be dangerous to the ship's stability.

† Seabees is the name universally applied to members of the Navy's mobile construction battalions (CBs).

this. I never gave it any thought, the fact that they'd even have a manifest of this cargo. Apparently they did have a manifest of the cargo that went aboard the ship, which I didn't learn till we just got out to Saipan.

A new skipper came aboard. Tom Bown got off. I don't know whether he was going back to another new ship or what. I lost touch with him for another 20 years. A new fellow came aboard, Joe Erlich. I was acting second mate still, and he was fairly young compared to Tom. He couldn't have been more than four or five years older than I was, which would put him in his late 20s. I was 24, so he was maybe 29 or 30.

Paul Stillwell: Real old guy.

Captain Shellenbarger: Real old guy. [Laughter] Today I can laugh about it, but in those days you'd go aboard a ship and licenses are always posted on merchant ships. You'd look at the master's license and say, "Gee, this guy's got his second issue of his master's license? Boy, he must be an old fart." That's exactly the words that you'd hear. [Laughter] And it's out of context, but I got my tenth issue of my master's license last November. [Laughter] I have proof that I've held a master's license for 50 years.

Paul Stillwell: That's neat.

Captain Shellenbarger: Anyway, we loaded all this cargo. There was a lot of heavy-lift cargo, earth-moving machinery, on deck.

Paul Stillwell: Why were you surprised that there was a manifest? Why wouldn't there have been?

Captain Shellenbarger: Well, this is something that at the time I never gave any thought to, because it wasn't something that I was involved in. I was saying, "Well, gee, under the exigencies of the war, they don't need one." But then, as I start thinking back, well maybe they would have to know what's on the ship, so they had to have a manifest.

Anyway, we proceeded to the Panama Canal, and this was my second time through. The first time had been on the <u>Colorado</u>, coming east. After we went through, we set off across the Pacific for Kwajalein. Now, this is the ship where the chief mate was the postmaster from somewhere in Florida, and I was acting second mate—third mate's license, of course. I had to do all the star sights. I didn't get along too well with this skipper, but I was stuck with him. That was because he's the one who insisted, "You're the navigator. I expect you to navigate." And this guy couldn't navigate. Of course, I'd been teaching navigation, so I took star sights in the morning and took star sights in the evening, put in a lot of extra hours. Of course, being the navigator you didn't get any overtime, but overtime wasn't a big deal in those days anyway.

But, anyway, we found our way out to somewhere near the island of Kwajalein, and we had charts that had been given to us.[*] I think they'd been printed in 1880, and I think they'd probably been surveyed in 1860. They were copies of British Admiralty charts and, of course, they didn't have the equipment and certainly no GPS in those days.[†] So we were hunting around, looking for Kwajalein, and it wasn't where we thought it should be. I knew damn well my star sights were right and we were there, and it obviously wasn't the right place.

This was when we saw this carrier come over the horizon with the four destroyers, and so we signaled and asked them if they could tell us where Kwajalein was. We were sure that they were ours and that's when the guy came back and blinked to me, "Follow me." Well, fortunately, they went by and left a wake astern.

Then Joe came up and asked me, "Do you think they're zigzagging?"[‡]

I told him, "How the hell would I know? I saw them from when they came until they passed us. If they'd been zigzagging they'd been changing course two or three times while we had them in sight." So they went by us at an angle, and we had to make quite a sharp turn. We saw their wake, and we lined up with their wake and we followed their wake, because shortly they were out of sight over the horizon. But in the meantime we'd

---

[*] U.S. troops invaded Kwajalein Atoll in the western Marshall Islands on 1 February 1944. Kwajalein fell on 6 February, and the entire atoll was declared secured.
[†] GPS—Global Positioning System, a satellite-based navigation system that provides terminals on earth with their geographic positions.
[‡] Steering a zigzag course was a means of foiling submarines by preventing them from setting up ahead of a course that a surface ship maintained for a prolonged period.

set a course and, sure enough, shortly real down low on the horizon we could start seeing masts and things, because this was late in the afternoon.

The next thing I knew, I saw the harbor entrance control post. They started blinking to us and wanting to know who we were, and so we told them. They said to proceed inside, and a pilot would board us.

Paul Stillwell: Did you have a harbor chart?

Captain Shellenbarger: We had no harbor charts or anything. We just went through the reef and through the buoys. They had some buoys there, so we got inside, slowed down, and a launch came alongside. It looked like one of the original Higgins boats.[*] This guy came aboard, and it turned out he was a Navy boatswain. Couldn't tell from any insignia or anything, because he was wearing just typical work gear.

Paul Stillwell: Dungarees?

Captain Shellenbarger: Dungarees, yes. And he said, "Okay," and he had a harbor chart. He said that there'd been a Hydrographic Office survey ship in there only about six weeks previously. Apparently they did their surveys and printed up those usable charts. As a matter of fact, he came back later and gave us a harbor chart for where our anchorage was. We dropped the hook there, and we stayed there a month, waiting for a convoy to Eniwetok.

So they did give the crew occasional liberty. You had to use your own lifeboats to go ashore. As I recall, they used to have 3.2 beer, and guys would go aboard and go over on one of the atolls. They told us where to go and have softball games and what have you. That was about all there was to do. As I recall, in Kwajalein they didn't have any movies. Sometimes the places where we had to go they'd invite us up and say that you could go to the movies with no problem, because that's the way things were done.

---

[*] "Higgins boat" was one name by which the Navy's LCVP—landing craft, vehicle and personnel—was known. It was designed for use in shallow water and had a bow ramp to facilitate the exit of troops onto a beach. It was 36 feet long, had a beam of 10 and a half feet, and could carry 36 fully equipped troops or a 6,000-pound vehicle.

One of the times in Kwajalein that I went ashore, Joe was in the boat with me. When you came back, you had to hook on the old manila falls onto the lifeboat and hoist them up. Well, of course, the two falls go to two different winches, to the gypsy heads. Well, somehow or other, one end of the boat got hoisted and the other one didn't. We were all hanging onto the thwarts as we were coming up, being two-blocked by the bow.* Oh well, that's one of the other instances.

Paul Stillwell: Did you rub shoulders with Navy men in some of these places in the Pacific?

Captain Shellenbarger: The only time we really rubbed shoulders with them was when we were ashore on these liberty things. There'd be a group of Navy people from other ships, and that was great, of course, because going ashore with us would be part of our gun crew. The armed guard officer would give part of them liberty. Of course, when you're living with people on the same ship, you form friendships. There were a lot of friendships between the two groups. No way that you kept separate from them, and to this day even in the veterans' organizations you find the armed guard is right there with the merchant crews.

Paul Stillwell: Well, I've heard about expressions of hostility from some of the Navy men. Did you encounter any of that?

Captain Shellenbarger: No, I never did. I never did, and I don't recall of any instances where we were. The only problem was the man I told you about, this chief mate on this ship.

Paul Stillwell: The postmaster.

Captain Shellenbarger: Yes. He was a comedy of errors, but, nevertheless, he had a chief mate's license.

---

* Two-blocked means hoisted all the way up.

We got to Tinian, where our heavy-lift equipment was supposed to be going. We didn't know anything about it until months later, but it was what was used to prepare the airfield for the B-29s, but, anyway, we were discharging these bulldozers.* There were a couple of cranes with dipper buckets. I know there were two big bulldozers, and they were D-8s. These were the big jobs because we had to handle them with the jumbo lift, heavy-lift gear. The chief mate was lowering this bulldozer. I don't know how it happened, but all of a sudden we heard the screeching of brakes and wires, and the D-8 went crashing into the deck of this LCT.† The LCTs could only take the one piece of equipment at a time, then they'd take it ashore. They would already have it running so it could just run right off the ramp and go ashore. This thing crashed down there, and I don't know what damage it did to the LCT. I was surprised when I learned that the skipper of it was a lieutenant (j.g.).

Paul Stillwell: I think that was standard.

Captain Shellenbarger: It was, but anyway, we had the Jacob's ladder down the side.‡ He came up the Jacob's ladder, and he had a .45 out. He was looking for the guy that had dropped the bulldozer in his boat.

Paul Stillwell: How far did it drop?

Captain Shellenbarger: I heard the crash and I was on the other side, and I came down. From what the guys that were there told me, they said it dropped about three feet. You know, when you're talking about what, 15-18 tons, something like that, you drop it three feet it's going to make a hell of a dent. Now, what damage it did I don't know but, boy, he was looking for somebody, and everyone was pointing at everybody else. We finally got him quieted down and took him in and gave him some coffee and a bunch of other stuff.

---

* Tinian in the Marianas Islands was the launching site for the flight of the Army Air Forces B-29 bomber that dropped the first atomic bomb on Hiroshima, Japan, in August 1945.
† LCT—tank landing craft, an open, barge-like craft that had a bow ramp for beaching. It came in various configurations and sizes; it was generally able to carry four to eight medium tanks or an equivalent weight of cargo.
‡ A Jacob's ladder is a portable ladder with wooden rungs; the sides are made of rope or wire. It is slung over the side of a ship when used, rolled up when stored while not in use.

Paul Stillwell: Did the chief mate have any redeeming qualities?

Captain Shellenbarger: No.

Paul Stillwell: Okay. Not even a nice guy?

Captain Shellenbarger: I'll tell you—frankly, he wasn't all there.

After we discharged all this stuff in Tinian, I got ashore, incidentally. Somebody took me ashore and we went in a Jeep. They told me, "With all these Japs around, you're crazy to be going ashore," and stuff like that. Because the chief mate wasn't doing his job. I was not only doing the second mate's, I was doing the chief mate's job in many ways. Something would come up, and they couldn't get hold of the chief mate, and they'd come to me as second mate.

Paul Stillwell: On your third mate's license.

Captain Shellenbarger: On a third mate's license, yes. It was nothing unusual because the third mate didn't have a license. He'd been previous boatswain on a ship, so he had no license at all. He was acting on what they called a waiver.

After that they moved us from Tinian to Saipan, because they didn't know where our cargo was going to be discharged. In Saipan they put us alongside this—I've forgotten the name of them, but they were big square metal things they put together with angle irons. Some of them they could put big outboard motors on and make barges out of them. Others they would put together and they would make piers out of them. So we went alongside this pier in Saipan, and Admiral Nimitz came aboard.* We saw this, and nobody give us any advance warning.

---

* Fleet Admiral Chester W. Nimitz, USN, Commander in Chief Pacific Fleet and Pacific Ocean Areas, 1941-45. In late January 1945 Admiral Nimitz, moved the Pacific Fleet headquarters from Pearl Harbor to Guam in order to be closer to the combat zone. He took with him only a relatively small staff, leaving the remainder of the staff in Hawaii.

Paul Stillwell: When was that?

Captain Shellenbarger: I'll tell you when it was because when we went into Guam it was New Year's Eve, so this had to be in December 1944. So we saw this big group of people coming down the dock. Nobody told us why we went alongside the dock. Actually, we thought we were going to discharge there because nobody told us. Then we got alongside, and this group of people came down there, must have been 30, 40 people, all in suntans,* and I went over to the gangway. Of course, I was acting second mate and chief mate, and I'll tell you the reason why later. But, anyway, I looked down there and I saw an officer in a uniform cap with gold braid on his visor. I'd seen pictures of him somewhere, and I ran back up and got a hold of the skipper right away. I said, "Hey, I think that this is Admiral Nimitz down there." And, sure enough, they came up the gangway. The rest of them all stayed down below, and I found out later most of them were newsmen, news people.

His staff was only maybe about five or six people because he came up and apparently his chief of staff or flag secretary or whatever came up and said, "The admiral would like to see the captain and check your manifests." And that's the first time I'd heard the word manifest.

So I took him up to Captain Erlich's cabin, and Joe said, "Go get ahold of the steward and see if we can offer them a cup of coffee or something," and they accepted. So they had coffee there with the captain, and then they broke out the manifest. This was when I talked to one of the officers there, and I said, "What's this. Are we going to discharge here or what?"

He said, "Well, they haven't made a decision yet, but you have most of our supplies for Admiral Nimitz's headquarters in the Pacific."

I said, "What do you mean?"

He said, "You know, our conference tables, chairs, filing cabinets, typewriters—everything we need to set up a headquarters." That was our cargo that we'd loaded in Davisville. So I guess he stayed about an hour. And, of course, in the meantime I was chasing down the steward, and it ended up I got ahold of the chief cook.

---

* "Suntans" is a term sometimes used for the Navy's khaki-colored working uniforms.

But, anyway, whatever they did, they decided. We stayed there at the dock that night, and the reason I remember is because they came down and said, "Any of you guys want to go to the movies up there they got a movie theater?" Some of our men went, and there was an air raid when the Japanese came over while they were at the movies. And, of course, the first thing they'd done is when we came in, they said, "If there's an air raid, you do not fire any of your armament."

Paul Stillwell: Ship's guns?

Captain Shellenbarger: No ship's guns. This was the first time we'd heard this. It was the fellow that brought us in and acting as pilot. He was a Navy chief boatswain, and he told us, "Well, the reason is, they've got antiaircraft guns here. They're 90 millimeters, and they're controlled from a central point." Now, whether that was radar controlled by that time I don't know. I know they used searchlights, but the 90 millimeters, boy, they put up one hell of a barrage. I think the antiaircraft batteries were Army or Army Air Forces.

I don't know how many Japs there were. Maybe two or three, for all I know. Maybe they were just reconnaissance. Of course, we always had to take cover because of shrapnel coming down, and the guys that had gone ashore to the movie said that they shut down the movie, and they all went into a cave somewhere. But the next morning we got orders to proceed to Guam. So this had to be right around Christmastime because it's only a short run down to Guam. On the way down to Guam we found out that the steward and the chief mate had gotten a bunch of prunes, raisins, and whatever and set up a still somewhere down below in the engine room with the assistance of one of the engineers. We assumed that.

I know that the skipper tried to get rid of the chief mate there, and they wouldn't take him. They had no facilities for anybody there in Apra Harbor. We came in and the pilot came out, and this was just before New Year's Eve, midnight. Of course, this was January 1945. And all of a sudden there was a 90-millimeter with all this armament firing and the pilot—they were all Navy men—said, "Sounds like an air raid. We'll stay outside until everything is over." At that time he had one of the early walkie-talkies, and he called somebody ashore and he said, "Well, we'd better stay here anyway." And then he told us, "That wasn't an air raid. Everybody was celebrating New Year's."

So, anyway, we went in and he anchored us, and we stayed there—I can't remember how long.

Paul Stillwell: Did they off-load the office equipment?

Captain Shellenbarger: They off-loaded everything into LCTs and these things that they put together and made barges out of them. They made flat barges out of these things, these big square steel boxes, and they bolted them together with angle iron. And then they had some of the boxes had sloping edges, so they could make a bow and a stern. And then there were certain units that had this motor built into the units, and they'd bolt one of those in each corner back on the stern, and you had a motorized barge.

Paul Stillwell: Sort of like an erector set arrangement.

Captain Shellenbarger: Yes. So we ended up discharging all of our cargo in Guam, and there we got orders to go back to the States. We had a few spare berths, and I don't really know what they were, back in the gun crew quarters. It seems to me that earlier when I mentioned the size of the gun crew, the armed guard officer had a cabin amidships, but the rest of the gun crew slept aft, right underneath the gun, and this was the deckhouse. The after house was designed with gun crew quarters.

As I recall, they used to have 14 bunks in there, and later on, when the armed guard had gone, we used those quarters right after the war to carry up to 12 passengers. So, anyway, we took two passengers back. They were a couple of people that they didn't have any other transportation for, and I'd sort of hoped one of them would be a war correspondent or something like that, but they weren't. They were just a couple of GIs that they were sending back to the States, because they were Army men. There again, they fitted right in with everybody else.

The only thing there was we'd been out there so long we ran out of provisions, so while we were in Guam they loaded us up with 10-in-1 K rations and what have you.

Canned potatoes. So potatoes and stuff like that were our ration going home. When we went to Guam, no convoy. I thought we'd get a convoy back to Eniwetok and then proceed independently like we'd done before. No, we went independently, but we did zigzag. We had zigzag orders, because when we got our sailing orders they sent them out, and we zigzagged and we had one of the fancy gadgets put on the gyro.

Paul Stillwell: Sinuous course clock?

Captain Shellenbarger: I guess so, yes, because the thing would be changing, and it would click-click-click-click like and then you'd click-click to click-click, and the helmsman followed this pointer.

Paul Stillwell: So it was almost constant helming.

Captain Shellenbarger: Almost, yes. The helmsmen hated it, but they told us to zigzag, I think, till we reached a certain latitude and longitude. And so we didn't use it that much actually, because when you're in convoy you never used it because the convoy would be changing courses. So we proceeded back to the States.

Paul Stillwell: What kind of speed could you make good with that combination of a slow ship and a sinuous course?

Captain Shellenbarger: I'd say we made probably about nine and a half knots good. This Liberty, the John R. McQuigg—you know, every one of them was built a little bit differently, and you could go on one built on adjacent ways and one would be a knot and a half faster than the other one. Don't ask me why, but they would. Maybe they had a little bit different blades on the propellers or something or other. Maybe they came from different places. It's kind of weird in a way.

Paul Stillwell: Well, people talk about warships having different personalities. Did the Liberty ships have different personalities?

Captain Shellenbarger: I would say yes. I would say yes.

Paul Stillwell: In what ways?

Captain Shellenbarger: Well, just in the respect that everything seemed to go well on one ship regardless of your crew. And you get on another ship, and it just seemed like everything was haywire. I think I was very fortunate. During that section of time I was very fortunate. With the McQuigg everything seemed to go well. I know that it sailed under about three other names after the war. Different people picked it up in different countries, and that thing wasn't scrapped till sometime in the late '60s.

Paul Stillwell: And all this despite a deficient chief mate.

Captain Shellenbarger: Well, this was the final thing. They insisted he stay aboard. In the meantime, I was doing his work. Of course, I was gaining a lot of experience, too, which was good. Not the way I'd want to have it happen. But when we got into San Francisco, he and the chief steward deteriorated drastically. When we arrived at San Francisco bar, there'd been a gale blowing. Of course, for us it was good because it was following, and because it gave us extra speed in spite of our wallowing back and forth in it. But I can remember—this is one of the things that stick in your memory—I can remember an aircraft carrier coming out of San Francisco. Now, we were outside, and they sent us a message saying, "Remain outside until the weather moderates." But I saw this aircraft carrier, and I didn't see any escorts there, but he might have joined them later on. But he came out into that sea, and he took green water over the flight deck.[*] When we finally got in and got the pilot, after the weather moderated, I think the pilot told us it was the Ranger. That somehow doesn't seem right.

Paul Stillwell: She was one of the old ones.[†]

---

[*] Green water means the ship has been taking solid ocean water over the bow, not just sea spray.
[†] USS Ranger (CV-4) was commissioned 4 July 1934.

Captain Shellenbarger: She was one of the old ones. She was the one that had the stacks that folded down, if I remember right.

Paul Stillwell: Yes, exactly.

Captain Shellenbarger: Yes, so it might have been the Ranger; as I recall, that's what the pilot said. I saw green water go over the flight deck of a carrier, and that's something you don't like to see. But, anyway, we got in, we got alongside the dock. Shipping commissioner came aboard to sign the crew off. Joe Erlich went up to the Palace on Market Street. I think it had a ballroom called the Rose Room. I think it was the Palace. He left the ship in the hands of the poor acting second mate, because on payoff day the chief mate was down in the dining room—you know those rails you lift to keep food from sliding off the table?

Paul Stillwell: They're on the edge of the table.

Captain Shellenbarger: Edge of the tables. He'd sit in a chair chewing on the rail like a beaver.

Paul Stillwell: So he really went round the bend.

Captain Shellenbarger: He really went round the bend, and they came down. They sent ashore for the doc, and they came down and they took him off in a straitjacket, because he was fighting them and everything. Well, of course, then I got to inventory and pack all of his gear. Oh, it was terrible to see something like that, and this was strictly from the stuff that he and the steward had been drinking. It had gone to his head, and the steward took off ashore, and we never did see him again. The waivers weren't effective once you got alongside the dock, and so the third mate went ashore and back to the union hall. He got paid off. They left me with a nucleus crew and an empty ship.

Paul Stillwell: You were the only officer.

Captain Shellenbarger: I was the only deck officer, except I had two of the engineers stayed aboard: chief engineer and I think the second engineer. The first had some pressing business to go ashore. Well, by that time, this was 1945, everybody was very efficient. The Coast Guard was having routine patrols of vessels to make sure that you were maintaining proper watches. I was the only deck officer on the John R. McQuigg, so I was thinking that "Gee, I want to get off of this thing. Am I going to be stuck for how long here?"

So the MMP union representative came down to the ship.[*] Mind you, up to this time I was non-union, because when you shipped out with the War Shipping Administration you didn't have to be union. I mean, you were assigned a ship, and that was it. So he said, "Why don't you sign up with Local 90 MMP here?" And I signed up with them and, of course, I had my payoff. And he said, "Are you the only mate on this ship?"

So I said, "Yeah, I don't know what's wrong. The skipper went ashore. Said he was going to come back, and I haven't seen him since payoff day. It's going to be two weeks. We've got a port payroll," because we still had part of the crew aboard. And I said, "I don't know what to do. I don't have the key to the safe or the combination or anything."

He said, "The skipper hasn't been aboard? He's supposed to be here every day." Well, this was interesting because the company I was working for was American-South African Line. A change in career. This is very important because this union representative was Captain May, a very nice gentleman, and I told him.

He said, "Gee, you haven't had any chance to go ashore?"

I said, "I don't dare go ashore. I'm the only deck officer here. I can't leave the ship. It would jeopardize what little piddling license I've got."

So he said, "Well, we'll take care of that." Mind you, this master was Joe Erlich. He beat me about every game of chess we ever played too. That's one of the reasons I didn't like him. [Laughter] But, anyway, Captain May came down the very next day, and

---

[*] MMP—Masters, Mates and Pilots Union.

he said "Have your gear packed." And, of course, you never sailed with that much gear in those days anyway. When it went down with the ship, it was gone anyway. So I got my gear, got it off, and he said, "Have all your keys ready. I'm going to go up and get ahold of the skipper and get him down here."

So Joe came down. I don't know what he'd been doing. But he came aboard, and I met him near the gangway, and I said, "Pleased to meet you, Captain. I would like to go ashore and make a phone call. I haven't been off here in two weeks, and this trip's lasted close to seven months."

He said, "Oh, yeah, sure, go ahead."

I said, "Here's the keys. I don't want to take them down to the dock. I might lose them." I got down to the end of the gangway, and I said, "Captain, I'm leaving. You now have the watch." Captain May was there, and I can't remember exactly what he said, but it was something to the same effect. Then Joe Erlich started blowing his top.

I said, "After this long trip you didn't even come down to relieve me to go ashore, and I didn't dare leave the ship." Because by that time the Coast Guard was coming around. I've forgotten what they called them. They were port watchers or something or other. They'd come around and check almost every day, and you never knew when they were going to show up. And if you didn't have a deck officer on watch you were in trouble.

So, anyway, I got a train and headed back to the East Coast. And, of course, this is something maybe I shouldn't be saying. The lady friend I'd met in New London showed up, and she was eight months pregnant. That was my first wife. I did the honorable thing. I married her.

Paul Stillwell: Do we want to put this lady's name in the record?

Captain Shellenbarger: No, I don't want to put that in the record. [Laughter]

Paul Stillwell: Well, let me ask you one more question. During all this time when the chief mate was so ineffectual, did Joe Erlich act as a mentor and train you in some of these things?

Captain Shellenbarger: I will say that. Yes, he did, because, after all, this was my first trip on anything, and I could go to him anytime and say, "Hey, Captain, what do we do now? This is something new to me." And he was experienced. He'd had experiences.

Paul Stillwell: Well, and it was in his interest to have you know these things.

Captain Shellenbarger: Absolutely. Oh, absolutely, yes. But, anyway, after my first daughter was born, April 1945, I went back to the American-South African Line. I went to the port captain and said, "I'm ready to go for another ship. I've had a couple of months off. My daughter's been born. I'm married."

Paul Stillwell: We're right at the end of the tape. I wonder if this is a good place to break.

Captain Shellenbarger: But, anyway, he told me I was fired. He said, "You deserted a ship in San Francisco and left the master aboard. He's given you all kinds of bad reports." [Laughter]

Paul Stillwell: Such loyalty. Well, I look forward to resuming tomorrow.

Interview No. 3 with Captain Franklin F. Shellenbarger, U.S. Maritime Service (Retired)
Place: U.S. Naval Institute, Annapolis, Maryland
Date: Thursday, 12 June 1997
Interviewer: Paul Stillwell

Paul Stillwell: Well, Captain, yesterday we had just finished up the description of your career in the Liberty ship during World War II. Then, after that, you got back to the States and were held prisoner for a couple of weeks and then set free. So if you could pick up the narrative at that point, please.

Captain Shellenbarger: Well, as I recall the comment I had, was the fact that I didn't go back to American-South African Line. I went to the port captain and told him that after my mishap or unfortunate occurrence or whatever in San Francisco when the McQuigg came back from the Pacific, he told me I was fired. Actually, I found out it was meaningless in those days. I mean, after all, the war was still going on in Europe as well as the Pacific.

Paul Stillwell: When did you get back to the States?

Captain Shellenbarger: We got back in February 1945, and then there was this period when I got married and my first daughter was born. In a very short period of time, a lot happened.

It was time to go back to sea. Having been at Fort Trumbull, I had a number of friends in the War Shipping Administration, and they had what they called a hiring office at 39 Broadway in New York. So I went over and saw a very nice gentleman named Welsh. I think he was a retired Navy man who'd gone to the Maritime Service. I'd met him in New London, and he told me, "Well, I can ship you out of this WSA office, but my recommendation is that it would actually be better for you to get connected with a good shipping company. I'll send you over to American Export Lines." So I went over to American Export Lines in April 1945.

Paul Stillwell: Had you joined a union at that point?

Captain Shellenbarger: I was still a member of MMP, the union I'd joined on the West Coast. However, at that time the union membership didn't really mean much. You could ship out of the hiring halls with the union, or you could ship through the WSA, or you could go the shipping companies, and there were plenty of jobs. Nobody worried about affiliation in those days.

But, anyway, it turned out that when I went to American Export Lines they had their own little company union, called the Brotherhood of Marine Officers. But that question didn't come up this first trip, because I just went over there and saw Tom Collins, the administrative assistant to the marine superintendent of American Export Lines.* I learned later that a railroad executive named Coverdale had been with the Export Steamship Company from the time it had been formed, I guess shortly after World War I. Later it had developed from Export Steamship Company into the American Export Lines.

They had done very well, actually, prior to World War II. They had four passenger-cargo liners known as the "Four Aces" that had been built in the '30s.† They had a very extensive network in the Mediterranean, and at that time American Export was an up-and-coming, you know, really well-thought-of company, right along with a lot of the others that went down the drain through the years.

I remember Tom Collins well, because through the years he became a very close friend. At that time I just went in and said, "Mr. Welsh has sent me over. Said you needed somebody."

He said, "Yeah, I've got a ship job for you tomorrow." By that time I'd upgraded my license in addition to getting married.

Paul Stillwell: So now you had an actual second mate license.

---

* Thomas F. Collins.
† These were the Excambion, the Excalibur, the Exeter, and the Exochorda.

Captain Shellenbarger: So I had an actual second mate's license. That's right. So he said, "I want you to go second mate on this Reverdy Johnson." Well, that name didn't mean anything to me until I got aboard and found out that it was one of the very first Liberty ships built, because Reverdy Johnson apparently was one of the signers of the Declaration of Independence. When I looked around, I could see that this was a much older ship and in many ways much better built than the John R. McQuigg. Had riveted seams. It had brass portholes, brass dogs. We had hanging oil lights in the cabins, little gimbals. Oh, do I wish that I'd got one of those through the years. And, of course, being one of the early Liberty ships it did not have a separate gyro room.* The gyro had been added later, and it was placed right in the middle of the chartroom. So to get to the chart table you had to squeeze past the Mark 14 gyro.

Paul Stillwell: How big was the gyro?

Captain Shellenbarger: Width of maybe three foot in diameter. Stood about three and a half foot high. And, of course, with associated switchboards and equipment on the side of it, it was not a small one. Later on some of the ships got—I think they're called Mark 18s. They were much smaller, though by that time the ships were being built with a separate gyro room. Our regular Export ships had Mark 14s, because that was standard for many, many years.

Actually I'd already had some experience. This is one of the things I learned on the Herbert, because there was a Mark 6, which is in a separate cage back in a crew's compartment, which obviously was an afterthought many years later after they were built. But the Reverdy Johnson, it turned out, was what they called a Liberty troopship. And I have never seen a picture of a Liberty ship quite configured as this was. I remember very well because it was the second Liberty I was on. It was quite a but different than the McQuigg. It had knock-down bunks. It could carry, as I recall, about 850 troops.

The number-three hatch, just forward of the bridge, was normally a very small hatch anyway. The booms came down, and they were crossed forward of the bridge;

---

* Gyro is short for gyrocompass, a piece of equipment that uses a gyroscope to produce true bearings on the earth's surface, as opposed to the magnetic bearings produced by a magnetic compass.

number three hatch did not exist. No derricks there. Abreast of number-three hatch they had a second set of lifeboats, so actually we had three lifeboats on each side in addition to our normal rafts and stuff.

Paul Stillwell: What do you mean knock-down bunks?

Captain Shellenbarger: They were pipe bunks with canvas, and we had racks for them in the holds. But you'd carry cargo going one way and then you could set up the bunks, and you could carry up to 850 troops in the hold.

Paul Stillwell: So the pipe stanchions must have been removable.

Captain Shellenbarger: The stanchions were removable. Everything was removable, and it looked like an erector set to put the thing together. There was a stowage place for them in each hold. And the number-three hold, being very small, I can't remember now what was down there. Were there additional water tanks? I don't recall that.

But the tween deck was fitted on one side with a troop galley for when you had troops aboard, and you had companionways going down in so that they could go across and come up the other side and back, and there also was one on the other side. As I recall, one was port, one was starboard, of course, had to be. And there was a little hospital there. As a Liberty trooper, we carried an officer; I've forgot the terminology, but he was a transport commander. I can't remember his name, but I remember him. He was an Army lieutenant. He had been a state policeman in Louisiana, and he'd been a member of Huey Long's bodyguard at the time Huey Long was assassinated.[*]

Paul Stillwell: Did he tell you about that?

Captain Shellenbarger: Oh, we heard it so many times I got sick and tired of hearing it.

---

[*] Huey P. Long, a Democrat, served as Governor of Louisiana from 1928 to 1931 and as a U.S. Senator from that state from 1935 until his assassination in 1935. He was known for his demagoguery and his dictatorial control of the state through his political machine.

Paul Stillwell: Any special insights you could pass along here?

Captain Shellenbarger: Oh, no, nothing that I can remember, because I'm sure he exaggerated so much, even as I do. Many times I exaggerate and forget things that sort of—

Paul Stillwell: Sort of fill in the blanks? A little embroidery.

Captain Shellenbarger: [Laughter] Okay.

Paul Stillwell: We all do that.

Captain Shellenbarger: Yes. But, we carried the transport contingent in addition to the Army people, which were the medics. They had a couple of their own cooks because our crew couldn't handle it. You know, when you get 850 people aboard you're feeding continually twice a day. And we carried a lot of extra space for stores for them. And usually when we left the States we were fully stored in anticipation that we'd be picking up troops somewhere along the way, on the way or coming back, because as I indicated earlier, normally these ships came back empty except for ballast.

Paul Stillwell: So would these be canned rations or battle rations?

Captain Shellenbarger: Yes.

Paul Stillwell: You wouldn't have that much fresh food.

Captain Shellenbarger: No, very little fresh. Later on, I was on a converted Victory where they used to carry frozen milk, frozen turkey, steaks and stuff like that for the troops coming back, but they carried 1,500 troops.* But in our case we did have a little bit of additional reefer space, and we carried a little bit extra anyway.

This is the first of my experience actually with the radar. We had an old SG radar.

Paul Stillwell: SG was a surface search.

Captain Shellenbarger: And we carried two radarmen to operate that. They were Navy because in our troop contingent there were these Navy radarmen. We carried three Navy radiomen. We didn't have any commercial radio operators on there. We carried two Navy signalmen and, of course, being an ex-Navy signalman I got on great with these guys. A lot of back and forth.

I went aboard the Reverdy Johnson in April. We loaded a lot of stores and stuff for England, and I don't recall whether this went to Liverpool or wherever it was. Going over, we were under way at sea on V-E Day, and that was, of course, a tremendous thing.† I have copies of about eight messages. Being a former Navy radioman and signalman, the chief radio operator came to me and said, "Here's something you might want for someday down the road," and he gave me the copies of these messages that we received declaring the end of the war, the fact we put our running lights on, congratulations from Lord So-and-so. I've forgotten, he was from the British. What did they call them? BAMS messages, I think they were, British-American Merchant Shipping. What we used to call in the Navy fox schedules. They came out in the blind, because no ship ever answered receipt. Everything was words twice, so anyway I have the copies today. I have mislaid the originals, but I do have the copies of those messages.

Paul Stillwell: Now, did these additional Navy people report to the armed guard commander?

---

* The Victory ship was a mass-produced cargo ship designed in World War II as a replacement for the Liberty ship. The Victory was bigger and faster and designed for post-war commercial use. A number of the Victory ships were converted for Navy use as attack transports.
† V-E Day--Victory in Europe Day, 8 May 1945, when the German surrender was ratified in Berlin.

Captain Shellenbarger: They reported to the ship's master, because he was the one in charge of security. The only time I ever saw a little bit of friction was with this guy from Louisiana. He used to say that he was in command of the ship, because he was the transport commander. And I can remember the skipper. He was a Norwegian, Captain Ole Petersen. I can remember up on the bridge once when a question came up. I don't know what it was. He turned to this guy and said, "You want to navigate this ship? Be my guest."

"Oh, no, no, no, no, no." [Laughter]

So Ole said, "All right. In that case get your ass off the bridge."

Paul Stillwell: That settled that right quick.

Captain Shellenbarger: That settled it real fast. He was a great guy, Ole was. Nice guy to sail with. I was second mate. The chief mate was Bill Frazier. He went into the Coast Guard and retired from the Coast Guard with four stripes. A lot of them did because shortly after that the Coast Guard took on what they called an augmentation program, and they took quite a few merchant marine people in, primarily for their inspection service when they took over the inspection service.

But that trip was very interesting. V-E Day on our way over. Of course, all the lights came on, the British ships especially. They'd been fighting a much longer war than we had.* Whistles blowing. The British ship in the column next to us tried to come over and pass us a bottle of whiskey, which was unsuccessful. [Laughter] So it was quite a thing. But, anyway, after we discharged we put into Le Havre, and we picked up a group of U.S. Rangers. We didn't take full capacity of 850 troops, as I recall. We took about 450 Rangers coming back out of the front lines. I never saw so much armament in my life. Every one of them was loaded down. Some guys had as many as seven or eight Lugers which they were trying to peddle to the merchant crew. So we brought them back. I think we discharged them in Boston.

---

* World War II began on 1 September 1939, when German ground forces invaded Poland. Two days later Great Britain and France declared war on Germany.

Paul Stillwell: Did you disarm them?

Captain Shellenbarger: How could we have disarmed 450 Rangers? No way. [Laughter]

Paul Stillwell: They kept their weapons at the ready.

Captain Shellenbarger: They kept their weapons until they got there. I understand that when they got ashore someone confiscated all the German weapons from them. I don't know what they did. I guess they took them off to one of the forts in Massachusetts—Devens or whatever. They were so happy to get out of the line and get home.

Paul Stillwell: Were they due to go to the Pacific after that?

Captain Shellenbarger: Probably. At that time they probably were going to give them leave of absence, and eventually they would probably go to the Pacific. That was what we were supposed to do, was to refit, but instead the Reverdy Johnson took a load of stuff over to the Mediterranean. And being a trooper, they said we'd probably pick up troops in the Mediterranean after we discharged our cargo and take them to the Pacific. Well, of course, that never happened because V-J Day came along while we were over there.*

We did a lot of bouncing around in the Mediterranean at that time. We got into Naples. Of course, the place was still shattered from the war. We went into the port of Leghorn early and, of course, in those days because of minefields, which weren't cleared, they would sweep a channel very close to shore. You'd only steam in daylight because the marks didn't have lights on them where they marked the channel. They were strictly daytime marks. So you'd anchor at nighttime, hoping you'd anchor in a place where there wasn't a minefield.

Paul Stillwell: Right.

---

* V-J Day--Victory over Japan Day, marking the end of the war in the Pacific on 15 August 1945.

Captain Shellenbarger: I know it took us two days to go from Naples up to Leghorn. We went into Leghorn, and I don't recall the exact date, but I know that we went ashore there, and we went up to the Army installation. They came aboard. Of course, we still had this transport commander and his contingent aboard, and I remember Leghorn very well. To enter it you had to go through a ship where they'd blown the center of it apart in order to get in. Then when you got in there were no docks. We tied up alongside of a sunken ship, which fortunately had sort of gone straight down so we could use his bollards and bitts to tie up to. And then we put a gangplank over to him and from there to shore, but it was interesting.

Paul Stillwell: Were these Rangers kind of rowdy on the way home?

Captain Shellenbarger: In a way, yes. I mean, after all, they'd come right from the front line and were just releasing tension and so on and so forth.

Paul Stillwell: I would expect so.

Captain Shellenbarger: Yes, you can imagine. A few fights. They had their own people to take care of the discipline that was necessary. A few weapons were fired off over the side occasionally at seagulls or whatever, but they were things you sort of expected.

Paul Stillwell: Were you in a convoy in that transit during which you got the message about the war ending?

Captain Shellenbarger: Yes, we were in convoy. That's why we had the British ship alongside trying to come over. It was in a convoy. It had left New York.

Paul Stillwell: Who was directing the ship's movements during this period?

Captain Shellenbarger: You mean aboard the individual ship or the convoy commodore?

Paul Stillwell: Well, both I guess. I mean, how did you find out where to go in the Med and so forth?

Captain Shellenbarger: When you were in convoy the messages would come through the convoy commodore, because he had additional people aboard, and he monitored additional circuits. It was usually a converted passenger ship of some sort that had your convoy commodore or at least a combination cargo-passenger. He'd have additional quarters—let's put it that way—because he would have additional radio circuits that he manned and he would get messages. And then they'd come to us by flashing light.

For instance, when the convoy broke apart as you approached the English coast, they would say so many were going to Scotland, so many would go down to Swansea, some would go into Liverpool. I've forgotten. Oban was one of the anchorages up in Scottish coast. That's where you'd go up to await further orders. There was a number of different places, and they would divert you, not by ship's name, as I recall, but by our position in the convoy. And certainly somebody must have known what cargoes we were carrying. Otherwise, how would they know where to send us with what particular cargo they wanted where?

Paul Stillwell: This goes back to the manifests that you mentioned yesterday.

Captain Shellenbarger: Yes, that's right.

Paul Stillwell: These were naval officers, weren't they, the convoy commodores?

Captain Shellenbarger: Yes. They were naval officers. Many of them had been retirees called back to active duty. The high-speed convoys, where they had the troopships normally—and this I learned later on, one of them was run by the admiral I'd served with when I was an enlisted man. He was David McDougal LeBreton; I remember his full name.* He was a convoy commodore of a fast one. See, you had slow convoys and fast

---

* Rear Admiral David McDougal LeBreton, USN, had stood number one in the Naval Academy class of 1904. Two of his classmates were well-known admirals in World War II, Husband E. Kimmel and William F. Halsey, Jr.

convoys. Fast convoys had faster troopships, whereas the real fast ships ran independently, zigzagging. As you're well aware, the Queen Mary and the Queen Elizabeth ran independently.[*]

I found out through later years of reading, maybe it was in the Naval Institute Proceedings, because I run into these names every once in a while and I say, "Gee, I knew that guy." I found that Le Breton was the convoy commodore of the convoy where the troopship Dorchester was sunk with the four chaplains.[†] Anyway, he was convoy commodore of that convoy, and that's the last time I ever heard of Admiral LeBreton because these people were pre-war, and they were getting along in years.[‡] Chances are that his service had been extended for the duration of the war.

Paul Stillwell: Well, they called back a number of retired officers.

Captain Shellenbarger: They called a lot of them back for that purpose and, of course, they were ideal for this. They had the experience and knowledge, even though they weren't that young.

Paul Stillwell: Did the convoying cease after V-E day?

Captain Shellenbarger: Pretty much so, yes. I would say that right after V-E Day, at least in the Atlantic, one of these messages that we received, which I'll give to you, speaks of looking for submarines that are flying certain color flags, "But be aware that some submarine captains may not abide by these things. Still proceed with extreme caution. Keep your gun crews on alert. Keep sharp lookout." If you saw a submarine flying a black flag or whatever it was, avoid them at all costs. As I recall now, when we made this trip to the Med, we weren't in convoy after that next trip.

---

[*] The passenger ships Queen Mary and Queen Elizabeth of the British Cunard Line were converted for use during World War II as high-speed troop transports. Each was capable of nearly 30 knots.

[†] Dorchester was a former passenger ship converted to serve as a U.S. Army transport during World War II. A German U-boat torpedoed the troopship in February 1943, and she sank with heavy loss of life. The incident became widely known in the United States because of the ship's Four Chaplains, Army officers who sacrificed their life jackets so that others could be saved.

[‡] Le Breton was born 12 August 1884. He served on active duty until his retirement in October 1947.

Paul Stillwell: Was the War Shipping Administration giving you your operating orders?

Captain Shellenbarger: Yes. They continued all the way right up till the end of the war. Of course, they gave the orders to the shipping companies who acted as agents for the ships.

Paul Stillwell: So these were not chartered. They were being operated by the shipping companies.

Captain Shellenbarger: They were being operated by the shipping companies for the government, War Shipping Administration. This was always a sore point through the years for merchant mariners getting veteran status. I mean, we were acting as gun crews; we were trained in the operation of guns. This was part of our training at Fort Trumbull. We had simulators. First simulator I ever saw was for a 20-millimeter with the Oerlikons, and we were trained how to operate the weapons. We didn't get the training on 5-inch or 3-inch guns, but we got training in the 20-millimeters and .50-caliber machine guns, stuff like that.

Paul Stillwell: Well, maybe it was a charter arrangement.

Captain Shellenbarger: I don't really know what the legal term was, but the ships were owned by the government. Every ship was taken over, not only U.S. flag, and this again is a sore point. Many foreign ships were taken over by the U.S. Government. For instance, there were Danish and Swedish ships that the Germans hadn't been able to get their hands on. Britain got a lot of them and operated them under their Board of Trade, I guess it was. A lot of them were taken over by the U.S. Government. Especially the oil tankers owned by Esso, Mobil or I guess it was Standard then, these other companies, because they had a lot of foreign-flag ships.

Some of them like Esso had a number of ships that had the German flag, but if they happened to be in a U.S. port when we entered the war, boom, that was it. Their crews were taken off, replaced by U.S. crews, and a lot of the Panamanian-flag ships had mixed crews. Where they didn't have enough of their own crew, they would put U.S. merchant sailors aboard. Now, I don't know if you're familiar with Arthur Moore's book.* It's a history of merchant ships lost during World War II.

Paul Stillwell: No, I'm not.

Captain Shellenbarger: You're not? I'll make sure you get a copy. Believe me, it's invaluable, because in there he did a tremendous amount of research. They talk about these losses of merchantmen. We were within one-tenth of a percent of what the Marines lost by percentage. Now, when they count all these foreign-flag ships that had U.S. sailors aboard, our losses for the merchant marine exceeded the Marines in World War II. They're talking on a percentage basis. But, anyway, this is what Arthur's doing now, and he's coming up with this information. For instance, some ship's name and date, there were eight Americans aboard that ship even though it was under a Panamanian flag. And in many cases they had U. S. armed guard aboard those ships, and the Navy has a record of those people. That's how Arthur's been able to locate the names of some of the ships because these companies have been long out of existence.

On that trip from Leghorn we brought back a small contingent, but it wasn't a full load of troops. As I recall now, it happened on about V-J Day, and everything just sort of fell apart, because what do we need all these ships for? That's what it amounted to, and shortly after that everything really changed. I was on the Reverdy Johnson until November 13, 1945, so I must have made another trip on her. At that time I got off the Reverdy Johnson, and that's when my first wife came up to Boston. We had an apartment in Brookline.

I went to an upgrade school, and I got my chief mate's license. At that time the inspection service was still pretty much operated by a former merchant man who had a Coast Guard license, but he also had a Coast Guard commission. And the inspector in Boston said, "Do you expect to come back here to upgrade to master?"

---

* Arthur R. Moore, A Careless Word . . . A Needless Sinking (Kings Point, New York: American Merchant Marine Museum, 1983).

I said, "As soon as I get my time in, I'll be back to upgrade." And the reason why is because one of my friends who had been teaching navigation at Fort Trumbull, had the desk right next to me, was a Captain Russell Perry. He had set up a little navigation school for refresher work in Boston called Bay State Navigation, and Russ had said, "How about coming up here to upgrade?" So I did.

When I went to the inspector and told him I'd be coming back there, he said, "Well, in that case, I'll go ahead and give you a number of elements from the master's exam. Then when you come back for your master's license, I'll have it on record here, and then you can do it in a much shorter time." See, in those days they were all written examinations—none of this multiple choice. Two of them are obviously wrong, and the other two are reasonable, so you've got a 50-50 chance of passing with knowing nothing. [Laughter] That's my attitude of them, but in those days you had to do everything essay and do everything written out. It took anywhere from a week to ten days to pass the exam.

Paul Stillwell: That was nice of him to do that for you.

Captain Shellenbarger: Yes, it was very nice of him, and it was a big help, because when I did come back for my master's license, I did it in three days. It was just the required elements that I had to do. So it worked out quite well.

That was November, and then from there my next ship was the Linn Boyd, another Liberty ship, but still with American Export Lines. I had cast my lot with them by that time. I ceased paying dues to Masters, Mates and Pilots and joined the little company union, Brotherhood of Marine Officers, which I stayed with until everything folded up in 1979.

Now we're getting into postwar things. First trip, Captain Gustav Moldestad. I had a chief mate's license now, getting my time in for master. I was the chief mate. We loaded coal, because this is the beginning of the Marshall Plan and, of course, a Liberty ship was ideal for coal.* We took a load of coal to Norway, and Captain Moldestad's

---

* At the Harvard University commencement in 1947, Secretary of State George C. Marshall made an address in which he outlined a plan for the economic rebuilding of war-ravaged Europe. Congress passed the European Recovery Act, and the program of American support came to be known as the Marshall Plan.

mother was still alive in Bergen. We went to a place called Fredrikstad, discharged part of our coal, and then we went up this river to Sarpsborg and I've forgotten where else. Lo and behold, Captain Moldestad said, "You're capable of relieving me. You take over. I'm going to visit my mother in Bergen. She hasn't seen me since before the war." Apparently he had an okay from New York. I never any problems. That was my first experience; even though I didn't have a master's license, I was still running the show.

Paul Stillwell: Bet it was a nice feeling.

Captain Shellenbarger: It was a nice feeling, yes. When we got up to Sarpsborg—at the end of the war, of course—we were greeted with open arms by the Norwegians.

    The agent tried to get us a little trip to Sweden. One Sunday afternoon he said, "I can arrange it. We've got a real fast train. Everything is going fine." I got a visa and everything. The purser and I got to the Swedish border, and they booted us off the train because they didn't want any part of us. This wasn't very far fortunately, so we rented bicycles and came back to the ship on bicycles. That was the only way you could get back. The agent made arrangements to ship the bikes back to destination at the border.

Paul Stillwell: Why wouldn't the Swedish honor the visa?

Captain Shellenbarger: It was a stamp on our seaman's passport, and they wouldn't recognize the seaman's passport. That was my impression. It had happened so fast, we were outside the train before I knew it. [Laughter]

Paul Stillwell: What a helpless feeling.

Captain Shellenbarger: Yes, but it was one of those little incidents that you've got to laugh at. And it was probably just as well. Who knows what would have happened if we'd gotten over the border into Sweden? Here I was, the acting master? Say I wound up in a Swedish jail? No way.

Anyway, when we left Norway, we came back in ballast. And somehow in there, there had to be another trip because we ended up going to France; maybe it was before the Norwegian trip. We couldn't go all the way up to Bordeaux and we tied up to a place below there in the Gironde River to discharge coal. There was my first experience of having to tie up with anchor chains, which happened many times later in India, because of the high tides. You have to take shots of chain from your anchors, pull them back aft by barge, hoist them back aboard, and make your stern fast with segments of your anchor chain.* And then your other anchor chain would be disconnected from the anchor. You hang off the anchor and send your forward anchor chain ashore. It happened there, and that was my first experience with it, in Blaye, which was the place where we discharged the coal. And, of course, coal was in much demand there.

So it must have been the trip before that when I went on the Linn Boyd, because when we came back from Norway we had 10 passengers. By this time the gun crew was gone, so we had the gun crew quarters available for passengers. There were eight pilots who had flown with the Norwegian Free Air Force under the RAF.†

Paul Stillwell: Were these pilots Americans?

Captain Shellenbarger: No, they were Norwegians, and they had two Norwegian young ladies. Now, there was a lot of conversation went back and forth in Norwegian, which we didn't know what it was about, but the Norwegian pilots all spoke good English. After all, they'd been flying for the RAF and they're taught English in school. The ladies spoke English. Eventually one of the ladies married our purser, and one of the pilots told me, "Hey, you don't want nothing to do with those two women. They're Quislings. The reason they're leaving Norway is that supposedly they're going to go live with relatives in the States, but they're Quislings. They collaborated with the Germans."‡ Now,

---

* In this context a shot is a length of anchor chain, usually 15 fathoms. A fathom comprises six feet.
† RAF—Royal Air Force.
‡ Vidkun Quisling (18887-1945) was a Norwegian Army officer and later the nation's Defense Minister. He believed in Nordic racial superiority and sought German support when his political fortunes waned. After Norway fell to Germany in 1940 Quisling became a figurehead leader in the country for the remainder of the war. He was tried for treason and executed in October 1945. His name became a generic term for those who collaborated with the Nazis.

whether that's true or not I don't know. From my viewpoint, they were two very nice ladies, especially Christine.

Paul Stillwell: And they were all sharing the same compartment?

Captain Shellenbarger: No, no. The two ladies were amidships.

Paul Stillwell: Oh, I see.

Captain Shellenbarger: The former armed guard officer's cabin had two bunks, so the women were up there, and the eight pilots were back aft.

As we left Norway and headed back, of course, by this time we were proceeding independently. Our orders said, "Go to Boston." We went through the Pentland Firth, because there were still too many minefields in the English Channel to zigzag around. We couldn't have been more than a day or so out of there when we got a message that said, "No, your orders are changed. You go to New York." Within hours the orders changed from New York to Norfolk. We proceeded another two or three days, supposedly headed for Norfolk.

In the meantime, I was getting heckled by these Norwegian pilots, who told me that I didn't know how to navigate and this and that and everything else, didn't know what port we were going to. They were supposed to be going one place. Well, I'll tell you what happened; we ended up in Galveston, Texas. [Laughter] And it turned out that at that time the ship was being transferred during all this juggling that was going on at the end of the war—this ship going to this company, that ship going to that company. The Linn Boyd was going to Lykes Brothers Steamship Company. After we delivered the ship, we got our transportation back to New York. The Norwegians were coming over to pick up some commercial aircraft for the nucleus of SAS.* Now, whether they were all pilots or some were pilots and some navigators—that I don't recall, but they were quite a bunch of boys. It was a lot of fun, really.

---

* SAS—Scandinavian Airlines System.

Paul Stillwell: In what ways?

Captain Shellenbarger: Oh, the jokes and stories and their war experiences. It was a lot of fun with them. They'd come around, and I was chief mate on the ship, and they really heckled me on that. Oh, boy. But as chief mate I was standing the 4:00 to 8:00 watch, three-mate ship, and I was doing the stars. I had a good second mate on there, and it was a nice ship. Very nice skipper, Captain Moldestad. He lived to be about 96 years old, and his son was in the U.S. Air Force. I think he became a colonel.

Paul Stillwell: These must have been bomber pilots if they had navigators among them.

Captain Shellenbarger: I think they could have been easily. Yes.

Paul Stillwell: Did you have charts that showed where these minefields were?

Captain Shellenbarger: You would have indications. Actually, they'd give you the limits of a minefield, and you had to plot them on your chart. In other words, the minefields ran from this point to that point to that point.

Paul Stillwell: Who would give you that?

Captain Shellenbarger: We'd usually get our sailing orders through the shipping company's agents. Presumably they came from the Navy. Who else would have them?

Paul Stillwell: So the Navy would give them to American Export?

Captain Shellenbarger: That's right, and then before we sailed we got all this information. Right up to the very end, before you left port on your sailing to the States, you would get what they called the captain's letter. And in there you had your sailing orders, and there'd be all kinds of attachments that we got: how much fuel we were expected to consume and not to exceed certain speeds due to fuel restrictions. And they would give us any special information about ports and the draft restrictions. And, of course, in those early days you'd get all the information on minefields. People to contact, which consulates to call at, and things of that sort.

Of course, under U.S. law if you go into a port as a merchant skipper, you are required to pay a courtesy call to the U.S. consul. And they usually had a merchant marine section where one of the vice consuls would take care of merchant marine matters. As a matter of fact, I've got about three or four passports that I've had renewed by consulates around the world. One of them that I sort of treasure was renewed in Taipei while they still had consular services, while we still officially recognized Taiwan as an independent country.

Paul Stillwell: Well, with this ship then turned over to Lykes, you were again without a ship.

Captain Shellenbarger: Yes. I left the Linn Boyd in June 1946, June 3. I went right back to New York and, lo and behold, I see that on the 13th of June I reported to the Coaldale Victory. The Coaldale Victory was one of those I mentioned earlier--a Victory trooper. This was a Victory ship. They had steam turbines, they were not reciprocating engines. As the war had progressed they had been able to build Victory ships with turbines. I don't recall—on the Coaldale, she was probably one of the 6,000-horsepower type. They had two grades of Victories. I don't know if you're aware of that or not.

Paul Stillwell: No.

Captain Shellenbarger: One was 6,000 horsepower; one was 8,500 horsepower. And the difference was primarily from an operational aspect was that the 6,000 horsepower—I may be wrong, but this is how I recall it—the 6,000 had a top speed of about 15 and a half knots, where the 8,500 would do about 17. Their top speed, of course. Most of the companies didn't recommend running them that fast, because of the expense of fuel consumption. However, the Coaldale had been fitted out as a trooper and those ships had extensive reefer boxes for additional troops. They carried 1,500 troops and they used of them for repatriating troops because now this is, what, 1946.

You're starting to get a tremendous inflow of troops. Believe me, the Queen Mary and the Queen Elizabeth couldn't handle all of them and, of course, they still had the Manhattan and Washington from U.S. Lines. I think they were troopers. The America, which became the USS West Point, which incidentally my sister Georgia was aboard. She'd joined the WAACs early in the war, and she was with a contingent.[*] They were the first WAC contingent to arrive in Australia. She was on a general's staff. She was a tech sergeant, I think—whatever it was. But I can't remember the name of the general. She told me too. General Somerville? He was with the services of supply or whatever. Anyway, the general in charge of supplies.

She was on his staff, and she'd been with him in Brisbane, she'd gone to New Guinea with him, and she was in Manila with him, and she came home from Manila. And this is an aside. She died in 1968. I'd say from complications that she received while she was over there. She got married when she came back and had four children. Her husband, I guess, was no great help. He passed away last year, but she died in 1968. There's only two of her children alive today.

But, anyway, this was a trooper, and we were all set to go overseas. They'd stored the ship and that was the first time I'd ever seen milk frozen. And they had cartons of milk, actually solid blocks, and they had the reefer boxes full of milk, pre-cut steaks, turkeys, all kinds of stuff they took. When these guys are coming home, they've been on K rations for years, they wanted to feed them well and they did. And they had extra crew members, and they, again, were fitted with these knock-down bunks so they could carry 1,500 troops, is what they told me in the crew.

Well, actually we waited at a pier at Staten Island—fitting out, loading, getting ready to sail, and all of a sudden it was canceled. They didn't need the ship. So I couldn't have been on that thing more than a month, just laying there, and from there the company sent me--yeah, it was just about a month. It was in July I went aboard a ship called the Honduras Victory, on which I remained roughly 14 months, and I'm still chief mate.

---

[*] The Women's Army Auxiliary Corps (WAAC) was established on 14 May 1942. In 1943 it changed from a civilian auxiliary into part of the Army itself, the Women's Army Corps (WAC).

Somewhere in there, I can't recall, I didn't make a note of it, I'd got my time in and I got my master's license. I'd gone back to Boston and got my master's license. Took only three days, because I went back to the same instructor. Must have been, because I'm pretty sure I had my master's license when I was up there on the Honduras Victory.

But, anyway, we made a lot of trips on the Honduras Victory, five or six. Two or three of them were with coal. One trip I remember specifically was coal to Alexandria, Egypt. Of course, it was still under British control. I went ashore, and I still have the passes from there.

And then again Export Line was starting to regenerate service to the Mediterranean. That's where their specialty was, package trade to the Mediterranean, carrying tobacco back and a lot, oh, you name it, what comes from the Mediterranean? Olives, raisins—just anything. So many I can't even begin to think of all of them. We carried the normal stuff going back. So these we started to regenerate, and with the Honduras Victory we started that.

We would normally start at Casablanca first port, Casablanca to Tangier to Algiers, Tunis, and Tripoli. AEL had the Eastern Med and the Western Med service. That was what they called the Western Med service, and from Tripoli we'd go up to Naples, Livorno, Genoa, Marseilles, Barcelona. Well, when you made that trip, this became a really quite hectic, because it lasted many years. I was on it with other ships. You'd start at Barcelona and you'd hit all the Spanish ports. You'd hit six or seven Spanish ports. Down to Malaga, through the Straits, back to Cadiz and then up the Guadalquivir to Seville, load olives. And back in those days we loaded them in huge puncheons weighing about 600 kilos each. From there because you had to have a minimum draft in the Guadalquivir, when you came out of there then you'd go to Portimao, a little port in the southern part of Portugal, and load sardines—skinless and boneless sardines. Then around up in the Tagus to Lisbon and Lisbon back to the States.

And was on that for a number of years. As far as history is concerned, I can't think of anything special in that time that would be of interest.

Paul Stillwell: Well, you were certainly building up experience toward getting your own ship during this period.

Captain Shellenbarger: Oh, yes. Definitely.

Paul Stillwell: Any observations about those Mediterranean countries and how well they were faring in rebuilding from the war?

Captain Shellenbarger: Well, one thing that as far as rebuilding from the war was that definitely they relied on assistance from the United States. As a matter of fact, some of our regular company ships even had special pictures in the paper about hands across the sea. And they put special slogans on the side of the ship, painted special signs on them, and what have you.

Of course, this particular ship, the skipper on there was a character. I joked with him, and I sailed with him for about 14 months. We got quite close, the chief mate and the captain, in a period of time like that. His name was Otto Trautman. He had been in the German Army during World War I, and he came to the States and followed the sea as a career.

He used to get upset with me because, with a German name like mine, I couldn't speak German, so he'd try to teach me German words, probably more than I ever got at home because my grandfather, who was from Germany, had apparently passed the word along in our family that there was no German to be spoken, which was a tragedy you realize in your later years. When he made the break, he wanted everything spoken in English. That was it, which sometimes I think maybe that's the right way to go. Who knows?

But, anyway, Otto and I became quite good friends. He was the skipper during this 14 months I was on the Honduras Victory, and I think we did a good job on the ship, at least from my personal viewpoint. We kept it up. We did a lot of maintenance, because the company had the option then when they started buying ships to replace their own fleet. They bought this ship, and they renamed it the Exton because the Export Line liked to have the syllable "Ex" in all of their ships' names. So they made the Exton out of it.

Paul Stillwell: What duties did you have as chief mate in addition to the navigation?

Captain Shellenbarger: Well, when you got on a Victory ship, you're going to four mates. And the chief mate on a Victory ship doesn't have much to do with navigation, because he's no longer a watch stander.

Paul Stillwell: I see.

Captain Shellenbarger: He becomes a day man, working a lot of overtime, cargo, cargo, cargo and maintenance of the vessel, of course. You're also the first lieutenant, but you've got the boatswain, and you've got the crew. In those days you had a crew of six ABs, three ordinary seamen to do deck maintenance, four on day work, two ABs and an ordinary was on a watch.* The two day men and a boatswain were day work, and they worked directly under your supervision. And, of course, during the day the ABs, if they weren't on watch, would be chipping and painting and maintenance. And we did a good job on the Exton, because when they started surveying the various Victories, they said, "Okay, we're going to take this one, and it's going to be the Exton," which it became. But, anyway, after 14 months there, it was time for vacation. By this time, it's 1947, and we're getting 30 days vacation a year. Prior to that you were lucky to get two weeks. Even then, with 30 days' vacation a year, was--what the Navy used to call it?—when the exigencies of the service permit.

Paul Stillwell: Yes, exactly.

Captain Shellenbarger: Well, this is true also of American Export Lines. If they didn't need you, you got a vacation. And the way they put it was, "Say, Chief, you're going coastwise, and we know you've got that 30 days' vacation coming, but how about taking a two-weeks coastwise? We'll pay you for the vacation, but would you mind working?" You got double pay, of course. You got your vacation time, as well as being paid for the job. Of course, they're playing on your ego because you're second mate maybe, and this

---

* AB—able-bodied seaman, as distinguished from the less well qualified ordinary seaman.

is a relief job as chief mate. And if you're chief mate, this is a relief job as master, and you building up experience and time. So they knew how to do it, and in all respects it was a damn good company to work for.

At that time they were running 84 ships at the end of the war, and they were in the prospect—their original Four Aces, which carried roughly 120 passengers, they had taken four of their so-called Exporter class right at the end of the war—they'd been troopships during the war--they took these four ships and they were rebuilding. They stripped them right down to the hull--I remember seeing in Hoboken Shipyard—a bare-bones hull and bare stack uptakes sticking there. And they completely rebuilt them as the second group of Four Aces. And they kept the same names: the Excambion, the Excalibur, the Exeter, and the Exochorda. Those were the four names that they'd had for their previous Four Aces, which had been built at in Philadelphia at Cramp's in the early '30s.

At the end of the war two of them had been sunk in the North African invasion, because they were troopers, naturally. One was sold to the Turks. We used to see it around the Mediterranean all the time. That was the leaning Harry Lee, called that because it always had a list.[*] I'd done a short tour of duty when I was with the admiral's staff. I got transferred over to the Barnett in one of our simulated practices in the spring of '41 or whenever it was.[†] But I remembered the Harry Lee, because we were a little flag contingent they put on board for I guess for about a week. We slept up in the forward stack, which was a dummy. It had been the dog kennels, still smelled of dogs. We had cots in there, and they'd just put the two 36-inch searchlights on either side of the forward stack, because that's what we were using. The 12-inchers didn't work worth a damn, and one thing we did was get their signal halyards out on a yardarm; this was our recommendation on that ship. This is going back again, because this developed later. They used to call me a freak. This was back in the Navy. Everything relates back to the Navy, so many ways. I could not go aboard a merchant ship and stand to see a triatic stay. You know what a triatic stay is?

---

[*] USS Harry Lee was built in 1931 as a commercial passenger ship and operated as the Exochorda by American Export Lines. The U.S. Navy acquired the ship 30 October 1940, converted her to a troop transport and commissioned her as AP-17 on 27 December 1940.

[†] USS Barnett was built in Britain in 1928 as the passenger steamer Santa Maria. The U.S. Navy got her on 9 August 1940, converted her to a troop transport, and commissioned her 25 September 1940 as AP-11.

Paul Stillwell: No.

Captain Shellenbarger: Between the kingpost or the mast there is a steel wire, cable that goes back to the stack, and on that are the pulleys for the little signal halyards. And this is what the merchant ships in so many cases back in those days would have for signal flags or for flying whatever like your George or your Hypo or for your pilot flags and various signals.* And, being an ex-Navy man, I couldn't stand it.

It got to be a joke because I was with Export so long. They'd say, "Shelley's been on that ship, because that ship has a yardarm." [Laughter] Because being BMO, the engineers and the mates all had the same union, we got along great together. And I would somehow or other con the chief engineer or the first. We'd get some pipe, and we would put a signal mast and yardarm up there. Because normally there was a kingpost or something there that you could put it onto. In many cases it was just a mast of some sort, and we'd put a yardarm, and I'd end up with a yardarm.

I had a friend, Captain John Cain, who was port captain. He'd say, "What the hell do you need all these blocks for? Every ship you go on you're putting a requisition for these little 3-inch blocks." And there was one block particularly that I was partial to, because this was the beginning of the nylon blocks and nylon sheaves. And I'd end up with a yardarm with at least two signal and sometimes three signal halyards on each yardarm.

It got to be a joke. They'd say, "Hey, there's the Exporter. Shelley's been on there, because they've got a yardarm. Exchester. Shelley's been on there because it's got a yardarm." And everybody that went on the ship after that would say, "Hey, that's great." And on the Excalibur in particular, because I was a long time on it. That was a passenger-cargo ship. I had been second mate on it and later on chief officer on it, a passenger ship. And, there again, when I was second mate I got together with the skipper and we got a yardarm—real fancy on there. The chief engineer was a good friend of mine, and he was a great machinist.

---

* George and Hypo represented two of the words in the phonetic alphabet of the era. George meant, "I require a pilot." Hypo meant, "I have a pilot on board."

Here again, I'm digressing, but he made beautiful brass belaying pins for the pin rails beneath the yardarms on the Excalibur. This one had six, three on each side. The chief engineer came up one morning and he looked at them and he blew his top. I had painted them. His name was Lawrence Washington Rivers; "Wash" we used to call him. I said, "Wash, if I leave those things up here in brass, and you know the Mediterranean. We'd come into port and with these ports they're going to be gone." Well, then he saw it my way, but he was livid after I painted these things. And then eventually what we had to do was we had to drill little holes through them and put like a pin through them so they couldn't be lifted out of the pin rail, because this is always a problem, especially in Korean ports and Naples.

Paul Stillwell: So you had your little miniature Navy contingent there on board.

Captain Shellenbarger: [Laughter] On board, yeah. But I enjoyed it. Yes, I enjoyed it. So, anyway, from the Honduras Victory I went to the Catawba Victory. The skipper on there had just come back from Japanese prison camp, Elmar Saar. He ended up in Sailors Snug Harbor, passed away there four years ago. He had been chief officer on one of the first merchant ships that was sunk at the beginning of the war, after we'd gotten into it. Had a ship called the Sawokla. The guy that got all the credit—and all the publicity— was the guy that was second mate. But Elmar was the chief mate.

They were sunk by a German raider, Michel, or whatever it was. The first shell hit the bridge and killed the skipper, Captain Carl Wink. I don't know what happened to the third mate, Stanley Willner, but the second mate was a fellow named Dennis Roland, and he was hero of the movie Bridge On The River Kwai, because he went in that contingent.*

However, the crew was picked up from the Sawokla, and Elmar immediately became captain because the skipper was killed. The crew was picked up by the Germans. They had a lot of British and other nationalities, prisoners aboard, and they had to get rid of them. Now, Elmar was Estonian, and in addition to Estonian he spoke Russian, he

---

* The Bridge on the River Kwai was an Oscar-winning movie, made in 1957, about the plight of Allied prisoners, mostly British, forced by their Japanese captors to build a railroad bridge in the rugged Asian jungle during World War II.

spoke German. He was fluent in a number of languages and he spoke German so when he was on the German ship he acted as interpreter for a lot of the POW crew, and he said that the Germans treated them decently. They treated them as prisoners of war, of course, but he said they treated them decently.

However, they had to get rid of them because they didn't have supplies naturally, so they went into Singapore and turned them over to the Japanese. Part of the crew went to Burma to build a bridge over the River Kwai, and the second mate went with that contingent. Elmar was sent with a group to a prison camp in Hokkaido. He said fortunately they had a few Japanese; he said they wouldn't have survived otherwise. He said the Ainu, the natives of Hokkaido, were terrible. The story they told about having to pick through excrement for grains of food. He said it was what they did to survive. That was it. And from the stories I hear about it, they're obviously true. By the same token, I know the other side of the coin too. I had a brother in Korea, First Marine Division, Chosin Reservoir, and they had North Korean prisoners.[*] They didn't turn them loose to go back to fight another day. He was a tank driver, a tank which had a flame thrower. Went through the compound and used napalm.

Paul Stillwell: I had not heard about that.

Captain Shellenbarger: This I heard from my brother. On their way back they were running short of fuel and they hit a mine. He was the only survivor of the tank crew. Had his hatch open. I don't know if it's good or bad. He came down on his head, and they sent him back. He ended up in the naval hospital in San Diego. From there he went AWOL. They put a plate in his head, but he was addled from then on. He became a truck driver and ended up disastrously. He ended up a suicide in a state prison in Utah. He went in the Marines, and his twin brother went in the Navy. His twin brother just returned to St. Louis at the reunion of the Pawcatuck, a Navy oiler, AO-108.

---

[*] In November 1950, in brutal cold, U.S. Marines fought a battle with Chinese Communist soldiers near the Chosin Reservoir in North Korea. In December the Marines staged a fighting retreat from Chosin and were evacuated through the port of Hungnam. The interviewee's brother was Private First Class Robert D. Shellenbarger, USMC, B Company, First Tank Battalion, First Marine Division. He enlisted 28 July 1948 and sailed for Korea on 16 August 1950.

Paul Stillwell: It's interesting what fate can do with different people in the same family.

Captain Shellenbarger: Yes. I think Richard, who was Robert's twin, was on the Pawcatuck during the Korean War. Then he ended up on a little yard oiler in the Bahamas? Who could ask for any better duty than that?

Paul Stillwell: That's right.

Captain Shellenbarger: That's where he was discharged from. But, anyway, he told me this was the Pawcatuck. because I was still sailing, of course, and I used to see the Pawcatuck in Norfolk, because I used to watch for it. This one time I know he came aboard with some of his buddies. They were in at the same time I was, and they came over and visited the ship. Of course, I was the ship master by then. These guys thought it was great. Here's a guy had a brother was a ship captain.

So, anyway, I was on the Catawba Victory for 1947, and then in 1948 I went back on the Drake Victory. Then I went on the Exhibitor. That was sort of a landmark when you went on one of that we called the "Ex" ships, in other words one of the regular company ships. You felt that, "Hey, I'm getting ahead in the company" On the Exhibitor I was just second mate and, of course, this was where everything started to cut back. When I went on the Exhibitor in May, 1948, you look at the license rack. You've got a master and four mates with masters' licenses there. A lot of them were merchant marine reservists who name came back to the company. The skipper had been a commander in the Navy, Jim La Belle. He was one of the few that didn't revert back to merchant practices, because he ran that ship like a Navy ship. I stayed on the Exhibitor with him, oh, until 1951.

Paul Stillwell: Now, what do you mean by saying that he ran it like a Navy ship?

Captain Shellenbarger: Well, he expected you to be in uniform—of course, this was a company regulation—when you were on duty. You were expected always to wear an officer's cap when on deck, so that you didn't look like another hired hand. The stevedores knew that you were a ship's officer on duty. He did make a concession that we didn't have to wear ties. He griped about it to me, but said, "After all, we're running to India."

This was the period of time where these long trips to India, four-five months, then come back in. I don't really blame my first wife. She ran off with a cop from Nassau County on Long Island. She left the two kids with her parents in West Virginia when I wasn't home. You know, this is not a life for a family man. Let's face it. That's why so many of my friends have gone ashore. And this is why my friend Joe Gross, went ashore but that's the way things happen. I felt that I had to earn a living, send that allotment home.

Paul Stillwell: And that was the way you knew.

Captain Shellenbarger: That's what I knew, and this is why it's fortunate that a couple of years later that I met my present wife. But, anyway, she was gone, the kids were living with the grandparents. I went to Florida after all this time on the Exhibitor, running to India. Long trips, very little time for vacation in between. Learning a hell of a lot with Jimmy La Belle, because with him I learned. Some of it wasn't real pleasant, but I respected him. Boy, I really respected him.

Paul Stillwell: What do you mean some of it wasn't real pleasant?

Captain Shellenbarger: Well, just to give you one little incident to illustrate. We're in the port of Colombo. I'm down checking out mail and special cargo. These were so-called the Exporter-class ships. They had a little hatch, which was the number-four hatch. Had two little square hatches on either side where you could put cargo in. Our strong rooms were down there. I think I was down there checking mail because that was quite common in those days; we carried a lot of mail. And you still had a tally counter there. We would tally bags.

But, anyway, this one draft was going out, and it was a case of pencils. American Export Line was notorious for the fact that you didn't get much of anything. Today you'll see me going around with four or five pencils in my pockets. Back in those days for a five-month trip the company would put 12 pencils aboard for the chartroom. Well, at the end of six weeks your pencils are all gone, so everybody carried their own pencils. This draft went out, and the sling broke. The case fell back in the hatch, and you've got a tallyman there, Ceylonese, part of the shore guys. The tallymen were a separate group anyway. They weren't regular longshoremen. The tallyman and I gathered up all the pencils.

We put them in the box, and I figured we got everything in there and the tallyman was happy. We got a cooper and recoopered the case. Number-four hatch is directly underneath the bridge wing. Jimmy was up on the bridge wing, looking down and watching this incident. After the draft went out and we got a clear signature on it, I looked around. Immediately under the hatch opening were the openings for our deep tanks, which carried bulk cargo and stuff like that. I looked around there and, hey, we missed some pencils. I guess there must have been about 20 pencils, and, boy, they were number twos. I picked them up, put them in my pocket, and I came up to the bridge about an hour and a half later.

I put the pencils on the chart table and said, "Hey, this is a windfall. We got some extra pencils." Jimmy came in, and he read the riot act to me: "You are stealing cargo." And he really reamed me out. That was his way of thinking. Now, I respected him. Obviously he respected me, because I ended up on two other ships with him and the reason I ended up with him is because he was always hardnosed in many ways. There were a lot of mates that couldn't get along with him, but I could.

There again, maybe it goes back to my Navy training. Who knows? But Jimmy would go aboard a ship as master. Tom Collins would call me and say, "Hey, do you mind going with Captain La Belle again?" He said, "The ship's ready to sail, and I can't get anybody that wants to sail with him. I can order somebody on there, but that isn't good. You know, you've sailed with Jimmy. You know how he is."

And so I ended up as chief mate with him on the Expeditor. (I got off the Exiria on the 25th of May 1953, and I went on the Expeditor the 26th, my birthday, at the age of 33.) I was with him on the Excalibur as second officer, and he was master of the Constitution when he cut an oil tanker in two off of New York Harbor, and he came to me and wanted my radar course.* I told him it was kind of late to be taking a radar course. He was put ashore for a year. He was with the company agent in Chicago for a year. And then he came back, but he no longer could sail on a passenger ship. You know, you've got 1,100 passengers on there, crew of 1,000. He was one of the up-and-coming skippers in the company, but he had this collision and he cut the tanker in two.

Paul Stillwell: What year would that have been?

Captain Shellenbarger: I'm trying to think of what year it would be, and I can pretty much gauge because it would have been the year previously because the ship that he called for me was the Expeditor. This would have to have been somewhere in '51 or '52 that it happened, because I know he was ashore in Chicago with the agent there, with the agency, and then he came on the Expeditor in July '53. That was when Tom called me. It was shortly after the ships were built, the Independence and Constitution, and then there was a change in the company's ownership.

Paul Stillwell: Well, back when you were in Exhibitor with him he must have had a considerable degree of confidence when he had a whole officer group made up of masters' licenses.

Captain Shellenbarger: Sure. And Jimmy also was noted for another thing, which I don't know whether it is his personality or not, but I became accustomed to it, and this again was why some of the people didn't like to sail with him. He had a tendency to sail far closer to any lighthouse than anybody I've ever sailed with.

In those days before radar we used a bow and beam bearing. As you were proceeding, you had a stopwatch. You took a bearing 45 degrees on the bow and a bearing on the beam. Well, when you're running a bow and beam bearing from 45 to 90 and you have to use a stopwatch to time with your speed, you're making speed and you're damned close in. I mean, we passed places along the coast of Ceylon and places where

---

* The Independence and Constitution were two passenger liners that American Export Lines put into service in the 1950s.

we were only a quarter of a mile off, and with Jimmy you did not change course without his permission—in the beginning.

Paul Stillwell: Why did he do that?

Captain Shellenbarger: I haven't the vaguest idea. Just part of his personality; he liked to cut corners. Let's put it that way. Now, he was always fortunate in that respect, because we had skippers in Export Line who would cut corners that didn't do so well. One of them off Cape De Gata in Spain ripped the bottom out of the Escambion by cutting too close. And that was just his personality, and that's the way he was.

Later on when I was with him on the Expeditor—remember this was a long time on the Exhibitor—he got to the point where he didn't cut it quite as close. He didn't lose any time. Another quirk he had was--this was kind of funny in a way--when we were on the Excalibur together I was second mate and the third mate was a fellow named Frank O'Byrne, Francis Xavier O'Byrne. And he had a master's license even then because he'd been skipper even as I had been earlier. And Jimmy.

We left Alexandria headed for, say, Gibraltar. He wanted to save time and speed. Can you imagine trying to sail a great circle in the Mediterranean from Alexandria to Gibraltar?* He used to cross the Atlantic and expect us to sail a great circle route. Frank O'Byrne came up one day, and I was busy calculating great circle. "What are you doing that for?" he said. "Here." And you had these big straight edges. He grabbed a straight edge, put it on the chart of the North Atlantic, bent it, and said, "Here, mark off the positions." That was our great circle. [Laughter] Frank and I were great friends.

Paul Stillwell: What did La Belle teach you from a professional standpoint?

Captain Shellenbarger: Oh, I certainly learned ship handling and seamanship from him. Of course, most of this period was, except for relief chief mate jobs, was second mate. I really enhanced my navigation during this period because he was a crackerjack navigator.

---

* A great circle route is one that would essentially be a straight line on the globe—that is, the shortest distance between two points on earth—but looks like an arc on a Mercator projection chart.

He had to be. Otherwise he'd have been piled up on the rocks years before. I don't know whether if he was like that before the war. He came out of the Navy as a commander. I don't know what he'd been commanding in the Navy. I never learned that.

Paul Stillwell: Well, I would be interested what you learned on ship handling, because I presume you had a single-screw ship and not much mobility.

Captain Shellenbarger: Oh, yes.

Paul Stillwell: What techniques did Captain Le Belle teach you?

Captain Shellenbarger: Oh. Not so much in ship handling. More on cargo and just operations and navigational skills, because he certainly taught me a lot of navigational skills. No question about it. I learned to use bow and beam bearings, which we did. You used those at 26 degrees, 26 and a half, 45s. These are primary piloting skills that we taught in Fort Trumbull that I hadn't used a heck of a lot but, boy, I sure used it with him. And this is before the days of radar, of course.

This Expeditor, incidentally, was the first ship that I'd seen with radar. It had something that looked like an oil well on top of the bridge because it had been a Navy trooper. The reason for that is because those Export ships were fast. They could easily cruise at 17 and a half knots. I had one ship, the Exiria, I took to the bone yard. They were the smaller ships, the four small ships. The Navy had two of them, the Army had two of them as Army transports, Navy transports. And the ballast in them, they used the deep tanks for fuel. They carried about, oh, 1500 troops, and they always ran independently because they could do 21-22 knots. And when I was on the Exiria and the Extavia I would normally cruise at 17 and a half because I had a schedule to keep. But when it came to running into heavy weather, you didn't make any speed at all because they had a bow like a knife, had no flare to the bow and once you started pitching you made like a submarine. You reduced speed or you had horrendous damage.

Paul Stillwell: You mentioned these long trips to India. What sort of cargoes would you be taking there?

Captain Shellenbarger: Well, this was right after the war basically, so there was a lot of manufactured goods going there. Occasionally automobiles and I can recall carrying deck cargoes of locomotives which we'd load in Philadelphia. We used to go up there, and they had a big sheer-leg crane, which would load a locomotive on one side. Tugs would turn the ship around, and you'd load one on the other side. Then you'd turn around and go back, load a tender or maybe another locomotive aft. Do the same thing again, because deck cargo is loaded after you've loaded general cargo, and the general cargo could be anything from foodstuffs. I spent a long time running to India. Second mate with Captain La Belle, and I was on the Exminster with Ernie Lorenz. I was second mate with him.

One of the incidents involved a time when the Exminster was carrying penicillin back in number six hatch. We were in Bombay, tied up to this berth, and we used to have policemen aboard. I don't know whether they were to prevent smuggling or maintain order, but it was during lunch hour of this particular day, and I was on duty, as second mate. I heard this noise down in number-seven hatch during lunch hour. The longshoremen had gone off for lunch. I said, "Hey, what's this?" So I went down in the manhole and went down the ladder. Lo and behold, there is an Indian policeman with his hand stuck in a crate. He looked at me and, of course, they don't carry weapons, they carry a lathy, this bamboo stick which they use for crowd control and what have you. It was lying alongside of him.

As I recall, he had something that indicated he was from the Yellow Gate police station, which was one of the dock gates. So here he was, and he had his hand stuck. So I don't carry it so much today, but normally I always had a little whistle. This dates back to your days when you used whistle signals for tugs. You used signals for on deck to attract attention and what have you, and I used to buy them by the dozen in Aden. They're British made and they're called an Acme Thunderer, a little whistle and they have very sharp sound, and believe me they can be heard.

So I blew my whistle, and one of the deck crew came up, and I said, "Hey, go get the chief mate. We've got a guy stealing cargo down here." Apparently the chief mate called ashore and said, "We've got a thief up here." When the chief mate came, there were four other cops with him from this dock. They took one look at this guy, and his hand was still stuck in the case. At the time I had no sympathy for him. He was pilfering cargo, and it was penicillin—crystallized, I think.

They took him up, and they put him on deck. And they started whaling him with the lathies, and they took him off. The very next day the skipper, Ernie Lorenz, he came to me, and he said, "Hey, you're going to have to go up to police court over on Ballard Pier. They've got a magistrate's court, and they've got this guy we caught pilfering over there."

The agent from Lionel Edwards was a very nice guy, really. I mean because we had a doctor who was a Parsi. He used to come aboard and check the crew. Every time you got to port if it was a big port, you always had a doctor come aboard to check out your crew ailments because while you did the doctoring and set bones and give shots and whatever, whenever you got to a port that had a doctor you'd get a doctor aboard to check them out to make sure that you were doing the right thing for one of them, even though it was part of your medical log.

Anyway, I had to go over there, and here was this court, magistrate, no jury, strictly a magistrate, hearing the evidence against this guy. Then, of course, I had to be sworn in and it was one of those things. "Do you swear on the Bible, the Koran or something else?" I said on the Bible, and it was the usual oath. I had to testify that I'd found this guy. Of course, they were referring to him by name. I said, "No, I recognize the belt buckle with his number, 526, [or whatever it was]." I said, "I found him with his hand in the cargo." And I didn't give any thought to it, you know.

Paul Stillwell: Just doing your duty.

Captain Shellenbarger: Doing my duty. And then we were finished, and I had to go back and sit with the agent, because he took me over there. I said, "Well, what now?"

He said, "Well, the magistrate will sentence him." And the magistrate sentenced him in English and in his local language, Urdu or whatever it was. Might have been Hindi, for all I know. But after the magistrate sentenced him in his language, I could see the guy, who was dark color, and he practically turned white. Then he said the same thing in English, "You are hereby sentenced to hard labor for ten years."

I asked the agent, "Ten years? That's a lot for pilfering."

"Oh," he said, "this was a major crime."

I said, "Hard labor?"

He said, "Oh, yes. That's hard labor in the Andaman Islands, a prison colony, and the average prisoner in the Andaman Islands does not survive more than three years." And then it's over. That's it. It's just one of those many things that happen to you through the years that kill you. You know, you remember.

Paul Stillwell: Yes, you would remember that.

Captain Shellenbarger: Yes, you would remember it. It's just one of the many, many incidents that, all of a sudden, as I'm doing this, memories start coming back to me.

Paul Stillwell: Yeah. Do you remember the upheaval in India during that period as they were partitioning and setting up Pakistan?*

Captain Shellenbarger: It was pretty much done with by the time I starting sailing out there regularly, but there was still a lot of nationalism and things you'd hear about, incidents here and there. There was nothing that I observed particularly, but, of course, later on after that period we would call at Karachi which was western Pakistan, and we'd deal with those people. Of course they're primarily Muslims, and we formed very good friends there.

One longshoreman in Karachi, every time I'd come in he would ask me if I'd had a son yet. I'd have to say, "No, no sons," and he was very much concerned. You know, it

---

* On 14 August 1947, sections of India were split off to become the new nation of Pakistan, an independent dominion in the British Commonwealth of Nations. India gained independence the following day.

is very important to them to have a son. The same thing would happen when we'd get to Chittagong. That was eastern Pakistan. We'd go up the Hooghly River, tie up with chains. You'd have to go to the mobile dock in Buj-Buj, B-U-J dash B-U-J. It was an oil refinery--or it wasn't really a refinery. It was just a distribution area. We used to carry a lot of bulk lube oil in there in our deep tanks. Go in the morning, tie up with chains to buoys and the shore. The drill of taking chains back aft, heaving them aboard, it's a four-hour operation. You'd tie up four hours, you'd pump your oil ashore, which took about six to eight hours, untie, another three or four hours because you had to have your anchors ready for moving up the river from Buj-Buj to King George Dock or Kiddapore. And if you didn't go inside the dock you had to tie up out in the reaches as they called them, Garden Reach, and those places where you tied up with the chains again.

Paul Stillwell: Why wouldn't a mooring line be sufficient?

Captain Shellenbarger: Couldn't withstand the bore. Are you familiar with the bore?

Paul Stillwell: No.

Captain Shellenbarger: A bore is an incoming tide in a relatively shallow area. They have it in the Bay of Fundy, a range of maybe 30 feet. When the incoming tide comes in over the water, it piles up, and you have literally a wall of water coming upriver or upstream. I have broken loose later on when I sailed around the world, we were running on the _Flying Fish_. We broke loose out there, and only our bow chains held us. Then we had to get tugs and go back and pick up all the debris, broken lines, because in addition to your chains you do have mooring lines because you have to tie up with mooring lines while you're working with the chains, and you had to got to get your chains done before the next bore.

Paul Stillwell: And sometimes you wouldn't get the mooring lines off and they would break.

Captain Shellenbarger: Yes.

Paul Stillwell: So I take it you had powerful enough winches aft to handle these chains.

Captain Shellenbarger: Oh, yes. They would, but when the chains came back on these little barges that they used for handling this, you'd have to send a wire down to bring the chains up and you're bringing the chains up through a chock which is normally used only for mooring lines, and so it was an operation, to say the least. Hard work. Laborious. And if you moored in the morning, do your job at Buj-Buj, unmoor in the afternoon, six hours later you're doing the same thing upriver. By the time you got finished, the crew was finished. I mean, they were worn out. Plus the officers had been up almost continuously. It wasn't an easy operation, but then once you got tied up in Calcutta you were there for three weeks because you went up on the spring tides, which are the highest of the highs and lowest and lows, and you had to come out on the spring tides.

Well, so what you did you went up and discharged your cargo, lay there, and loaded cargo. Most of the time it was jute, gunnies, tea. I've forgotten most of the other stuff, but we sometimes would load manganese ore but not there so much as we did down at Vizagapatam. Because that was after we got out of the Hooghly. But quite often we'd stop at Vizag on the way in. Madras. Gee, I can't remember what we used to load there. Shellac, all kinds of stuff. And then on our way home we'd stop in Colombo, Ceylon, and start loading all kinds of nuts and stuff like that. We used to come back with vast quantities of cashews and pepper. Oh, we carried a lot of pepper, spices, and what have you.

Paul Stillwell: How did you spend three weeks in Calcutta?

Captain Shellenbarger: Chasing the coolies. Going up the Chowringa Road. Going to the movies. Drinking beer. They had a British seamen's club there where we were always welcome. And I don't know whether I should say this or not because she's become almost a saint, but we chased Mother Teresa and her cohorts off the ship.[*] Oh, they used to haunt us up there. This is before she became famous worldwide.

Paul Stillwell: Haunt in what way?

Captain Shellenbarger: They used to come aboard and there'd be about six of them at a time come aboard. Well, we called it panhandling. Of course, they were raising alms for the poor, which was a good thing, but nevertheless they would come aboard with the crew and they would interfere with the operations of the ship. You just can't have those people aboard, not to mention insurance problems. When people come aboard a ship that's working, it's a dangerous place to be. You've got to remember this is a cargo ship. You've got cargo swinging back and forth. You've got it on the dock. It's not a good place. They did it on all the American ships, because that was where the money was. The Isthmian Line ships, the Export Line ships, Waterman used to run ships in there. And, of course, the attitude of the typical American sailor is, "Hey, you want a buck? We'll give you five. What the heck? Another payday's two weeks down the road." I didn't realize till many years later that sure, this was the same Sister Teresa. She spoke very good English. Boy, she'd give us what for: "You have no charitable bones in your soul. We pray for you people nevertheless."

Paul Stillwell: I've always had this image of Ceylon as a very exotic place. What was it like in reality?

Captain Shellenbarger: I never got outside of Colombo but once, and that was only after I became sailing master because when you're chief mate, you work the cargo when you're in port. This was all before containers.

---

[*] Mother Teresa (1910-1997) was a nun known throughout the world for her charity towards the poor. She led the Missionaries of Charity home in Calcutta, India.

Paul Stillwell: Break bulk.*

Captain Shellenbarger: Break-bulk operation, and this is what I became an expert at. The only time you ever got ashore when you're chief mate was when it was raining, and the cargo had to cease because of rain, and that was the case now and then. As chief mate you couldn't get too far away because the skipper was ashore. Well, once I became master I took advantage of it, and I'd be guest of the consul maybe.

Beirut, there was a vice consul there, a lady, very nice lady. She and her husband were in business there, and I partied with them a number of times. She had something about Cheese Whiz, and I'd go back and I'd have to bring cases of Cheese Whiz. I don't know whether she traded it or what she did with it, but every trip I'd have to come in with cases of Cheese Whiz. If you go in as master you'd go to the consulate, and if they're going to be in for two, three days, they like to visit with somebody that speaks English and comes from home. They want to get the little tidbits of news that you might have. They'd invite you to their homes and they'd take you out to hotels and places and you'd see a lot more. But you didn't do that until you became master.

I made a lot of good friends and acquaintances. One of them was the agent in Beirut, and I became quite friendly with him. I was at his home a number of times. I just happened to pick up Shipping magazine here last year and found that he is now head of the French company called C.M.A., which just took over the French government containership operations. They have an office in Secaucus in New Jersey, and I have left word that when he shows up there that I would like to visit him. I haven't seen him in over 20 years. And I consider him a good friend. I went there on almost my last trip. I can't remember the name of the port because the port of Syria that we normally went into was Latakia, and then they built their new port in between Latakia and Beirut, but it's still in Syria.

Jacques Saade is his name. He was actually Syrian, but he had an office, and he was the agent in Beirut because in those days everything went through it because it was

---

* Through the 1950s, the standard method of handling shipboard cargo was called break-bulk, in which individual items were loaded and unloaded separately by winches and gangs of stevedores. From the late 1950s onward, merchant ships switched to containerized cargo that could be unloaded from the ship by cranes and immediately be hauled away by trucks or railroads without being restowed.

the Paris of the East and a beautiful place, Beirut, so I've been to some really nice places there. Used to go for a nice walk there with the chief engineer.

Paul Stillwell: I have a question going back to when you were loading those locomotives. Was there concern about stability with that much weight on deck?

Captain Shellenbarger: No, because in those days we had a lot of general cargo below decks, heavy stuff. We'd carry a lot of machinery, tool chests. A lot of tools went overseas in those days. A lot of vans, vehicles, things that we'd put in the tween decks. And our tween decks were rather shallow, and there again comes one of these funny incidents.

I remember this time that we loaded a bunch of vehicles that lacked about two inches of clearance to get into the tween deck. Most of our longshoremen came with the company from Greenpoint when Export was over in Greenpoint in Brooklyn. One of them was the hatch boss in number-three hatch. He was the heavy lift expert, Luigi Romero. Anyway, we went down and discussed the problem, and I don't recall whether I was on deck or not, but whatever it was all of a sudden somebody came to me and said, "You know what Luigi's doing? He's getting those cars in there."

I said, "How's he doing it?"

"He's letting the air out of the tires."

Well, after he got them in there they brought in a portable pump and blew the air back up. I think I had finished the cargo and I was getting off, because I was thinking, "Well, what are they going to do when they get over to the other side and they have to start getting those cars out? Is anybody going to remember they have to let the air out of the tires to get them out of there to get under the hatch coaming?" So many things like that all of a sudden come back.

But the locomotives, there was no question on stability, because we had very good port captains who were cargo superintendents. And they realized that when the mate has asked for a certain way for certain cargoes to be secured, they should do it. When we started loading locomotives, I told them, "No wire lashings." Wire lashings will slip in a seaway. You use chains and shackles and turnbuckles and that's the way you secured them, because they don't slip. As the ship worked, you had to keep tightening them up every day, but you didn't ever use wire. And then later on I carried locomotives out of Erie, Pennsylvania, on the Extavia or the Exiria, and those ships were so tender. Those were two of the four ships that I mentioned that the Navy used as transports.

Well, right at the very beginning of the war, before they used them as transports, on delivery the government had requisitioned the Extavia from Export and turned it over to the British Board of Trade. And, there again, was how I learned about this Empire name because they had named that ship, of all things, the Empire Widgeon and turned it over to the British. The British, at the end of one year, which was a bareboat charter or a lease, turned it back to the U.S. Government.

Because when I went on the ship cleaning out the files one day I found this letter from the British Board of Trade saying that they much admired the ship, due to its speed and everything, but due to its inherent lack of stability they were returning it to the U.S. Government. And, believe me, when you were on those ships, those four ships, you were very, very conscious of stability and how you loaded your cargo. When they told me I was taking locomotives out of Erie, Pennsylvania, I was very upset, to say the least. We took them to Turkey, but we made sure that the ship had a lot of heavy cargo down below before I put them on board.*

And, there again, you loaded them on one side, turned the ship around, loaded the other side. And in those cases they were diesel electrics, and they took all the trucks off, which had the electric motors which are quite heavy in themselves, and then put them down below along with a lot of other heavy gear. I don't recall what we had down below but I know it was--the ship was stable, plus the fact that I insisted on we take a maximum of fuel which we did.

Then again, as I recall that trip because of possible stability problems, this company always left up to the discretion of the master. If you said you needed to go into a port and get fuel for stability you went and got it. That was it. That was one of the good things about American Export Lines. They didn't second-guess you. If they had

---

* A ship's stability, the capacity to come back upright from a roll, is adversely affected by topside weight.

confidence in you, you justified that confidence and you did it. And if you didn't do it, when you got back you were fired. That's the way companies operate.

Paul Stillwell: But it was to their interest to have that confidence, because if they gambled wrong they could lose a ship.

Captain Shellenbarger: They could lose a ship. That's right. It worked out very well actually, plus the fact that when we were in Erie on that ship, my wife came up.

Paul Stillwell: Was this trip to Erie after the opening of the St. Lawrence Seaway?*

Captain Shellenbarger: Yes. I spent about six years running in and out of the seaway. Have we got time now to start on the Savannah?

Paul Stillwell: Sure, but let me ask you one more question. You talked about the agents in these various ports. What was the function of the American Export's agent in all these different places you went?

Captain Shellenbarger: The agent in these various ports arranged customs, and they would arrange for stores, such as fresh food, etc., and a doctor if you needed one. We sent them a radio message ahead of time telling them our ETA.† And they would arrange customs, tugboat, and pilot. We'd always update our ETA right up to the last minute by sending a radio message, and, of course, this was back in the days of Sparks. Later on you'd do it by radiotelephone. And, of course, then later on, why, when we got into the pilot station we'd call the pilot on the VHF, but when you got in there they had arranged gangs of longshoremen, because they knew what cargo you had, and they'd say okay.‡

And then they'd come back to you and say, "All right. You're going alongside

---

* On 26 June 1959 President Dwight D. Eisenhower of the United States and Queen Elizabeth II of Great Britain joined in ceremonies at St. Lambert, Canada, near Montreal, that marked the official opening of the St. Lawrence Seaway, a man-made project to connect the St. Lawrence River with the Great Lakes.
† ETA—estimated time of arrival.
‡ VHF—very high frequency radio.

berth so-and-so in Genoa or Livorno or Naples or wherever." Say, "We've arranged for five gangs at such and such a date to start." And this was the duty of the agents. And then when you got in there if you had any stores, needed to replenish your stores, they would arrange for the ship chandler to come down and take care of the stores. If you had any personal things or if you needed a doctor for some of your crew. They call them husbanding agents is what they are, rather than a general agent.

A general agent might be, in our case in the Mediterranean we had our own office in Genoa. We'd have a district director. We had a general office in Piraeus. We had a general office in Alexandria. We had one in Madrid to handle all the Spanish ports. But then in each port you'd have the husbanding agent who was a local man. And, of course, when you call at places frequently you get to know a lot of them quite well. And you'd do little favors for them through the years.

You'd go through the Suez Canal two or three times and, of course, you get a pilot saying, "Oh, I remember you when you were second mate on these ships." I know one case that they'd do you a lot of favors, you'd do them favors. We had a Turkish agent in Istanbul who had relatives in Piraeus. He tried to conceal that. I don't know whether the Turks knew or not he was Greek. But he changed his name to a Turkish name, hoping to conceal the fact or make the Turks think he was a Turk. I don't know.

But I know that in his case I learned I would carry a briefcase from Istanbul back to Piraeus for him. Customs didn't worry me. But after I found out that this briefcase was loaded with gold and currency, I told him, I said, "Tony, no more." I said, "What if I get caught out here? You know. Even though it's in a company car taking me over to Haidapasha, you know, on the other side, if I get caught I'm done for. Nobody gets out of a Turkish prison. Not alive."

Suez Canal. Yugoslav pilot. He had a brother pilot in Masawa, and in his case I got 10%. He used to ship U.S. dollars down to his brother because he couldn't get them out of Egypt any other way. You know, this is the kind of thing that goes on in the world.

Paul Stillwell: Sometimes known as cumshaw.

Captain Shellenbarger: Yes, various names. And, by the same token, when you come to Suez and you get ready to go through if you haven't got the proper number of bottles of whiskey and cartons of cigarettes, you may sit there for weeks. "Oh, there's something wrong with your papers. I'm sorry, Captain. You can't make this next convoy." And that goes on today, because up until a year or so ago I was still working on a lot of foreign tankers and talking to these people and discussing my experiences through the years with them. It hasn't changed. If anything it's gotten worse.

Paul Stillwell: Well, in keeping with the time line, this is probably an appropriate place to tell about meeting your second wife.

Captain Shellenbarger: Oh, yes. [Laughter] Okay. This must have been about 1951; I had gotten off a ship. That's when I came back from India that trip and found my first wife had gone. I had to hire a detective to track her down. Found out she'd left with a Nassau County policeman. Actually, it turned out that she'd gone to Alaska with either him or somebody else, whatever. She left the two girls with her parents in West Virginia.

Due to the laws of New York you've got to catch them in the act for adultery, so I got a leave of absence from Export Line and went to Florida. Now, I had industrial arts experience in high school, and I've always carried my own tools on a ship, very familiar with machinery, worked with the engineers and what have you. I got a job making fishing reels in Miami Springs, because I had to establish residence in order for the courts to issue a valid divorce down there. In the meantime, the detectives caught up with my wife, and she'd been served papers. She agreed to a divorce. Agreed to be represented, let's put it that way.

I was in Florida for five months, very busily making fishing reels while my lawyers are working on it. Had the hearing, and I got a divorce but, of course, due to the fact that I had been spending my career at sea, and though Fred Greiten, my boss, over at the Fin-Nor shop was very unhappy about it, the court said, "No, this guy's going to go back to sea. Therefore he should not have custody of the children." And they gave my wife Mona custody of the children. She went her way and I went mine. And for a good many years all I did was send a check to West Virginia to support the children, and I will say that it was a nominal sum compared to what a lot of people were hit with. And, as part of the settlement, the house in Long Island was transferred to my first wife. This was an agreement that I was quite happy with.

Then I went to live with a friend who later on became captain of the <u>Independence</u> out in Hawaii, Vincent Antworth. Vinny and I shared this apartment in Brooklyn on Pierrepont Street with another friend of his. I didn't know him too well, but a fellow he sailed with was an engineer. At different times the three of us would be in this apartment; we all had keys to it. We shared the rent and whoever happened to be in town at the time would stay in the apartment, and that was our address. That was our place of residence. And this particular time I came in from a ship, Vinny was on a different ship, and Vinny had been there before me. He was one of the original renters of this place. It was on the fifth floor of a walkup.

We were both in together, probably waiting for jobs, and we'd had a few beers. Also the other guy had left a few empty beer cans around, so there was this huge paper bag full of empty beer cans. And, of course, it being a walkup, you had to take your garbage down below to the main entrance to put them in the garbage cans. When Vinny grabbed this big paper bag full of beer cans and went out the door, the thing had gotten soaked with beer dregs and the bottom fell out of it. Now, there might have been only a few as maybe 15 or 20 beer cans, but it sounded like 100 of them going down the open stairwell, so here were beer cans, boom, boom, boom, boom, boom, all the way down.

We went and got a couple more bags, and we were going down the stairs picking up beer cans. We got down on the second floor, and here were two ladies with their heads sticking out, wanting to know what the hell's going on. It turned out that one of them was Mary Ivil, and she shared an apartment with the other lady. They used to hold parties, several groups in the building. Vinny had met them at a party, and she knew him so he introduced me to them. Well, one thing led to another. First thing you know, Mary and I were going out together without the other people, and I guess one thing led to another.

Paul Stillwell: I never heard of that as a way of meeting a future spouse. [Laughter] So how long have you been married?

Captain Shellenbarger: Well, we've been married since January 15, 1953. We got along fine and as a matter of fact we took over an apartment on Remsen Street, right near there. Fellow that was next-door neighbor to us on Pierrepont Street, his girlfriend, he was the best man and she was the best lady, because Mary had only two or three friends. She worked for Anaconda Copper. She had been born in Dublin and came over as an immigrant. Then she got a job and worked here. Her first husband was a man named Arthur Corry. He had gone to Canada and joined the Canadian Army. He was an officer in a tank battalion and had been wounded. She had met him at a dance. His uncle was among the first naval aviators to be killed.* The USS Corry (DD-463) was named for his uncle.

The marriage didn't work out for various reasons, and so it was annulled. The Corry family owned WPAT, a radio station in Paterson, in northern New Jersey. And the few things that she tells me about them apparently they treated her very, very nicely, even after the separation. They had a place in Florida because she's spoken of being there. And like I'm joking about it, but that's it. We have never discussed very much of our prior lives before our getting together, because I had a life and, of course, she knew that I had two children and was supporting them. In my case I knew that she had been married, and that was because that was required for the marriage license when we got it in Brooklyn.

Paul Stillwell: Well, I can understand why both of you—having been burned once—would maybe go for this trial period before getting married a second time.

Captain Shellenbarger: That's right. And it worked out wonderfully.

Paul Stillwell: Great.

---

* Corry Field is part of the Pensacola Naval Air Station; it was named in honor of Lieutenant Commander William M. Corry, USN, naval aviator number 23. On 3 October 1920 he was injured in a plane crash from which he was thrown clear. He went into the flaming wreckage to save the pilot; he died of burns on 7 October. Corry was awarded the Medal of Honor for his heroism.

Captain Shellenbarger: It worked out wonderfully. Well, of course, you're going to have little arguments now and then, but I don't think in almost 45 years that we've had any real arguments. That's amazing and when I stop and consider that I've seen other families, other people, it's rather amazing, really. I still think we get along pretty good together.

Paul Stillwell: Some marriages last and some don't.

Captain Shellenbarger: Yes, some do and some don't. It's one of those things. I've been lucky. It's a really wonderful second marriage.

Paul Stillwell: Well, we've talked quite a bit about your experiences as a first mate or chief officer. Could you please bring us into your experiences with the Savannah, please, and maybe a little background on the ship as well.*

Captain Shellenbarger: Yes. Actually, my last major assignment as chief officer or chief mate—States Marine called them staff captains—was on the Savannah. I was on vacation, and I think I indicated earlier that we quite often were called back on our vacation. I think this was one of the years that I was paid for over 400 days during the year. This was primarily because I'd had this experience as chief officer on the Aces, the combination passenger-cargo trips. At that time they intended to certify the Savannah for passengers. It was originally fitted out to carry 60 passengers, and due to my experience there the company said, "Go to Galveston. You'll be down there most of the time ashore."

So I said, "I'll take my wife with me?"

And they said, "Oh, yeah. Sure." So this was a great deal for me, and Mary and I drove to Galveston. I had a date to get down there to relieve the previous chief officer. Actually when I got there I found out that there was really nobody there other than a

---

* NS Savannah was the world's first nuclear-powered passenger-cargo ship as a joint venture of the U.S. Maritime Administration and the Atomic Energy Commission. She was nearly 600 feet long, displaced 22,000 tons, and had a top speed of 24 knots. From 1961 to 1971 she steamed some 450,000 miles, including sea trials and goodwill trips. She carried cargo from 1964 to 1970 after a few years of at-sea tests. She was retired in 1971 and later spent several years as a museum at Patriot Point, South Carolina.

captain who worked for the Maritime Administration. He had been a captain I think with States Marine.

David McMichael was the fellow that was there on the Savannah, and he had been with the Maritime Administration during the launching of the vessel. The ship was launched in 1959 at New York Shipbuilding, in Camden, New Jersey. The sponsor was Mamie Eisenhower.[*] I'll start right off with one of the things that happened there, because it sort of leads up to my time on the ship.

Anybody that wants to look at the record will see who the naval architects were, and my personal opinion is they did a lousy job designing the ship.[†] First thing they did was fail to take consideration that there had to be access to the top of the reactor to replace tubes. When they made the original plans, they had the bridge and all the control devices over the top of the reactor. Made a nice looking diagram of the ship, but it wasn't practical. So they had to revise the plans while it was still on the ways and move the whole bridge structure aft. Well, that freed up the reactor hatch, which was number-four hatch. Then by moving it aft they went over the top of number-five cargo hatch, which meant they had to go through the bottom of the swimming pool to get into number five.

Well, we had passenger ships, Independence and Constitution, where you did have a sealed bottom of a swimming pool which could be undogged and lifted up for access to that cargo hatch, but in the Savannah's case they decided no, they would just put two big side ports into number five, and when they loaded them they'd use elevators, which they did. So the ship ended up with nine elevators instead of seven. And eventually it wasn't practical to use them for cargo, and they ended up as strictly for stores. Starboard number five became a deck storeroom; port became an engineers' storeroom.

But, anyway, the next big boo-boo was something I saw while we were in Galveston, which was the homeport. I was out on the pier one day, looking at the draft marks. I came back to the boatswain, a fellow by the name of Marvin Dittmars, and I said, "Hey, something is wrong. I don't see how it could be." The draft marks weren't just painted on. They were welded in place. I said, "I took the amidships draft marks.

---

[*] Mamie Eisenhower was the wife of President Dwight D. Eisenhower.
[†] The ship was designed by George G. Sharp, Inc., of New York.

They're out about 7-8 inches. The forward and aft draft marks look okay. What's wrong?"

So then I went to Captain McMichael and asked him about it. He said, "Well, this is one of those stories that isn't well known. It was never publicized and for obvious reasons." He said when the ship was launched, he as a representative of MarAd rode the ship down the ways.[*] And he said that somebody failed to take consideration of the fact that they built this reactor shielding on the vessel roughly amidships—weighing well over 3,000 tons in one spot. When it went down the ways, the stern became waterborne and the center of the ship didn't. When it hit the water, the ship sagged something like, according to Dave, about 18 inches. He said, "We thought the ship was going to sink right there in the Delaware."

Tugs came alongside. They heard the tremendous crashing of bulkheads buckling. Elevator shafts out of alignment. Of course, most of the paint at the time was primer. He said it was falling off the bulkheads, and he said it looked like the ship was on fire. Of course, everybody knew there was no source of fire or anything on it. New York Ship had the graving dock ready for it, because that's where they were planning to move it anyway. So they immediately shoved it in the graving dock. Of course, they had to move the blocks because of the sag of the ship, and the ship sat there for two years. The delivery of the vessel was delayed for two years while they had to rebuild the ship. In that time they reduced most of the sag from 18 inches down to about seven inches. They took about ten inches of the sag out of it.

Anyway, the operator who'd been nominated to operate the ship was States Marine Company. They did not have any experience with passenger ships. Of course, this was all a political thing, probably some of their senators or what have you. They'd been nominated to operate the <u>Savannah</u>. They had already selected the engineers and the deck officers for the <u>Savannah</u> when it was launched. They said, "All right. They'll be there for fitting out, and they'll learn about the ship as they go along." Well, here the ship was delayed.

I think Ted Blankenberg was the chief officer in the original crew. He was master on a States Marine ship that came into the shipyard while I was in the shipyard in

---

[*] MarAd—U.S. Maritime Administration.

Galveston. He came over just to say hello, and I told him, "Captain, we found all your books and stuff like that."

He said, "Well, they had nothing else to do with us except to send us to school." So the deck and engineer officers of this nucleus crew for the Savannah were sent to Hanford, Washington, the Fermi Institute, Oak Ridge. Spent, oh, two or three months in each of these different places all over the United States because they had to do something with them.

Of course, they were on the payroll. They've already been nominated to go on the Savannah, and he said that they didn't actually move the ship out until it was delivered about two years later, in which case I think they took it down to Yorktown, and it stayed at Yorktown for a long time. They started its trials out of Yorktown and, I think they made one trip to Hawaii. They went through the Panama Canal; they did very little steaming with it. Came back to this pier which had been built especially for them in the Todd Shipyard at Galveston.

Paul Stillwell: Why would it need a special pier?

Captain Shellenbarger: For the support. That fact that is was a nuclear vessel. They had a pool for spent rods from the reactor. They had a special 75-ton crane for handling the heavy lifts and do all work on the Savannah, because remember this was an experimental ship. They were changing this, changing that all the time. They needed support services because you needed shore power. Most of the time we were on shore power. Let's see. I went down there in August, I guess it was, of 1963. Now I hadn't been there more than a month when I got a call from Herb Hanson, who was the manager of the program. He said the Atomic Energy Commission regulations were that anytime the ship's master left a radius of 20 miles from the vessel, he must be officially relieved. Well, by this time I had my master's license. He said, "Therefore you will become acting master anytime Dave McMichael even goes to Houston." It's more than 20 miles from Galveston to Houston, so every time he left we had to count the money and turn the ship over to me. So I became acting master, and I have a letter appointing me as acting master of the Savannah.

One of the fellows that came on later on the ship from Export Line said, "Well, "Dave McMichael wasn't the real first Export Line man who was master of the ship."

I said, "Oh? Who was?"

He said, "I was."

I said, "John, I have a letter saying that I was appointed acting master. What do you think about that?"

He said, "Oh, no, I don't believe that. You weren't acting master."

I said, "Well, suppose I could prove it."

He said, "I'd bet you $100.00 you couldn't."

We were both masters then. I said, "I'll meet you tomorrow up in Tom Collins's office." This is Collins I was talking about, the administrative assistant. He handled all the assignments for the deck men. So I came up with the letter, and he paid off. [Laughter] Because I had the letter saying that I'd been appointed acting master, which didn't mean a heck of a lot, but it's one of these anecdotes.

Within the first six weeks, I don't recall the exact dates now, but a little hurricane formed while Dave was away. I came in to the ship in the morning and at 10:00 o'clock a guy came down from Todd's and said, "We've got to prepare for a hurricane. We just got notice in the yard that there's a small hurricane forming down off Brownsville. They expect it to proceed due north and hit somewhere around here sometime during the night."

He said, "Well, during this we can anticipate that you'll lose power." Now, one of the requirements on the Savannah was that when you were running your reactor you had four primary pumps circulating the coolant around the rods, and that had to be extremely pure distilled water. That's why you had all this problem. One of the things was they had a barge called Atomic Servant with all kinds of purifying equipment on board. That was one of the reasons for being in there at that pier. When the rods were in and the reactor shut down, one of your primary pumps always had to run about quarter speed to maintain the slow circulation. Otherwise, you'd end up with a meltdown. They were concerned about losing electrical power, so he said, "Well, you'd better get your diesels ready." So that's when I went to the chief engineer and asked him, I said, "How much fuel you got?"

He said, "Not a hell of a lot."

So I called the yard right away and said, "You'd better get some diesel fuel in here."

They said, "How much do you want?"

I said, "Well, about 20,000 gallons." That's what the chief had said. You know, for safety's sake. Well, in two hours I had tankers waiting on the dock, and I got my 20,000 gallons of diesel fuel to run our two 1,500-KW generators. Basically we wouldn't have needed both of them, but I thought that, well, good idea to have both of them ready.

At that time we had the B&W men there as the nuclear engineers.[*] Now, to go back a bit, I don't think I mentioned the fact that the reason for its lay-up there and the reason American Export Line took over was because of a union problem that States Marine had between the deck and the engine. It's been documented many times about how they fought with each other. The engineers wanted more money than the deck men and vice versa. The squabble ended up at MarAd, and the Atomic Energy Commission got fed up with them, and I think it was sometime in May they'd come down. This is all hearsay to me because actually I got it from one of the nuclear engineers, George Kulynych, who taught me the basics of the ship.

Turned out he was one of the designers of the reactor, and he'd been sent down from Lynchburg, Virginia, to take over. The reason they were sent down was the engineer said, "Well, we've got a hot reactor here, and there's nobody around who's qualified as engineers for this." So MarAd apparently told them, "Pack your bags," and I guess they told them 9:00 o'clock in the morning be off by 5:00 P.M.

Mates, no problem. They got them, because Dave McMichael was there and another guy with a deck license. The engineers said, "No way." Four o'clock came in the afternoon, and they told these guys, "Look, your reliefs are on the dock."

And they said, "Oh, impossible. There isn't anybody licensed for these."

"Well how about these guys? They built the reactor." They had six men there from B&W as reactor operators, because they had to keep two men on watch at all times with it. So when these guys left, they only had an hour to get off the ship, and they left tons of books because they'd been to all these schools.

---

[*] The Babcock & Wilcox Company produced the ship's nuclear reactor, which was cooled by pressurized water.

Paul Stillwell: And they didn't expect to leave that ship.

Captain Shellenbarger: They didn't expect to leave. And they told them, "Be off the ship or we'll have marshals take you off." These were in the other engineers' union.

Paul Stillwell: Did the U.S. Government own the ship?

Captain Shellenbarger: Oh, yes. The ownership was always with the U. S. Government. Still is today and this is something I learned from Tom King only recently, the fact that the U.S. Government still retains title because of this fact. Even though the reactor space is sealed and the rods have been long gone, there's still a certain amount of radiation available in there, and because of that the Nuclear Regulatory Commission says the government for insurance purposes has to retain title and it's in the James River.* It's still government property. Surprisingly, it's still painted white.

Paul Stillwell: What was the point of being painted white? Was that of some significance?

Captain Shellenbarger: Oh, no, other than the fact that somebody thought it would look good for a ship that's going around advertising the fact that the United States has a nuclear merchant ship.

Paul Stillwell: Well, it attracted attention that way.

Captain Shellenbarger: Attracted attention. Sure. Actually the lines on it—I think it's a beautiful ship.

Paul Stillwell: Yes.

---

* James River, Virginia, is a storage site for inactive ships owned by the Maritime Administration.

Captain Shellenbarger: You know its lines. I look at it and I think of it. [Pointing to a picture of the ship]: Here's the problem I was talking about. There's one, two, three, four cargo hatches. There's the nuclear. That's the reactor hatch.

Paul Stillwell: Right in front of the superstructure.

Captain Shellenbarger: Right in front of the superstructure. I saw some of the original plans, and originally that superstructure was designed to be right behind number-four hatch. Then they had to slide everything aft one hatch and, of course, that put it back here.

It was a show-place ship. Beautiful bar, dining spaces, a dining room, real plush cabins, completely outfitted hospital. I had a doctor there, Dr. Peters, who was a specialist in nuclear medicine. I think he was a Navy-trained man. We also got a retired chief machinist that had been in the Navy, but he'd retired and then he came with us to assist this merchant ship. And this was a pressurized water reactor.

All I can say is it was a very interesting period. I was on it a relatively short time, but I learned fast. George Kulynych would hold tutoring sessions with me in the evening a couple of hours. I'd go aboard the Atomic Servant, suit up, and go into the reactors. Things were pointed out to me and then, of course, a lot of things I learned on my own, because after all when we went aboard we had to get the ship ready for sailing.

One of these engineers is still in Washington running his own business, a consulting business. Stan Wheatley. He was one of the original engineers on the ship. He did not go along with this group, and because he protested so much his union kicked him out. Then he went to work for Todd, and because he'd been on the ship our company immediately said, "Hey, we want this guy." And he became our chief engineer. So Stan was there as our chief engineer.

In the meantime, a class at Kings Point had a mockup with deck and engine men there learning about the ship; I think it was four or five months.[*] Their engineers got their atomic energy certificate for operating this reactor. That might be of interest, the fact that when you receive a license to operate a reactor it is for one specific reactor. You

---

[*] U.S. Merchant Marine Academy, Kings Point, New York.

can't just get a license to operate reactors and go to any reactor and operate. Your license is good only for one reactor. And so these people were licensed for the Savannah's reactor.

Now, I don't know how it is in the Navy, because there they obviously must move around from ship to ship. And whether their reactors are similar on another ship I wouldn't know. Frankly, at this stage of the game I really don't care, but it was really fascinating at the time to learn about these things.

George Kulynych was the designer of the reactor. He would have made a brilliant teacher, maybe he was, because he put things in plain layman's language. Because I remember the first thing he told me, "Hey, you've come from a steam turbine ship." He said, "We're a steam turbine ship. You have boilers to produce steam. We have a reactor that produces steam. The only problem is that the reactor produces nuclear contaminated steam and has to be converted to nonnuclear steam for the turbines."

I don't remember the figures now, but I know it was very high. Steam pressure was something up around 1,800 hundred pounds per inch.[*] The temperature was in that same neighborhood. One of the figures was around 2,000. He said, "That contaminated steam which is produced with these primary pumps circulating to the reactor, once you go critical you start producing a tremendous amount of heat"—and how! But, anyway, he said, "That steam goes through a heat exchanger, which looks like a big condenser."

But that was the real critical factor, because that's where the nuclear plant converted the steam that ran the turbines, and this was of interest to me. Oh, I've always been mechanically inclined anyway, and that's one the reasons I ended up there, because I'd worked with a port engineer on one of our ships under new construction. John Bone was the port engineer handling that project. I think he was the one that actually was instrumental in getting me there because he knew of my mechanical bent.

Anyway, the turbine in the Savannah was a DeLaval, and it operated on saturated steam. Now most of your steamships that I was familiar with used superheated steam. There you're only talking about 850 pounds pressure and temperatures way up there. So this was saturated steam that they used, and it was a special design turbine for that

---

[*] The steam pressure in a conventionally powered U.S. Navy ship of the same era was 600 pounds per square inch, moving to 1,200-pound ships in the early 1960s.

purpose. George said, "All we do is produce the steam, because it is a nuclear reactor. And then we've got this auxiliary machinery that we've got to think about, the primary pumps and the various pieces of equipment."

I can't remember now, but they used to circulate the distilled water through some kind of filters, because every bit of sediment or whatever that happened to be in this distilled water accumulates radioactivity, and that's what makes it really bad. Whereas, with the plain distilled water you can circulate it and you don't have the contamination and things like that so if you don't have a leak or anything you can control it much better. These are the matters that I learned in a hell of a hurry, plus the fact that we had the two 1,500-KW generators. We had a 750-KW up in the stack area, which was another emergency generator because it was vital that if we had a scram, in other words the rods went in, we still had to keep the primary pumps going to circulate this superheated water.

The shielding around the sides was cement, steel, cement. And underneath the double bottom, up in that area, was about six feet deep, and that again had distilled water in it, and water is a good shield for radiation. But in order to prevent rust and contamination—my information is that this area is still in relatively good condition—they put zinc chromate in the water. It's chromated water because this was one of the deck department's jobs, so I'd have to send the carpenter down. He not only checked the bilge wells, but he also checked the shielding water underneath the reactor.

I mean, there were so many things that's going on. They'd told me that I was going to go in the second nuclear class at Kings Point, but then they could see the program was phasing down, running out of money. The government was starting to cut back. They said, "We want to get that ship out operating. Training program, forget about it, and this and that." So I guess it must have been about two, three months, and in the beginning of '64 I went ashore as assistant ship superintendent. And because I was able to read blueprints and do these things, I was put in charge or removing these monsters back in number-seven lower hold, Bessler boilers. Being a nuclear ship and going to various places in the world they didn't want any vestige of anything that looked like a stack, so they had two collapsible stacks back in the after house.

Paul Stillwell: These were boilers for auxiliary steam?

Captain Shellenbarger: For auxiliary steam, yes. In case you had to scram the reactor and you lost your steam there, this was to produce steam for the take home and operate your main turbines. How much it would produce I never learned, because I was too busy working with the shipyard, supervising getting those boilers out of there. Then after we got them out we had to check the hatch to make sure the hatch covers could operate—that they hadn't been budged since the time the ship was built. Had to get them in operation, and I had to check the steam lines going from the boilers up to the engine room, up through the shaft alley, went through a couple of bulkheads. We had to get those sealed, and there was quite a bit involved with that. But it was, once again it was something different. I'd been on cargo ships and doing a lot of other things. This was something different, and it was very interesting.

Paul Stillwell: What could you do for auxiliary steam after those boilers were taken out?

Captain Shellenbarger: They didn't depend on that. Primarily they said that auxiliary steam was to run the turbines and in case of emergency take home. What they did was mount this monstrous electric motor that was geared into the reduction gear, and supposedly that could be operated by one of the 1,500-KW generators to run this motor, allegedly to drive the ship at six knots. My information and from what little bit of experience I had, you were lucky if you got three knots out of it. The thing just couldn't do it. I mean, this was a big ship. I don't recall the exact dimensions, but it wasn't small.

Paul Stillwell: What kind of speed would the Savannah make?

Captain Shellenbarger: My understanding is that they measured the power level by how far your rods were pulled out and while I was on it we never went to full power. I left it, I guess, in March '64. I made one or two trial trips on it in the Gulf of Mexico. One of them I know was about three days, three and a half days, while I was assistant ship superintendent, but I understand that later on they got to 85% power level and could do about 17 and a half knots. I don't think in our trial trips that we ever got much above

45% power level, and that we were doing about 14½-15 knots. And, of course, you don't have to worry about fuel. Inexhaustible fuel. Refuel every five, six years. One of my friends who stayed on was Bill Hunter, who came with me as chief officer later. He was the last master on the Savannah. He and Pete Block were the last two.

Paul Stillwell: How long did that last? When was the ship finally taken out of service?

Captain Shellenbarger: We ran it about seven years. American Export Line formed a separate corporation, because this was strictly a government operation, a government-owned ship. I think Bill told me it was actually just about seven years that we operated the ship under the FAST Company, First Atomic Ship Transport was the acronym, FAST.

Paul Stillwell: So from about '63 to '70?

Captain Shellenbarger: Something like that, yes.

Paul Stillwell: Was the ship under way at all while you were the acting master or the first officer?

Captain Shellenbarger: Not while I was acting master. No, under way we didn't do any trials until I became assistant ship superintendent. We went critical while I was there. In other words we did dock trials and things like that. We went critical. As a matter of fact, I think that was around Thanksgiving Day in '63, because it was right after Kennedy was assassinated.[*]

Of course, that was a big unfortunate event while we were there.

Paul Stillwell: Especially in Texas.

---

[*] John F. Kennedy served as President of the United States from 20 January 1960 until he was assassinated on 22 November 1963.

Captain Shellenbarger: Yes, I was on the bridge wing. I think Dave McMichael was there, so I was chief officer at that time but I was working with a contractor from Houston. He was renewing some deck above, up on the bridge, and I think Marvin came up with the news that the President had been shot in Dallas. I think it was about the fourth or fifth time I'd seen the guy, and he said, "I'll bet that bastard Johnson had something to do with that."[*] And, of course then later we found that Kennedy had died.

Paul Stillwell: Why was your tenure so short in that job?

Captain Shellenbarger: Well, because they had decided to get the ship under way with the crew. The crew had showed up from their training sessions. When I was relieved, I went ashore as an assistant ship superintendent. Then they were going to close down this particular operation in Galveston and only have people there when the ship was in Galveston and, of course, they wanted to get it running. That was the idea. You know, there's money going into the ship and nothing's happening. You're not getting any exposure, which is what they wanted.

We got people from Germany there. I took more sightseeing parties around from Germany and Japan. The Japanese ship, the Mutsu, we had a whole group there that I had to take around, describe this and that and everything else. The Otto Kahn, which was the German ship which was smaller than the Savannah. I didn't realize that until I saw it later on in Casablanca with diesels in it.

So what happened was that they came to me and they said, "Well, you can stay with the Savannah program or get your own ship as master." And, of course, that was something I'd been waiting a long time for, my first ship as master. I'd been on the Exiria as second mate with my good friend, Charlie Reilly, and I was familiar with the ships. I'd sailed chief mate on the Exceller. These were the four small ships I was referring to. Fast, very tender, but I felt confident in my ability as chief officer to handle the cargo on them, so they said, "Okay, you're going to go out as master on the Extavia."

---

[*] Vice President Lyndon B. Johnson became President upon Kennedy's death.

Paul Stillwell: Was this because the people coming from Kings Point were considered better trained?

Captain Shellenbarger: I would say probably yes.

Paul Stillwell: So did they have the deck officers go through a nuclear training program also?

Captain Shellenbarger: They had a nuclear training, but, of course, it was entirely different than the engineers, because, you see, under the deck department, you had six nuclear health technicians and the doctor in your department. They were just considered deck men, and they had to go around and check all monitoring devices, and that was part of the deck department. We used to go through cases of flashlight batteries for the various detection equipments, the hand-held stuff, because you had to run continuous monitoring all over the ship. Had all kinds of drills. They might have considered that. I never gave it much thought, because when John Bone came and with the letter of commendation from Admiral John Will thanking me for my services in putting the ship into the service.* More important, an assignment as permanent master on the steamship Extavia. That was it, finally.

Paul Stillwell: Was this a normal overhaul you were involved in after the period the Savannah had been out operating?

Captain Shellenbarger: I wouldn't call it a normal, but because it was in the shipyard and it was at its own dock they figured, well, here's a chance to do a lot of experimenting. They were always experimenting with different things even right up till the end. I understand from Bill Hunter telling me that they were talking about the rods that were inserted into the reactor and removed by a hydraulic system. This was always a matter of great concern to the powers that be, because hydraulic fluid is flammable.

---

* Admiral John M. Will, USN (Ret.), was president, chief executive officer, and chairman of the board of American Export Lines, Inc.

Paul Stillwell: Was there a concern about it getting contaminated also?

Captain Shellenbarger: No. The concern was that if you had a leak that hydraulic could get down—you've got a reactor running—and BOOM!!

Paul Stillwell: At some pretty hot temperatures.

Captain Shellenbarger: At about 2,000 degrees Fahrenheit underneath there, and this was always a big concern that this reactor would start a fire. So they were experimenting with electric-drive controls to lift and lower the rods. But the thing is that with the reactor that when you have a scram situation, where you've got to shut down as quickly as possible, you've got to withdraw all support for your rods and let them drop in there, because reactors will cease reacting when you drop the rods in. Whatever the material these rods are made of, they're X-shaped, and when you drop the rods in, that stops the reaction. Mostly. Not all. You always have the residual reaction and, of course, that's the reason for keeping your primary water circulating to a certain amount, because they used to tell us that if that pump broke down completely and you didn't have any primary pump, they said you've got five days to get it running. At the end of five days the heat buildup will be sufficient to melt through the bottom. [Laughter] They had a term for it but I don't recall it.

Paul Stillwell: How was she just as a ship per se, in terms of handling and riding?

Captain Shellenbarger: Well, the only times I rode it, of course, were on the two trial trips. The one was just an out and turn around practically. I think we were out less than 24 hours. The other time was about three and a half days, where we actually ran through certain points. The weather wasn't bad, but it was a little bit choppy and the ship--and, of course, I was on the bridge as an observer because by that time I was assistant ship superintendent, and I thought it handled beautifully. I never had the chance to actually conn it, but I was on there as an observer and she rode beautifully.

Bill and Pete Bloch were the later masters that I knew on it, because they were the ones that relieved Dave McMichael when we took over full operation, and they both spoke very highly of it. They said that the astern response was almost like a diesel, because you had an unlimited amount of steam. You didn't have to worry about firemen jumping up and changing burners in your boilers.

Paul Stillwell: What about her capability as a cargo ship? They certainly had a problem with that hatch that was inaccessible.

Captain Shellenbarger: Well, that was just written off. They said, "Okay, that's number-five hatch. We'll stick with six and seven." Six was the bottom of the swimming pool, so I don't think they ever did a hell of a lot with it. I don't really think they carried much cargo there, but they had the four hatches forward, and after we got the boilers out, that seven hatch was a fairly good-sized hatch. But the ship never paid for itself; that's for sure. It made a number of trips to the Mediterranean, North Europe for showing the flag more than anything else. It even went into Japan with their phobia against nuclear ships. They went into Taiwan a number of times, and they used to go into Morocco. I don't know if I spoke for the record. I told you about Bill Hunter being master on the ship and the baksheesh that he wasn't aware of.

Paul Stillwell: I don't know if we got that on the tape, did we?

Captain Shellenbarger: Well. He was with me as chief officer on the Export Courier, because I was on the Courier for almost six years as master. And at this time and Bill was the chief mate, and we were in Casablanca a couple of days. The agent came down. Nick Esterhazy was the guy that was like a supercargo there. He said, "We're going up to the consulate, check with the consul." That was one of the ports where the consul would send down word if you were in port, to get up there and report. So we'd go up to the consulate in Casablanca.

Nick said, "On the way we'll stop at the tug office for the usual."

I said, "Okay, fine." In Casablanca, the Moroccan unit of money is a duran. So we went over, and I picked up my usual tug fee for the number of tugs that you have for entering and leaving port. I got back to the ship and said to Bill, "While we were on the way, we stopped at the tug office and picked up the baksheesh."

He said, "What do you mean? What for?"

I said, "Well, for the tugs and their service."

He said, "I was in here on the Savannah for five days. I had tugs standing by continually."

And I said, "Well, hey. You know, everything's going pretty slow. Nick will take you over to the tug office. You have to go over and collect in person." Which you did. You had to sign for it.

He came back, and he had almost, as I recall, almost $1,200 in Moroccan money. He said, "Oh, we're going to leave today. What am I going to do?"

I said, "Get up to the souk? Get up to the market," I said. "Buy brass. Buy some carpets, because if you try to exchange it anywhere, it's going to be worthless." You know, there are certain currencies in the world you can't exchange.

Paul Stillwell: So this was essentially a bribe for using the tugs.

Captain Shellenbarger: For using the tugs when he was master on the Savannah. And when I spoke to Nick, he went to the phone and called the tug owner and he said, "Sure, we've got a record here, the Savannah with a Captain William Hunter. The money's here. Let him come over and get it."

Paul Stillwell: Oh, I see. It was a retroactive deal.

Captain Shellenbarger: Yes, retroactive. He'd been in there over a year before, and, of course, it was surprising because they held it on the books for a couple of years.

Paul Stillwell: They were honest about bribing.

Captain Shellenbarger: Very honest about bribing. It's a way of life. It's a way of life. That's it. It's one of the things a lot of people in this part of the world don't realize. It's a way of life, and if you don't do the way the locals do you're not going to do business. The huge corporations that work worldwide know that. But then they pass a law in this country that says, "Hey, you can't do that." If you can't do that, you don't do business. You're out of business. That's what it amounts to. It's very true in Italy. That's it.

Paul Stillwell: Captain, you mentioned this group that came when American Export took over the ship, the nuclear engineers who had been involved in the design. Who employed them? The government?

Captain Shellenbarger: They were employed by the government, and, of course, because the government owned the ship, we as American Export Line acted only as agents, so the government was paying their wages.

Paul Stillwell: Just directly in that case.

Captain Shellenbarger: Actually, they were probably paid by B&W, because they were B&W engineers and probably the government reimbursed Babcock and Wilcox, who were the designers in their nuclear plant in Lynchburg. I assume that's what it was. Of course, I have no way of knowing that.

Paul Stillwell: Did these nuclear engineers have to join the union?

Captain Shellenbarger: No. No. They were working directly for the government, in the government's interest, and they didn't even join our union because they were only temporarily there until our men were trained to take over as reactor operators. During this period of transition, when we were getting the ship ready to go, they sent down the marine engineers. Because on watch in the engine room you had the reactor operators who had their control room, and then you had your marine engineers who took care of the turbines and the auxiliaries, condensers, and stuff like that.

You know, in your condenser you have to have cooling water, which changes your steam back to water, which goes back into the boilers. In our case it was recirculated back to the heat exchanger, and under way once you'd get up to a certain speed you'd drop a scoop underneath the ship and you'd pick up the water. You don't need a pump. But when you're alongside the dock and do anything like this, you've got to have a circulating pump circulating your cooling water and your overboard discharge, so you had to have marine engineers. So they sent me down six marine engineers, two to a watch, because on there they wanted a backup for everything. Where a normal ship would have one engineer, we had two. Like they had two nuclear operators on watch at any time.

As I said, it was on Thanksgiving Day in November 1963 that we went critical for the first time, because just prior to that Stan Wheatley came to me and said that they had to do something in the reactor. I can't remember what it was, but he had me get ahold of the boatswain, and we rigged something. They had to lower something down in the reactor to gauge something or other. This gadget they lowered in there to take a reading apparently had lines on it, and it was critical that they didn't drop it. So he was very concerned, because it had to be non-metallic. So I told him, "Well, you'd better go over to a fishing outfit and get some monopole fishing line," which is what we used to lower this gauge down in there. It was something that some special team was there to measure, possibly radioactivity.

Paul Stillwell: High-tech fishing line.

Captain Shellenbarger: Yes.

Paul Stillwell: Well, the use of two men is sort of suggestive of the Rickover approach.[*] Did the Navy have any connection with this?

---

[*] Hyman G. Rickover was considered the father of the nuclear Navy. He ran the U.S. Navy's nuclear-power program for many years, from 1948 until he eventually left active duty in 1982 with the rank of four-star admiral on the retired list. Rickover Hall at the Naval Academy is named in his honor, as is the nuclear-powered attack submarine Hyman G. Rickover (SSN-709), which was commissioned 21 July 1984.

Captain Shellenbarger: No. They had no connection, other than the fact that we had this one Navy man there assisting us. And he had been apparently with Rickover because he was an ex-submariner. As I recall it, he was a chief machinist, a chief warrant officer.

Paul Stillwell: Well, there have been dozens of nuclear submarines since the Nautilus.[*] Have there been any other nuclear merchant ships since the Savannah?

Captain Shellenbarger: None.

Paul Stillwell: Why not?

Captain Shellenbarger: Money. Money. And yet, strangely enough, somebody ran a survey. They said in 1973 if they'd had a nuclear ship that was fairly up to date, it could have operated economically during the oil shortage. Remember, the Savannah became an antique. It was designed and built in the 1950s. I mean, that's ancient with science today. As a matter of fact, when I left in 1964 George Kulynych told me, "With what we've learned with this experimental reactor today, we could build a reactor half the size with twice the power and do it very efficiently." Well, of course, if it's anything like that design it takes an awful large amount of money, and Congress wasn't about to go along with it. They said they wanted no part of it. Even today you look around, and our country does not want atomic power.

Paul Stillwell: That's true.

Captain Shellenbarger: They don't want it. And you take a look at France. The figure that sticks in my mind is something like 85 to 90% of their electric power in France is produced by nuclear power.

---

[*] USS Nautilus (SSN-571), the Navy's first nuclear-powered submarine, was commissioned 30 September 1954. She was 324 feet long, 28 feet in the beam, and displaced 3,533 tons. She had a top speed on the surface of 22 knots and undisclosed speed submerged. She was armed with six 21-inch torpedo tubes. Because she did not have to come to the surface frequently to recharge batteries, the Nautilus revolutionized submarine warfare.

Paul Stillwell: I had no idea it was that much.

Captain Shellenbarger: It's tremendous. I was astonished. It was one of these specials that I watch occasionally on public television, and they were talking about the various countries that use it. Even Japan. Now, later on, when I was master of the Export Courier, I carried nuclear fuel rods to Japan for their reactors. That's power-producing reactors. I took a special load of fuel rods to the island of Taiwan. Loaded them in Norfolk. They were produced at a huge plant somewhere in South Carolina. They came up in these containers, specially fitted, and they came in on tractor-trailers with guys with tommy guns sitting on top of them. So they put them aboard the ship and told me, "You're to take care of these things all the way across the Pacific, through the Panama Canal," and they handed me a .38.

Paul Stillwell: [Laughter] You were going to ward off the pirates.

Captain Shellenbarger: Yes, I was going to ward off the pirates. [Laughter]

Paul Stillwell: Well, I'm presuming that the government charged some freight rates for any cargo it hauled in the Savannah.

Captain Shellenbarger: Oh, I'm sure they did, yes.

Paul Stillwell: But it was probably a drop in the bucket compared with the cost of the ship.

Captain Shellenbarger: That's right. It would be a drop in the bucket. It was strictly to show the flag and to tell the world, "Hey, we've got an atomic merchant ship," and then they just let the whole thing drop. Actually, it's debatable in my mind whether it would become economically feasible, but with the price of fuel today and the fact that that is not an inexhaustible resource, somebody should be thinking about these things. Maybe there are other alternatives. I don't know. I won't be here to worry about it.

Paul Stillwell: Well, as you say, the ship was designed in the break-bulk era, and then all too soon the containerization took over.

Captain Shellenbarger: Containers, sure. If you'd build a ship today, it would have to be a nuclear-driven containership, because I ended up with my career with containers.

Paul Stillwell: Well, the Navy can afford nuclear power for submarines because of the military value. It doesn't have to earn that back in revenue.

Captain Shellenbarger: That's right, and as far as I'm concerned, I think it's been proven that nuclear power is a very feasible way to go. Costs a lot of money but, boy, you stop and consider the efficiency.

Paul Stillwell: Did you have to take special precautions to avoid contamination of the water around the ship?

Captain Shellenbarger: Our only special precautions were to monitor all overboard discharges practically continuously, because we had sensors. Just like every man in the crew—the minute he came out on the dock he had to pick up his badge, and they were read weekly by our health physicists. They had special devices called dosimeters.

Paul Stillwell: Did you have any problems during your time on board?

Captain Shellenbarger: No, we had no problems. We conducted our regular drills, evacuation drills and, of course, during this hurricane that hit at 2:00 A.M. in the morning I'd put out every line, taken in the gangways. And I wish I'd kept a copy of the Galveston paper, which said that the center passed about 30 miles east of us. The highest winds we got were about 78 knots. Four to five foot tide. Above high water level. Flooded out the causeway so that they couldn't get access to the shipyard. Pelican Island's where the shipyard was. Today I think it's the University of Texas.

Todd is long out of business, of course. I know that my wife and I had a second-floor apartment over in the Bayshore Apartments. The lady downstairs came up and stayed with my wife when they thought the water might come into the first-floor apartments. It didn't reach that high, but I understand that the place was alive with rattlesnakes that got flooded out of their holes. I was able to round up enough of my crew to get them aboard, and we stayed aboard the ship during the hurricane. After it was over, I got a nice letter of commendation for what I did as acting master. I had every piece of rope we had on the ship to moor us to the dock. They used to laugh about it. They said, "If the Savannah blew away, it would take the dock with it." [Laughter] That was an exaggeration.

Paul Stillwell: Did you have to get any special security clearances to work in that program?

Captain Shellenbarger: No. There were no special security clearances, other than the fact that we had to be trained. And, of course, in my case I was trained on the job. It's a period of life which I look back on it and I say, "Yeah, it was great." It was something very interesting, different.

Paul Stillwell: Certainly was.

Captain Shellenbarger: That's what I enjoyed about it. It was very different. We had a lot of people visiting. They'd come aboard sometimes on a Saturday. We'd have to go aboard and escort different groups around. Show them the ship. Sometimes Dave McMichael would do it. But half the time he was in Washington doing something else with MarAd, so I was acting master about half the time I was there. It was quite interesting.

Paul Stillwell: Did you hear any other stories about the ship's subsequent operations, other than the trip to Morocco and the baksheesh?

Captain Shellenbarger: No. I don't really recall ever hearing any. I just talked to Bill Hunter about the ship and the operations, and everything seemed to have been pretty much routine. I know that once in heavy weather something happened that the reactor scrammed automatically. Nobody hit the button to pop the rods in place, but they just all of a sudden dropped in and, of course, they lost everything as far as the reactor was concerned. But the emergency generators came on line right away, and they went to work. Apparently within a few hours they had everything up and running again. I heard this from one of the people who later on became port captain. At that time I think he was a second officer on the ship. So these things happen.

But then once I got on the Extavia, why, as far as I'm concerned, my seagoing career really took off from that point, because that was the end of my actually sailing as chief mate. From then on I never went back to chief mate. I stayed master. That would be from 1964 until 1979.

Paul Stillwell: Well, please tell me about that, starting with Extavia.

Captain Shellenbarger: Starting with the Extavia. Oh, brother. Somewhere, in one of my diaries for 1964, I wrote, "This could easily have been the worst year of my life." The first trip when I went on there as master we went to Norfolk and loaded grain for Russia. Now, I'd had some coastwise experience, ship handling and what have you. But this is the first time that I was the master backing a ship into its slip into the grain elevator at Lamberts Point. To say I was nervous is an understatement; I was shaking in my shoes. The tug captain said, "Cap, don't worry about it. I've done this many a time."

I said, "Single-screw ships?"

He said, "Yeah, sure." Because the only way you could back in this long slip, you know, in a single-screw ship, full ahead, full astern, hard over, hard left, because every time you back down your bow goes to starboard. It's a single-screw ship, so once it starts going you'd back, you'd straighten it out again, then you'd back some more, straighten out. It's a good thing I had observed this, because this is what I ended up having to do in Chicago because in Chicago they wouldn't give me any tugs to go into Navy Pier.

Well, anyway, we loaded the grain and I had a mate, Gus Svokos. Later on he became skipper, and I've lost track of him. I wish I hadn't, because he was with me a long time. Family, Greek descent. His wife was arranged for him by his family. Brought over from the island of Chios to marry him. When we used to go into Izmir, he'd go out with the binoculars to look for his wife's village up on the mountainside. On one trip she rode the ship with us when my wife couldn't make it into the lakes. Once we got to Montreal our wives could join us, ride the ship into the lakes and back out again, which meant about six weeks aboard. So Gus's wife came aboard one trip. They got somebody to take care of the kids and, boy, she enjoyed it very much. She didn't make the round trip. She went to Chicago. But, anyway, she rode all the way in.

Paul Stillwell: What happened to that load of grain?

Captain Shellenbarger: This load of grain was destined for Ilyichevsk, a port in the Black Sea. I had some other miscellaneous cargo, but the bulk of it was grain for the Black Sea. Now, Export ships, because they'd been in and out so many times, we never took a pilot through the Dardanelles. We did our own piloting. It's permissible under Turkish law. Primary reason for that is if you have an accident in Turkish waters with a Turkish pilot, the Turkish government has a number-one witness against you. You're automatically at fault, and the pilot bears no responsibility whatsoever.

So Export ships were under standing orders, "Hey, you do your own piloting. Don't take a Turkish pilot." So the only time we ever took a Turkish pilot was up in the Bosporus. I don't know how familiar you are, but this was weird to me the first time I learned about it. Due to the currents in the Bosporus coming out of the Black Sea, ships upbound against the current stay to the left, and you don't observe the Rules of the Road in the Bosporus. It's strictly upbound ship and downbound ship. And at that time they still had the nets across on top of the Bosporus from the Black Sea.

Paul Stillwell: What was the purpose of the nets?

Captain Shellenbarger: Those nets were supposed to keep out midget submarines and so forth. This was something that apparently is left over from World War II and this is 1964. Nevertheless, they still had nets there. They didn't open and close them, but the nets were there with an opening in them. That's what it was, so when you went through the nets you had to stay between those buoys. And, of course, you're at an angle to the current.

Anyway, I told them I wasn't taking a pilot through the Bosporus because I had been up and down through there as chief mate many times. And we get up in the Black Sea, and I looked at the orders and they said, "Contact Moscow, and Inflot will let you know what port you're going to discharge your grain at."

They came back and said, "You go to the port of Ilyichevsk."

I said, "Ilyichevsk?"

Before I left Norfolk, naval intelligence contacted me, because I'd done some work before. When I was on the Aces, we used to go into Alexandria, Egypt, and they'd come aboard in Beirut and hand some me films and say, "Take pictures in Alexandria, since you're a Naval Reserve officer. And when you get back to Beirut, give us the film." It was special fine-grain film. "And any pictures you take we can blow them up and see the secrets." At one dock we could look right down into one of the Russian submarines that was lying there. So we'd go back on the fantail and take pictures.

Anyway, when I left Norfolk, they came aboard and said, "Well, you're going to a Russian port in the Black Sea. Here's some film." And this is always something.

I said, "Hey, you give me the film, but I'm supposed to use my own camera. If worse comes to worst, and all they do is confiscate the film, they'll confiscate the camera too. That's my camera." Never got any satisfaction from ONI on that.*

But, anyway, we got into the Black Sea and they'd given us orders to go to Ilyichevsk, and I looked in the sailing directions, and I couldn't find Ilyichevsk anywhere. It wasn't there. So I sent a message back to Moscow saying, "Please give me the coordinates, latitude and longitude, for the port of Iljicovsk." Here they give me a latitude and longitude on the Black Sea coast. It's about 30 miles from Odessa, down toward the southwest, towards Bulgaria.

---

* ONI—Office of Naval Intelligence.

I got in there somewhere around the middle of the night. I don't know if you're aware of it or not, but the Black Sea's very shallow there, so we were taking soundings continually. I went in, and I saw this glow of lights over there, and the next thing I said, "Hey, there's a channel there, a buoy markers, lights flashing." So I went up and got fairly close, and rather surprisingly I wasn't challenged by any flashing lights asking me who the hell I was and what I was doing there. So I dropped the hook, turned on all my lights, and the next morning a tug came alongside with a pilot, dock master to take me in. Spoke very good English. He said, "Oh, I spent 15 years in the States." And very friendly.

I said to him, "You're going to take us in?"

He said, "Yeah, I've got to take you into a lay berth. Your discharge berth isn't ready. You're going to have to lay at this lay berth for about four or five days."

I thought immediately, "Well, that means demurrage. The charter party will pick that up."*

He said, "Oh, by the way, you see the tug captain down there?"

I said, "Yeah. Rather handsome lady."

He said, "That's my wife!" [Laughter] She was skipper of the tug that brought him out.

Paul Stillwell: How convenient.

Captain Shellenbarger: Yes. And actually she helped dock the ship when we got in. So we became quite friendly with him and, of course the usual carton of cigarettes and what have you. After we docked, he came down to the cabin to have coffee or tea or whatever. That's usual in these foreign ports. So we talked about this and that and everything else and after I got a little friendly with him I said, "Well, you know, I haven't any charts for this place. I never heard of it."

He said, "Oh, that's strange."

Then I said, "Can you do anything about it?"

---

* Demurrage is a charge paid for detaining a ship beyond the time allowed for loading or unloading.

He said, "Sure. Tomorrow I'll come over and bring you a chart of the harbor." And then he did, brought me a beautiful chart of the harbor, and then he explained how it had been built. He said there was a little lake inside the coast and they'd dredged it out, built the harbor, put the piers in, cranes, rails, everything. Then they dredged the channel from the harbor out to the Black Sea and opened it up.

And I said, "Gee, that's strange that nobody ever heard about this."

He said, "I don't know why not."

Well, anyway, to make a long story short what happened was I headed back. We loaded our usual ports, started loading at Turkey and Piraeus, the Greek olives and the almonds and the sultanas, big golden raisins that we used to load at Izmir. And then we loaded in Italy and Spain and came back.

When you left early in the spring with a load from the East Coast, this was the lake service. You came into Montreal, proceeded into the Great Lakes, and I got to Chicago the first time. Here I had to back the ship down at Navy Pier. There were about six berths there, as I recall. I think we were back about number four and had to get the ship in. No bow thrusters on those ships. That was something that came much later. But I got in there without banging into anybody else.

I guess the second day there, a lieutenant commander from ONI came aboard: "You got any pictures?"

I said, "Yeah, I got quite a few pictures. I got a chart of the harbor."

And this is what always struck me as so strange. He said, "How did you get all this?"

I said, "I got it from the pilot."

He said, "You got it from the pilot?"

I said, "Sure. And not only that, when they dedicated this port, the pilot tells me the naval attaché from Moscow was there at the dedication." So this is how one hand didn't know what the other hand was doing. So I gave him the whole business and told him, "It's a beautiful port," and it was. Beautiful port.

Paul Stillwell: That's a funny way to make a harbor.

Captain Shellenbarger: It is. It's a funny way to make a harbor.

That, of course, there was my first job as master. Anyway, Gus Svokos got off after about two trips, and I got a new chief mate. Later that year we made our regular cargo run. Their Western Med service, as we called it. We left Livorno, Italy, at midnight. At quarter after 4:00, we just cleared the island of Gorgorna. I'd gone down about an hour before, just gotten to sleep, and there was this god-awful crash. I ended up on the deck. I went up on the bridge. The second mate, who was on watch supposedly, was getting off the settee in the chartroom. That's the only time in my seagoing career that I ever struck a man. As he was getting off the settee in the chartroom he said, "What happened?"

Paul Stillwell: And he was supposed to be on watch.

Captain Shellenbarger: He was supposed to be on watch. Well, the words I used were, as they say, unprintable and I hauled off and floored him. I was in such a rage I couldn't contain myself. Here was a man that was supposed to be responsible for the ship and lives of the people on it. In the meantime the ship that we had hit, the Luigi Martini, Italian, had a big flare on his bow. After this guy picked himself up off the deck and I told him to get his ass off the bridge, I said, "Get ahold of the chief mate. Send him up here. He's going to be on watch."

I went out of the bridge and, of course, we'd crewed that time in Chicago, and we had lakers because that's what you got mostly in the summertime, lakers. Fellow name of Sullivan was on the wheel, and he said then, "Captain, I didn't know what to do." He said, "I hollered for the mate. I couldn't get him. I thought he'd gone below to the toilet, the head." He said, "I can see this guy over here. It's a clear moonlit night." Perfectly calm which was unusual. We were in the Gulf of Lyons by this time, just past Corsica. He said, "I saw the guy coming. He was over on the starboard bow." And this guy who was steering was an old-time sailor. He knew that this other guy had the right of way.

Paul Stillwell: The Italian had the right of way.

Captain Shellenbarger: The Italian has the right of way. Here was this bright green light coming at him. He said, "I'm waiting for the mate. I want to change course to the right." We were doing 17½ knots. These were fast ships, you know. And he said, "I didn't know what to do. I'm hollering for the mate, and he never showed up. At the last minute, I put the wheel hard left."

So I said, "Sully, it's a damn good thing you did, because if you hadn't, we'd have cut him in two or he'd have cut us in two, one or the other."

As it was, we were turning hard left and, of course, at that speed we were moving fast. The flare of his bow hit us up forward, just behind number-one hatch, and raked us, came right down and sliced through our amidship house. We had quarters on the starboard side. The collision took out our gangway. Took our starboard lifeboat and crumpled the tops of the cabins of a couple of the guys. Only the chief cook and the boatswain were on the starboard side, but the rest of it was like a recreation area and the bulkhead was in over their bunks. The boatswain, I guess, took it in stride. The poor chief cook dirtied the mattress, and he was so embarrassed.

Immediately I got Lane Wilkins, the mate, to go down and see if anybody was hurt. And I got somebody, one of my crewmen who could speak Italian, to holler out to the other ship, Luigi Martini, because I could see he was Italian. I asked if there was anybody injured over there. No. "Are you sinking?" No. This is a required thing you have to do after a collision. So I told him who we were, the name of our ship, the port of registry. I got his name and his port of registry and owners. That's what you do in these cases.

Paul Stillwell: Just like after an auto accident.

Captain Shellenbarger: Just like after an auto accident. The only thing is you don't have to exchange insurance cards. So he said, "No, I'm seaworthy. I'm proceeding on to my destination," and he gave me his destination; I think he was going to Sardinia.

And I said, "Well, we're proceeding to Barcelona," which we did, and, of course, at Barcelona I had to get a seaworthy certificate. And I'd taken the second mate off watch and notified New York, and Lane Wilkins went on watch. That was my chief mate. It was a four-mate ship, so you always had a mate that you could put on watch. Lane was the nicest guy you could ever have known, 42 years old.

We got to Montreal. The marine superintendent came up from New York. The insurance people came aboard. Nothing was said at the time, not much about it, other than the fact that obviously we had been at fault and Captain McLaughlin, marine superintendent, gave us a survey of damage with the insurance people.[*] This was shortly after the merger. Isbrandtsen had taken over the company. We left Montreal.

Incidentally, while we were in Montreal my wife and Mrs. Wilkins had flown up together because we were going to be about two, three days in Montreal. We went out to dinner that night. We started up through the locks and went through St. Lambert, Beauharnois, got up to Snell, got through Eisenhower, and were headed for the next lock. I've forgotten what the name of it is, but it's a guard lock and you only go up about a foot or so. We were passing Thousand Islands in the Lakes. Once we got through Eisenhower Lock, I took the mate off the bow and just left the boatswain up there for emergency purposes. The purser came on the bridge, and he said, "Captain, I think the mate's having a heart attack."

I said, "How could that be? He's only 42 years old."

He said, "Nevertheless, I'm sure that's what it is. He's got a pain in his jaw and down his left shoulder, and he's sitting on his bunk. He's shaking with chills."

I said, "Oh, for Christ sakes." The radioman happened to be up there. We had VHF by that time, and we'd just checked in with the Coast Guard. I said, "Sparks, call the Coast Guard and tell them we need emergency help right away. We've got a man with a heart attack." I called the bow and told the boatswain to get back and get the boom rigged and get the Stokes basket ready.

The pilot said, "There is a hospital right over there. I can hold it. We've got three-and-a-half knot current here." Steam turbine ship—put her on dead slow, and you can hold her in position." He said, "I can hold it here. You take care of it." I went down, and we had him in the emergency room at Thousand Island General Hospital in 25 minutes. You can't do that in New York City.

---

[*] Captain C. H. McLaughlin.

Paul Stillwell: That's right.

Captain Shellenbarger: He died in the emergency room. Massive heart attack. And, gee, you know, it really hit me hard. Well, we had a lot of different things happen. Proceeded on. I got a new second mate in Toronto. They shipped him right up from New York, and I got a new chief mate. The second mate I'd shipped back from Lisbon actually. That's where I flew him back because he was deadwood on the ship. Collision. Dead chief mate. I arrived in Chicago still in a state of shock.

I told the second mate, "We've got to settle these men's accounts, especially the chief mate. Because he died on board, you ought to take care of his effects, finish his payroll." I also told the second mate, "Lane had not given me any overtime sheet from the time of the collision. Been too busy doing this, doing that, and didn't think anything about it." He would have normally done it just before payoff to the paymaster.

So the second mate went back through the logbook, and I said, "Figure out when the chief mate, Wilkins, would have been on overtime." So he wrote up an overtime sheet and gave it to me. I just signed it. I didn't look at the damned thing.

Well, that thing came back to haunt me two years later, because poor Margaret, his wife, got caught up with a shyster. I use the word shyster because that's what he was. They sign up with a lawyer, they sue, and then they're stuck with the lawyer until it's settled. And he gets a percentage. They sued the company and me personally, each for a million and a half dollars, charging that I had worked the chief mate to death.

When we ended up in court several years later, these overtime sheets were presented to me with my signature on them, showing that Lane Wilkins had worked between 22 and 20 hours every single day from the day of the collision. I rounded up the second after this had been presented in court, because I couldn't refute that. I said, "What in the hell is wrong with you?"

He said, "Well, you know, I felt sorry for Wilkins's widow, and I thought I'd pad the overtime to give her some more money."

I said, "Well, you don't realize what you did to me." Fortunately, there were other circumstances, a lot of other things. The fact that we found out, of course, he did have a previous history, and in the autopsy they found that his coronary arteries were blocked.

You couldn't get a pencil lead through some of them, they were so small, because I saw some of the cross sections. Here was a guy, only 42 years old, and it was probably congenital with him. But it was a terrible trip, terrible.

Paul Stillwell: That's why you say it was the worst year of your life.

Captain Shellenbarger: Oh, it was terrible. There were other years things happened, but that to me, everything, one on top of the other.

Well, paid off. I got relieved in Chicago. I went home, and this was still '64, early '65. I got called into Captain McLaughlin's office, and he said, "Well, we don't have a job for you. You had a ship involved in a collision. You were at fault. You were the master. You should have known that this man was a drunkard." That's the way McLaughlin operated. He was an Isbrandtsen man. He was a great buddy of Jacob, who was the son of Hans, who was the owner of Isbrandtsen Lines. They were the ones that had, you know, that had control of the company at that time and that was it.

I was out actively looking for a job for almost six months, because I thought I was fired. All of a sudden, one day I get called up, "Hey, we've got a master's job for you."

Tom Collins called me up, and the port captain, Captain Hardy called me, and I said, "What the hell is this? I thought I was fired."

He said, "Oh, that's the old man's way of punishing you for something. He considered that you had a miscue." We've had people in our company, and I knew two cases where people had gone in a cabin and pulled a revolver out of the safe and blew their brains out. That's not a way to do business. I never forgave McLaughlin for that.

Paul Stillwell: What happened to the second mate who'd been sleeping on the settee?

Captain Shellenbarger: I don't know.

Paul Stillwell: You don't know if there was any disciplinary action?

Captain Shellenbarger: He had his license revoked completely. That I do know. I gave a deposition, because I was unavailable at the time he had his Coast Guard hearing. But Tom Collins told me. He said he was fired and that he had lost his license. It was completely revoked. It wasn't suspension or anything like that. It was revoked. There could have been a lot of men killed because of this guy. The company wouldn't buy them, but I'd bought these little CB radios to talk to the bow and the stern, and when I talked to him on undocking he sounded sober. He must have gone right directly from undocking down to his room and started downing whatever liquor he had available.

There again, I was noted throughout the fleet as a man who not tolerate drunkenness on the ship. I didn't prohibit drinking, because it's almost impossible in merchant ships to completely prohibit it. Today you can, yes, because you've got the force of the law and the Coast Guard and they're ready to back you up. In those days you didn't. But I didn't tolerate anybody that was drunk. I fired a chief engineer in Yokohoma and flew him home because he was drunk. Promoted the first assistant. Didn't even have a chief's license. If the man was incompetent, I wasn't going to have him endangering the ship or the crew. A lot of people called me hard-nosed, but I'm not ashamed of it.

Paul Stillwell: A rough year of indoctrination at being a master.

Captain Shellenbarger: Sure was. Sure was. But then I had a lot of good years afterwards.

Paul Stillwell: Well, let's hear about those too.

Captain Shellenbarger: Well, I had time on the Export Agent, the Export Aide, carried 12 passengers. I ran in and out of the lakes quite a bit. That's when I had the locomotives. We loaded them in Erie, Pennsylvania, which I've already told you about.

After Captain Hardy called me in and told me this was McLaughlin's way of punishing me, they sent me out the end of June. I went on a ship called the Flying Spray. This was one of the original Isbrandtsen ships. The design was a C1-A. The C1-Bs had quarters for 12 passengers. The C1-As didn't. They were designed and they were built in different shipyards during the war, the C-class ships, but they were small. Didn't have a hell of a lot of power. They could do about 14½ knots, but they didn't have any backing power. I didn't know it at the time, but I learned it in a hurry.

So Hardy told me, "Back in the lakes." So I went up there on the <u>Flying Spray</u>, and after two trips in and out of the lakes you got what they called a "B" certificate. You went into Montreal, and you took an oral examination on the Great Lakes Rules of the Road. And the fact that you'd made two round trips in the lakes, the Canadians just issued you a little yellow certificate called a "B" certificate, which meant that you were competent to pilot your own vessel in practically all Canadian waters. You were expected to dock and undock your own ship in Toronto, Hamilton, Sarnia and all these places around in there. They did this also in U.S. ports.

There were certain places that you were not permitted. In other words, you could take the ship in on your own to the number-one dock at the Welland Canal from Lake Erie. Then you had to pick up a pilot, he'd take you through the locks, and he left you in Port Colborne, and then you had to pick up another pilot in the Detroit River, up until you got into Lake Huron. They were the areas where you had to carry a pilot.

The rest of the time, if you had a "B" certificate you did your own piloting, your own docking and undocking and everything. So, anyway, Hardy told me, "Part of your punishment was this period that you thought you didn't have a job. Then the <u>Flying Spray</u> is the rest of the punishment." Because this ship was notorious for its lack of backing power. I found out that in the history of that ship it had had four bows put on, because it had hit docks, and I almost hit the lock at St. Nazaire with the ship. Fortunately, the pilot, the French pilot who was on there had had experience with the ship previously, and he said, "Captain, I'm going to start backing down here."

I said, "Way out here?"

"Yes." As it was, we came up against the chain. [Laughter] Fortunately, the chain held. I can laugh at these things today, but, boy, I sure didn't laugh in those days.

Paul Stillwell: I'm sure that's right.

Captain Shellenbarger: And this was different from the others I'd had before. The Extavia had been into the Mediterranean, but this was a run from the Great Lakes to North Europe. The Flying Spray went to go into Southampton, Antwerp, Bremen, Bremerhaven, Hamburg. Of course, this was 1965, only 20 years after the war, and of course, there were still submarine pens and everything at all these places. As we went by a beer garden on the Elbe, headed up to Hamburg, the German pilot said, "As we go by this place, they always play the national anthem of the ship going by. "They will dip the flag, and you can dip your flag too."*

Well, I'm ex-Navy, and as you can tell, I still have a lot of Navy in me. And sometimes I can have a short fuse. I said to the pilot, "It will be a cold day in hell before any ship I'm on will ever dip a flag to a beer garden." Well, that's the way it was. I wasn't about to dip my flag, the American flag, to any beer garden, especially a German beer garden. Not that I have an attitude toward them, because I didn't. It was just a matter of principle. So it was just one of those things, I guess. No way I'm going to dip my flag because to me that's for rendering honors between ships. Dipped the flag many times to naval vessels and had it returned to me. But to a beer garden? That was just one of the things that happened on the Flying Spray.

Of course, I went into Southampton and for the first time met some of Mary's relatives. Her sister came down with her niece and nephew and visited. And the niece's children, which we correspond with today and telephone. We haven't been over to visit in a long time, but we stay in touch. Of course, this would actually be Mary's grandniece, because it was her niece's children. And, of course, her sister was still there. I can remember when I went into Southampton we always had two or three days in Southampton, and they would come down to pick me up and I'd go up to Aldershot. That's where they lived.

Paul Stillwell: Well, I guess one question I should have asked earlier. What was the outcome of this legal case in which you were sued for working the chief mate to death?

---

* To dip the colors involves a merchant ship lowering her national flag about a third of the way down as a salute to a passing warship. The warship then responds by dipping her colors, a means of acknowledging the salute.

Captain Shellenbarger: Well, to start off the first part of this thing, Isbrandtsen's law firm said, "Oh, you're going to have to defend yourself. We're not about to defend you. We've got our own case."

Of course, I popped on it right away. I said, "Hey, if I lose the case, you're going to eventually lose yours. I think we'd better get together on this."

So they immediately got together and said, "Okay, we'll defend you along with ourselves." Because they were sued for the same amount at the same time. I felt very sorry for Margaret Wilkins. She'd got taken in tow by this shyster, who had her tied up and insisted that she could not settle. The company offered her a quarter of a million dollars just to settle the case—$250,000.

She called me, and I told her, "Margaret, you shouldn't be talking to me. I'm a defendant in this case."

She said, "I don't know what to do. The lawyer won't let me settle."

I said, "I'm sorry. That's your problem. I've got a big problem of my own." That's the way I had to look at it, and I did feel sorry for her. She had four small boys. I mean, the guy was only 42 years old. Four small boys, and my feeling was not so much for her. Bitter feelings for this guy, and he is still in business in New York. But it was settled in our favor. Unfortunately, she didn't even get medical expenses or anything. She didn't get a single penny, primarily because they ruled that he had concealed his medical condition. There were a number of other things. And I will say that this one attorney for the firm was good, because he proved to the satisfaction of the court that it would have been physically impossible for Lane to have worked those hours. Physically impossible. The second mate, in his zeal to help the widow, said Wilkins had been working on cargo papers, doing things that would have been physically impossible for him to have done because he was standing a watch. So that was part of it.

Of course, I felt very badly about this guy who was such a good mate, and he was a good friend, even though I'd known him for a relatively short time. He was such a friend in fact that when he and his wife came to Montreal, we all went out and had dinner that night at the Beaver Club. Of course, Mary and I were staying at the Queen Elizabeth, and that's where the Beaver Club is. It's a good restaurant there. They were very devout Catholics, and they left us and went to some shrine in Montreal. But I tell you, it was a miserable year.

Paul Stillwell: Did she get any death benefit from the company?

Captain Shellenbarger: Nothing from the company. Whether he had private insurance, that I don't know, but he got absolutely nothing from the company. Nothing. Because the terms of the agreement she'd signed with this lawyer was that all or nothing. There's a name for it and I can't think what it is. It's common in maritime circles. The lawyer will say, "You have to sign this agreement. We sue for a certain set amount of money. If we win I get one-third." I think they're limited by law to a certain amount, so they sue for these fabulous amounts so they get a sizable chunk of it. It's all or nothing. That's it. Now, there have been other cases where you've had injuries aboard ship, where through no fault of their own they were injured. And sometimes then they sue for alleged negligence or whatever else, and then they get what the law calls maintenance and cure, in which case they get reimbursed for the time that they've lost, any medical expenses and things like that. But that's the way the law reads.

Paul Stillwell: Well, if a man is injured in that kind of situation, does he have to sue in order to collect?

Captain Shellenbarger: No. He doesn't have to sue, but in many cases they do. As a matter of fact, even after I left the Export Courier in '79 I was on a court case in Philadelphia for over a week for an electrician that had been on the ship, allegedly fell down a ladder and allegedly there was grease on the ladder. Of course, it was proven that he had sued various steamship companies a total of 17 times through his seagoing career going from one company to another suing. Some people make a career of it. [Laughter]

So that was the Flying Spray and the Extavia. After my period of penance on the Flying Spray, I was assigned to the Flying Fish, February 1966. We had 12 passengers aboard for a trip around the world. The ship had reasonably good accommodations—not air-conditioned, but they were nice. We left New York fine. Got into somewhere in the

Mediterranean. I don't know where it happened, but shortly before we got to Suez, going into the canal, one of the passengers, an unaccompanied lady, came to me and said the purser during the night was standing outside the door of her cabin breathing heavily. And that was the term she used. [Laughter]

So I said, "Well, we'll see what happened." When we got to Port Said, I was waiting for the transit of the Suez Canal. I sent the agent ashore, and he brought a vice-consul aboard and questioned the lady and questioned the purser, and he denied it, of course. One person's word against the other. I found out later that he had been molesting her. Not physically but emotionally, let's say, and so we asked her, "Well, do you want to go ashore, continue, return to New York, or whatever? The company will pay for whatever you want to do."

She said, "Oh, no. I'd like to stay." So she stayed. She was rather attractive, not too elderly. Eventually things got worked out, and I didn't find this out till much later. The way it got worked out was she went to bed with the chief mate. So he did his duty for the company and took care of her problems. [Laughter]

Then I had another problem. There was a sandstorm in the Suez Canal, and the pilot walked off shortly after we left Ismailia. Said, "Oh, you've been through here many, many times, Captain. No problem. Follow the ship ahead."

I said, "Christ sake. You can only see about half a mile here. "You can't leave now."

He said, "Oh, yes I can. You signed my chit." Which I had. Normally you sign them when they come aboard. Of course, the accommodation ladder's down there and there's his pilot boat waiting alongside. He'd called on his radio, and he said, "Don't forget to leave the line handlers." You see when you go through the Suez Canal you take line handlers aboard with their boats. If you have to tie up in the canal, you put the line handlers over with their boats to take a line ashore so you can tie up temporarily.

So blowing up a sandstorm. Lousy visibility. Our radar wasn't working very good, and it was one of the original old Raytheons. It had about a 7-inch screen on it. It wasn't working very well, to say the least. So we got down to Suez, and shortly before we got there I got hold of the mate, and I said, "Hey, get those boats away." So we got the boats and the line handlers off, and then I stumbled out through the Suez Harbor.

I went through the Gulf of Suez, through the Red Sea, with anywhere from half to one-mile visibility with a very imperfectly operating radar. I was on the bridge continually till after we left the Gulf of Aden on the way to Karachi, Pakistan. We dropped anchor off Karachi, got a signal station. They sent us word that the pilot would not be out for maybe a week or ten days. The port was congested, which happens quite often over there in that part of the world. Sometime in that period, I don't recall the exact time, I collapsed; I folded up. That was the beginning of my medical problems. This was the first incident I can recall of having this tachycardia, and I still think it was strictly stress.*

Paul Stillwell: That would be understandable.

Captain Shellenbarger: When I collapsed, the mate picked up anchor, took over the ship, and sent a message in right away that I'd had a problem. I don't really know what happened because I was out of it. Surprisingly, I survived the tachycardia. I was blacked out. The purser brought up nitroglycerine. That's probably what took care of it. We didn't have oxygen on that ship. Dr. DeSouza had come out, finally got word. He was our regular doctor, had come aboard. So, anyway, we stayed there for about three weeks, as I recall, discharging a lot of cargo and loading some other cargo, and proceeded on our way to Colombo in Ceylon and Singapore.

I saw a doctor in Singapore, and he said that I was fit for duty. Saw our regular doctor in Hong Kong, Dr. Franklin F. P. Li, I think it was. Very nice guy. He'd been trained in the University of Edinburgh, Scotland. Served internship with the University of California. He was a good friend. He put me on a medication, which I took for a good many years, so everything worked out. I've still got the problem. It's been almost 30 years, since 1967. Doctors still can't say what triggers these attacks, but I still carry nitroglycerine.

People think it's bad. Who knows what's going to happen? But, anyway, these were come of the incidents that happened on the Flying Fish around the world. I made a second trip around the world on the Flying Fish, and that time when I left Singapore we

---

* Tachycardia is a form of irregular heartbeat.

ran into a typhoon in the South China Sea. And when you're in the South China Sea, with this little piddling radar, you can't pick up the atolls or anything anyway, because they're too low. There we got blown about 60 miles off of our predicted course line. Just by luck, the moon came out in the middle of the night and with what little bit of horizon we got I shot a bunch of sights and said, "Jesus, we're over there in dead man's land. We're near the atolls and stuff near the Philippines." We changed course and kept our fingers crossed, and, sure enough, the next morning we made landfall; we lucked out. Of course, the passengers, needless to say, didn't know about this. [Laughter] Most of them were too damn seasick anyway in the typhoon.

Paul Stillwell: What would be the motivation for an around-the-world cruise in a merchant ship?

Captain Shellenbarger: I don't really know. You get the people who really enjoy it.

Paul Stillwell: So it would be set up for the benefit of the passengers? I mean, you didn't necessarily have a cargo route the whole way across, did you?

Captain Shellenbarger: Oh, yes. Sure. We were operating strictly as a cargo vessel, loading and discharging cargo. As far as we were concerned, the passengers were just baggage. And when they go aboard, they understand that this is a cargo ship, and there is no fixed schedule as far as ports, or getting back at a set time. So therefore you get a bunch of retirees, in most cases, or single people.

In our case, the Flying Fish was originally the Robin Wentley. We had her name changed when it changed over to the Isbrandtsen Line. Used to run to South Africa. We had a beautiful dining room. The overhead was about 14 feet with two big skylights in it. We had two verandas on either side with sliding windows. In bad weather we could put sliding steel plates over them, but they could be opened so we could get air ventilation in. We had screens for those so you could keep the flies and bugs out. And the overhead skylights were screened, so you'd get a nice circulation of air through the verandas, through the dining room, with this high overhead. So, even in the worst of weather, even in Calcutta and places like that, you'd always get a little breeze going through.

On either side of the veranda there was a cabin forward and a cabin aft, so you had two people, two people, there's eight. And you had a small inboard cabin for a single on either side. So you had six berths on each side of the vessel, each side of the dining room, and that made up your 12. In my case, being the master, I had a little cabin on the deck above. I had a bracket which the chief engineer had put outside the porthole of my cabin with a fitting on it, and I had an air-conditioner there with a special line. On the ship we had DC, but we had a big AC generator in the emergency generator room just aft. So, being the sort I am, I had a special line from that AC generator to my air-conditioner, so I had air-conditioning in my cabin. I was the only person on the ship that had air-conditioning. Of course, it was kind of noisy, and I didn't run it that much, but it saw service because I was on the ship for over a year.

Paul Stillwell: Who set up this chain of cargoes? Was that the operations office in New York?

Captain Shellenbarger: Yes, that would be the operations office—special cargo department. They would book cargoes long ahead of time, saying the ship would be in there within a certain period of time.

Paul Stillwell: Do merchant ships have crossing-the-equator initiations in any way comparable to what Navy ships do?

Captain Shellenbarger: No. You know, it's strange. On that round-the-world trip we did not cross the equator. You come very close to it.

Paul Stillwell: Singapore's close.

Captain Shellenbarger: It's very close, but you don't cross the equator. I got my crossing-the-line ceremony in the Helena on our cruise to Buenos Aires.

Paul Stillwell: But I guess your answer is "No," that the merchant ships don't do this.

Captain Shellenbarger: No, they don't have these ceremonies and, of course, we crossed the International Date Line, the Golden Dragon.

Paul Stillwell: Right. And Golden Shellback if you cross the Equator at the International Dateline.

Captain Shellenbarger: That's right. Merchant ships don't have that. I'm sure that I could send in the names of merchant ships and get certificates for them from the Naval Institute, which I know they have a whole lot of certificates.

Paul Stillwell: Right.

Captain Shellenbarger: But it's kind of late in the game to get those. When we crossed the line in the Helena, we not only got our regular certificates but we got a postcard with the dateline information. On it was a small certificate, and I had it sealed in plastic afterwards, but I had sent it to my girlfriend who lives up in Owego, New York, the one I mentioned earlier. And she returned it to me and I had it plasticized, and that's about the only thing I've got covering my crossing the equator in 1939.

Paul Stillwell: Did they have a wallet-size card?

Captain Shellenbarger: They didn't have wallet-size cards in those days, no.

Paul Stillwell: They became handy to prove to somebody in a subsequent ship that you had done so.

Captain Shellenbarger: Sure, that you had done so.

Paul Stillwell: To revive the topic we were talking about at noon, you had known Kurt Carlsen who became famous in the early '50s in that line in the Flying Enterprise. If you could tell me about that association please.*

Captain Shellenbarger: Well, of course my association with him came much later and principally because he was a ham radio operator. That's how he was able to stay in communication on the Flying Enterprise. In 1976 I got a ham license, WB2FHW. Later on I changed to KC2PS when I upgraded to advanced class. Carlsen was W2ZAM. That was his call sign. What happened was that I got in touch with him. I'd worked him on the air, and then finally met him because he had been with Isbrandtsen, and later he was working for American Export-Isbrandtsen. Therefore, we knew each other and that we were both hams and there weren't that many in the company. One time Kurt said, "Well, we'll meet one of these days." He meant an eyeball Q-S-O, because on the air you have conversations with people all over the world, but you never meet them. One of these days, I met Kurt and we became quite good friends.

He and I had been sent down to the Savannah. Somebody—and I think it was John Bone, the guy that was running the program for Export—decided that Kurt did not have the passenger ship experience that I had had in our passenger-cargo ships and I relieved Kurt Carlsen. He was only there two weeks, and I relieved him. He had originally been sent down there to take over, but I was sent down to relieve him. Kurt was not happy about it. At that time he was riding a motorcycle, and he took off on the motorcycle in a cloud of dust back to Perth Amboy, his home.

Paul Stillwell: From Galveston?

---

* On 21 December 1951, the U.S.-flag cargo ship Flying Enterprise, operated by the Isbrandtsen Line, left Hamburg, Germany. On 25 December she ran into a severe storm 300 miles off England. Cargo shifted, the ship was holed amidships, and she heeled over with a severe list. On 31 December rescue ships evacuated the passengers and crews, but the ship's master, Captain Henrik Kurt Carlsen, stayed aboard and received considerable media attention for his efforts to stay with the ship in an attempt to save her. A British salvage tug took the Flying Enterprise in tow, but the towline snapped during a new storm, and the ship sank on 10 January 1952.

Captain Shellenbarger: From Galveston, yes. Now, this was 1963. And eventually there were various other ships. Lo and behold, the man that I was relieving on the Export Courier was Kurt Carlsen, and he thought that was his permanent job. I had more seniority. He had to get off the ship, and he'd just bought a new ham rig in Yokohama. He was showing it off very proudly to me.

Well, anyway, poor Kurt and I parted ways. We were still friends; we still talked on the air. He retired shortly after that. I think he had some health problems, but he apparently got away from them because I talked to him once when he was working at Perth Amboy Yacht Club. He was running the launch back and forth. And, of course, he was Danish and the Isbrandtsens were Danish.

Paul Stillwell: He had been a master before you. How would you be senior?

Captain Shellenbarger: He had been a master with Isbrandtsen, but Isbrandtsen bought into American Export Lines. Export Lines was the parent corporation, and my seniority was with the Brotherhood of Marine Officers, and Kurt came in later with Isbrandtsen, and therefore his seniority was down. That's how the union worked it and, of course, even though we were a company union we were still a union. An association of licensed officers.

Paul Stillwell: Well, he had come to great public attention in the early '50s when he was the master of the Flying Enterprise. What was the perception of him in the marine community after that?

Captain Shellenbarger: My perception of him was that he was a very competent ship master who had a tendency to not be as aware as he might have of some sea conditions. When I relieved him on the Export Courier, he had made a trip back from the Far East; this is what the run was at the time. When he left Yokohama, he took a great circle course to the first port, San Francisco. Well, you can't take a full great circle. You've got to modify it. Otherwise, you'd go overland. But he came out and went right up through the Aleutian Islands. That's the worst part of the Pacific, and you take a terrific beating, and he had unnecessary damage to his containers on deck. And that's not the way to operate a ship.

And some of the people on it, they said, you know they stayed on the ship to come with me, and they said with Kurt on there, he used to go up on the bridge, the wind spray flying around, and he said, "This is being a seaman." That's for the birds, to say the least. But he was certainly a competent ship master.

Paul Stillwell: Well, you mentioned at lunch, though, that the problem in the Flying Enterprise came because he didn't check to see that the cargo was stowed properly.

Captain Shellenbarger: Well, you know, this is a difficult decision to make. When you're not there, you wonder, because the chief mate's job is to take care of the cargo. Not the master. But with Isbrandtsen if the cargo shifted, hey, you're the master just like in the collision. With Isbrandtsen you're the master, you're responsible. Just like it is in the Navy.

Paul Stillwell: In the Navy there's no question.

Captain Shellenbarger: No question about it; that's it. Same way in the merchant marine. You're the master. If a man dies, you'd better have an answer to why he died on the ship.

I've had a couple of guys die on ship, and they had no relatives. To this day I've got papers from the embassy in Madrid about a fellow that died in Alicante, a fireman that I'd sent ashore and knew he was having a heart attack. He died in a doctor's office. We notified New York, and he had no next of kin. He had a sister apparently that they located, and she wanted no part of it. They said bury him wherever he is. And that was it. So what happened, years later I got a bunch of papers from the embassy in Madrid saying that I was the next of kin of this Panamanian seaman, because I was the master.

I had another man die in the port of Tunis. He was my B.R. Took care of the officers and an elderly gentleman, black. But he had served in the U.S. Army in World War I. He had no next of kin except a cousin, and they said bury him at sea. So the guy had died and was taken ashore in Tunis, which is the capital of Tunisia, and they had a marine section at the embassy. The man died aboard, and when I got in port I called the doctor. Of course, I knew the man was dead, but we've got to make sure they're dead before we do anything. It's the master's responsibility. But I got a doctor anyway, and he said, "Sure, the man's dead." Of course, he was already cold.

So they took him ashore, they embalmed him, which turned out to be the proper thing to do. The vice-consul came down to me, and he was in charge of American maritime affairs at the embassy, and I told him, "Well, I'm going to have to take him out to sea and bury him. I want to make arrangements for a coffin and whatever. He's already been embalmed."

This vice-consul said, "Hey, I was looking through the guy's papers. He's got an honorable discharge, U.S. Army. Why can't we bury him here in a military cemetery? We've got a lot of veterans of World War II here. You've got a military cemetery with a detail that the Army provides." You know every cemetery had to have a detail to take care of them. He said, "I'll make a contact and see if they will accept him for burial as an honorably discharged veteran." And they said, "Yes." So we were in port for another day. I would say that about a third of our crew went up. They buried him with military honors. Believe me, we were happy. He had served in World War I. He was an elderly gentleman going to sea, and that was his time to go.

Paul Stillwell: That was a good outcome.

Captain Shellenbarger: It was an excellent outcome and saved me one hell of a lot of paperwork and heartache.

Paul Stillwell: Well, we're right at the end of the tape so that's an interesting note to end on. Thank you very much, Captain.

Interview No. 4 with Captain Franklin F. Shellenbarger, U.S. Maritime Service (Retired)

Place: U.S. Naval Institute, Annapolis, Maryland

Date: Tuesday, 18 November 1997

Interviewer: Paul Stillwell

Paul Stillwell: Well, it's a pleasure to see you again, Captain. We've got a beautiful fall day out there, and we're inside here recreating the story of your life, as it were. Last time we went through some unhappy memories when you were talking about your service as master of Extavia, and you had a collision and you had an officer die on board. Then you had the rehabilitation period in the Flying Spray and the around-the-world cruise in the Flying Fish. Anything to add on those?

Captain Shellenbarger: All right. I got off the Flying Spray November '65, and I had vacation accumulated from that, and it seems to me I took some extra time off, and by this time I was back in good graces, so there was no problem with that.

    This was one of the beautiful things working for American Export Lines, even during the period Isbrandtsen was running it. You had a lot of flexibility as far as the jobs were concerned. You didn't have to go to a hiring hall and check in with the union, because it was a company union. Everything was done by phone. They'd call you up and say, "We've got a job. Are you available? If you can't make it, when are you going to be available?" Things like that and it worked out beautifully.

Paul Stillwell: Let me ask you about shifting cargo on these long cruises you made. There would be ports where you off-loaded some cargo and took on other things. Would that be done by the ship's crew, or would you get stevedores?

Captain Shellenbarger: You would be in port and you hired special long-shore crews, which in many cases you'd have to take cargo out of the ship, put it into a barge. Or if you're alongside of a quay you'd put it on the quay and have to be hauled away to the shed because of weather conditions. Then, of course, you're working in these foreign ports.

Your costs were not like they would be in the States, and in every case that I recall it was always worthwhile. And later on we'd have to do the same thing occasionally with containers when it was a container operation. You'd have to take containers out, set them on a barge, load some other containers, and then put these back on board, because they were going off at the next port, and the stuff that you were loading might be going all the way back to New York.

Paul Stillwell: So presumably the freight fee far outweighed the stevedore fees.

Captain Shellenbarger: Yes, it did. Yes. Made it worthwhile.

Paul Stillwell: Well, I would suspect there'd be a few times, though, where you couldn't fill up everything wouldn't there?

Captain Shellenbarger: Oh, yes. There would be times we'd come back with empty spaces because there was just no cargo for it. And later on the break-bulk trade just sort of fell apart, and there were more and more empty spaces. One of the ships, you'd come back where normally you could be carrying 7,000 tons of cargo, you'd be only carrying maybe 2,500 tons or 3,000 tons of cargo because it wasn't there.

Paul Stillwell: It was there, but it was going by other means.

Captain Shellenbarger: Yes. That definitely was it. Of course, this again might be of interest to somebody, the fact that these ships, American Export Lines and a lot of the other companies have gone because they did not change fast enough. And it started in World War II with the Conex boxes. You know, putting cargo inside of a steel box, where it's protected, and it was not pilferable. It was protected and you'd load these boxes. Of course, Conex boxes were a horror because you couldn't secure them properly. You had to try and lash them down there and everything.

Once you went to the containers, where you had cell guides, blocks, they'd put them in place, you'd lock them in place, and that was it. And the cargo was protected. Not only that, but you could work in the rain. With general cargo, like bales or anything like that, you had to close the hatches when it started raining or anything like that, so the whole operation of carrying cargo changed through the years.

Paul Stillwell: That was a revolutionary change.

Captain Shellenbarger: Very revolutionary. I would say it was as much of a revolution as changing from sail to steam.

Paul Stillwell: I had not heard that comparison, but that's appropriate.

Captain Shellenbarger: It is, when you stop and consider what was happening and is happening today. We joke about it now when I go aboard these tankers. At one time, when I was sailing, nobody wanted to sail on tankers because they were in maybe two or three days and, of course, the thing is that when they tied up at tanker terminals you were a long way from town, so it would be hard to get crews. So the tankers always paid higher wages in order to get crews. A normal freighter would be in port maybe two, three days. Today it's the tankers that have the time in port. They're quite often in for 24 or 36 hours.

Paul Stillwell: Just because they're so big?

Captain Shellenbarger: They're so big, and they've got so much to pump out. A containership today comes into port at 8:00 o'clock in the morning and leaves at 4:00 o'clock in the afternoon. He's discharged all of his containers, reloaded, and he's on his way. This is why the people on those ships today normally they work four months on and four months off, at least on American ships. Foreign ships, they work ten months on and two months off. They're gone from home ten months. I've talked to a lot of Koreans and Filipinos. Of course, in their case quite often they'll be coming back to the same ship after two months.

Paul Stillwell: That's a tough life.

Captain Shellenbarger: It is. It's a tough life.

Paul Stillwell: What do you recall about the passengers on some of these long jaunts?

Captain Shellenbarger: Around-the-world trips we carried 12 passengers. They were almost always retired people. In that year I made two round trips, and they all ran over five months, because it was a very flexible schedule. In a few cases people got off in Japan. They were mostly couples, and I remember one was the former CEO and his wife of a dairy company in Massachusetts. I think his name was Hood, because I'd get invitations on my vacation to visit some of these people at different places, which, of course, I never could. It was interesting. Very interesting.

Paul Stillwell: Well, let me ask you, just curiosity. I've noted that there are a lot of diversions on board the cruise ship or passenger ship for the passengers. When there are only 12, how do they spend all that time?

Captain Shellenbarger: Being the fact that most of them are retired, they do a lot of reading. They have shuffleboard, and we always had a shortwave radio. We had tape recorders with a lot of tapes, and then later on my understanding is that the ships that still have these facilities they have a lot of videos. And I see that on a lot of the tankers and things like that. There are a lot of videotapes.

Another thing that I found that a lot of the passengers on these ships, they did a lot of playing cards. They were playing games like hearts, bridge. There were always bridge games going. They always found a lot of things to do. And, of course, we did have our little dinner parties. I didn't have it on the Flying Fish, but later on, on one of the what we call the A-class ships, the Ambassador Agent, I had a 16-millimeter sound movie projector which I'd go get maybe 25 or 30 films from Universal in New York, where they'd give us the best rate. We'd show movies maybe once or twice a week, and if it was something we'd want to repeat maybe a couple of months later, why, we'd see some of them two or three times. Paid rent for the movies and then exchanged them for some more for the next trip.

Paul Stillwell: Well, I presume the attraction had to be the port visits, because you can read, play cards and watch TV at home.

Captain Shellenbarger: That's right, yes. And, of course, there again was the fact that in the ports, general cargo ships, we'd spend maybe three to four days in Hong Kong. We spent probably one day in Singapore. We were a long time in Karachi always. A couple of weeks. Passengers would take off and go to Delhi. Can't remember the name of the place where the guy built the temple for his wife.

Paul Stillwell: Taj Mahal.

Captain Shellenbarger: Taj Mahal, and then they maybe would rejoin the ship in Bombay, or sometimes they'd rejoin us at Colombo. I remember one couple that left us in Bombay once and rejoined us in Singapore, because when they left we weren't too sure they were going to be able to make it because they were uncertain about the plane schedules. The agent in Bombay said, "Well, don't worry." He said, "They'll be there." They were. So this was part of their round-the-world cruise. And, of course, all these things were extra expense, at their expense, but it was great for them because it give them a chance to have a base of operations and continue.

Paul Stillwell: It was during that period in the mid-1960s that the United States was pulling a lot of Victory ships and what have you out of mothballs and finding crews and sending them out to Vietnam. Did you get involved with any of that activity?

Captain Shellenbarger: Not directly. But with the Flying Fish one time we loaded 300 pigs on the after deck in Saigon, going to Hong Kong. You're aware that the Chinese love pork. And they had two attendants to take care of them. Of course, they were only on there about three or four days, and it took us three months to get the smell of the pigs off the ship. Oh, it was unbelievable. At that time I was on these ships running to Japan and Korea. Once we took a load of military cargo to Manila, where it was picked up, transshipped in other vessels. The company had other vessels, Victory ships, that they'd pulled out of lay-up and they put crews aboard. Our company had about 15 ships running into Vietnam during the Vietnam War.

Paul Stillwell: So those were probably specific charters though by the government.

Captain Shellenbarger: They were chartered by the government for specific things, and the majority of them were carrying ammunition—bombs and ammo. And, of course, the tanker companies were carrying fuel.

Paul Stillwell: Well, I'll bet some of the ones going to Vietnam had beer in them also.

Captain Shellenbarger: I don't doubt that.

Paul Stillwell: But they got a lot of amenities over there—I mean, bowling alleys and radio and TV setups that had to go in ships.

Captain Shellenbarger: They had to go in ships. That's right. I don't know what they'd do today. They don't have the ships.

Paul Stillwell: Send it airmail.

Captain Shellenbarger: Yes. Well, let's see. I'm trying to think of what else happened. We made so many ports. The first experience, of course, in the Flying Fish was going through the Inland Sea and, this was back around '66. Because they still didn't have much in the way of pilots there. You did most of your own piloting in the Inland Sea. It was beautiful if they had beautiful weather, but if it was bad, foggy, why, it's not a pleasant place to be.

Paul Stillwell: The Strait of Shimonoseki.

Captain Shellenbarger: Yes.

So I guess the next ship was the Exiria. That was running from the Great Lakes to the Mediterranean, and this was one of the so-called Bath ships.* Six-hatch. The four ships had been old troop transports during World War II. I'm trying to remember which one it was. They were delivered in the 1940s by Bath, the company, and they had the same power plant as their seven-hatch jobs. They were about 50 feet shorter, but they had the same power plant, and they had slightly less beam so that gave them a speed of about 21-22 knots, so it was ideal in those days for a troopship.

So when the government took over all four ships, two of them were assigned to the Navy and two to the Army as transports. They put about 3,000 tons of permanent ballast in the bottom of the holds. As commercial ships, they had deep tanks in which you carried lube oil, vegetable oil, things like that. But as troopers this was ideal for extra fuel, because they were using a lot of fuel running them at top speed. A friend of mine was second mate on one of them. It was Navy charter, and he said they consistently operated at 21 knots.

Paul Stillwell: I presume the reason for the ballast is that people are a lot lighter then cargo.

Captain Shellenbarger: Definitely. And I went on the Exiria afterwards. Of course, this was some years later, '67, '68, after they had reconverted it back to commercial. I found old records on board indicating where they'd used the one deck as a hospital, and right opposite was a troop galley, and they had the companionways. There were some plans there. The troops would go in one end and go through the galley and come back up the other side. Of course, they all got their own mess kits. They ate on deck. And they had the latrines between a couple of hatches, because they carried about 1,500 troops.

---

* The Exiria was a 420-foot-long dry cargo ship completed in February 1942 by Bath Iron Works, Bath Maine. She was eventually scrapped in 1968.

Paul Stillwell: Not really a civilized way to cross.

Captain Shellenbarger: No. [Laughter] You know, it's strange. Through the years, later on, I've gotten letters from people telling me that they'd seen some record somewhere where that I'd been master of such-and-such a ship and they remembered that ship when it was a trooper. It's strange these things that happen. One of my correspondents was in San Diego until the time he died. I sent him pictures of the ship, and he was really interested in pictures of the ship because this Exiria was scrapped just after I had it. I took it to Valencia, Spain, where it was scrapped, and I had pictures of it taken there in its final days tied up stern-to at the breaker's yard in Valencia.

Paul Stillwell: Well, please describe that, because I know that a lot of Navy men develop an emotional attachment to a ship. How is it in the merchant service?

Captain Shellenbarger: To a certain extent, I think, in some place like American Export Lines where you had the same people sailing for the same company for a long period of time, you do form sort of an emotional attachment to certain ships, especially if you've been on them for a long period of time. Especially the senior officers. I was only relief master on the sister ship to the Exiria; it was the Exceller. The chief engineer had been on that ship from the time it had come out of the shipyard. He had started on that ship I think as a second assistant, first assistant, and then chief. And he was on that ship until the day he retired.

Paul Stillwell: How many years?

Captain Shellenbarger: It had to be at least 25-26 years on that ship. Now, I spent six years on my last ship, and I formed a definite attachment to the Export Courier. I still to this day keep track of where it is, and I know it's laid up in Beaumont, Texas, in the reserve fleet there.

Well, I think I mentioned it some time ago that during the Gulf War they called me up and told me my old ship was in Sunny Point.* Did I want to take it out? It was fully loaded, ready to sail. And I thought. I said, "My age? My condition of health?" I still hold a valid master's license. I turned them down, because all I could think of was the ship's getting older, all these things that it needed, it probably would break down. And then after it came back I talked to somebody on the ship, and he said, "Oh, no, they did all kinds of repairs. They retubed the boilers. They fixed up all the pumps. They put a whole new electronics suite on the ship. All new radars and everything." The thing that got me was he said, "Oh, yes. Navy style. We have two chairs on the bridge now—one for the captain and one for the mate on watch."

And I said, "One for the mate on watch?"

Paul Stillwell: That's not Navy style.

Captain Shellenbarger: [Laughter] It wasn't my style either.

Paul Stillwell: No.

Captain Shellenbarger: There was one chair on the bridge, and that was mine. [Laughter]

Paul Stillwell: Well, how did you feel taking the Exiria into Valencia, knowing that she was going to be scrapped?

Captain Shellenbarger: I'd been second mate on the ship with Charlie Reilly, who's a friend of mine who's still alive. He'll be 89 next February.† And there was sort of an emotional feeling there, though I knew it had to go because it was starting to fall apart. But from Genoa to Valencia, our last passage, we did 19 knots, so it was one of those fast

---

* In January 1991 U.S. and Allied Coalition forces attacked Iraq to get it to retreat following its August 1990 invasion of neighboring Kuwait. The holding action in the meantime was Operation Desert Shield. The conflict itself became known variously as Operation Desert Storm and the Gulf War. Coalition forces won the war in February 1991. At the time Captain Shellenbarger was 70 years old.
† Reilly turned 94 on 22 February 2003. He lives about ten miles from Captain Shellenbarger and telephones him frequently.

little ships, you know. We did 19 knots and primarily the reason was because they told me when I left Genoa, they said, "Try to arrive in Valencia with as little fuel as possible."

I said, "But suppose I run out of fuel outside the breakwater and have to be towed in?"

"Oh, no. Don't let that happen."

Paul Stillwell: They don't want a towing charge.

Captain Shellenbarger: Yes. And I said, "Well, what's the story?" Well, any fuel you had in the ship, imported into Spain and not exported, you paid a fine. And, frankly, I'd sold practically everything else that was movable on the ship, because the marine superintendent at that time had been an old friend of mine, Frank O'Byrne. He'd been on the Excalibur, on the passenger ship. He'd been third mate, I'd been second mate, and Frank had sent me a message. I'd left Montreal when we got the word the ship was going to be scrapped at the end of the passage overseas and that we'd be flying the crew back, and that I was to stay there until the ship was delivered in Valencia.

Frank told me, "You're going to be in Casablanca. You're going to be in Lisbon. You're going to be in Algiers, Tunis. Get rid of all the excess ropes, canvas, and stuff like that that you can. Get as much as you can for these things." He said, "There are certain items [and he gave me a list] that you're to land in Naples to be used on other ships of our fleet." A lot of tools and things like that. I know we had a brand-new arc welder in the engine room. We transferred it to another ship.

I ended up in Genoa with something like about $40,000 from stuff that I'd sold which when you went into the breaker's yard everything on board became his property, because when the chief engineer came up from down below he had the engine room clock tucked under his arm and I told him, "Chief, why didn't you get rid of that thing in Genoa?" Now you're going to have to smuggle it out through Spain and Spanish customs."

He said, "Oh, I didn't think about that in time." But I understand he did get back to the States with that clock. How he did it I don't know, but the engine room clock on those ships was something like this you know. Enormous.

Paul Stillwell: Like two feet in diameter.

Captain Shellenbarger: Eighteen inches at least.

Paul Stillwell: Well, going back just a moment to the <u>Flying Fish</u>, your question about maintenance and repairs comes up. How much would you get done during the course of an around-the-world voyage and how much would you save till you got back to the States?

Captain Shellenbarger: Well, in those days, talking about in the middle '60s, we were running with anywhere from 36 to 38 men in the crew, so you did a lot of your deck maintenance with the ship's crew. However, I think this was true of most steamship companies, and I know it was true of American President Lines, because they had round-the-world service westbound where we were eastbound, and there were certain ports like Calcutta, when you were in Calcutta, Kaohsiung in Taiwan, Pusan in Korea, which now they call Busan for some reason.

What you'd do—there was always in general cargo ships a certain amount of dunnage, scrap, and stuff like that. You'd sell it, and then you put it into the ship's funds, and out of the ship's funds you would hire painters, chippers, laborers in these various ports. I've had a ship completely scaled, two coats of red lead and two coats of paint in, say, a month's stay in Calcutta. And do similar things in Pusan, Kaohsiung, and you always had a certain amount of money that you passed on to your relief, that was passed on to you. It was kept in the captain's safe, and it was used for these purposes. But you'd do a certain amount of it, but major repairs, engine room repairs would have to be done because they'd have to be done by certified people, and there were certain places we'd get done.

Round the world, we tried to avoid Japan because everything was so damned expensive there. Hong Kong was a very good place to get repairs. I presume it still is, because they do a lot of shipbuilding there. Taiwan, they had shipyards. They have shipyards in Keelung and in Kaohsiung, the two major ports. There's another port now, which I understand they were building while I was out there, T'aichung, which is on the west side of Taiwan. And I understand there's a couple of others there that they've built up, because it's a fantastic nation. I don't know if you've ever been to Taiwan.

Paul Stillwell: Just briefly.

Captain Shellenbarger: It's fantastic. On one of our ships, I think it was the Export Ambassador, I had occasion that I was able to save them a lot of money in Taiwan. This was earlier. When you do the Chinese a big favor and save them a lot of money, they don't forget it. I was six years running out there, and every time I came into Keelung later on, I had a chauffeur, an interpreter, and a limousine at my service.

Paul Stillwell: You must have done a really big favor.

Captain Shellenbarger: I did. They couldn't get a hold of a district manager in Japan, Johnny Hsieh. There were two brothers, one who owned the Hsieh agency in Hong Kong. Johnny was the younger brother, and he was our district agent in Yokohama, and they couldn't locate him. It was a question of customs, whether we were able to sail or not. The fellow I'd sailed with was our local manager in Hong Kong, Frank Jung, Chinese-American, born in San Francisco.

So what happened was in Keelung the agent came down and he said, "I've got 40 containers here, all less-container lots." You know, less than full containers and there are a lot of shippers involved. Forty 40-foot containers. And there was a longshoremen's strike in the States. We were sailing directly from Hong Kong to the Panama Canal, because I remember averaging 19½ knots on that ship. But, anyway, they couldn't get a hold of Johnny, who had the authority to say, "Okay, go ahead and load the things on the vessel."

So the agent came to me from ATRANSCO, Allied Transportation Company. They were our main agents in Taiwan, and they came down and, "I got these 40 containers. They've been passed by customs for the previous ship. They didn't have space for them. They're here and at Chinese customs, once they've passed, they're in a yard. You can't take them out again. They've been passed by customs. They're ready for export. This was for Christmas, a lot of toys and stuff like that, electronic goods, and they said, "If we don't get them, we're going to lose all those shippers because that stuff's going to be stuck here till after the first of the year, and then nobody wants it. So, is there any way that you can get it on your ship?"

And so the mate and I went around and said, "Hey, we can do this." I think we had to shift about 15 containers that we already had aboard. We knew that Hong Kong was going to be our last port, so we took a taxi right up to Taipei, called Frank Jung in Hong Kong, and I told Frank what the situation was. I said, "They've got these 40 containers. "If I can get them aboard, in Hong Kong I'm going to have to shift some other containers."

He said, "Hey, this is a policy thing. We don't want to lose those shippers. If you think you can do it, yes, do it."

I said, "I don't want to take the authority as a ship master because after all we've got district agents out here. But you're the sub-agent in Hong Kong." Our agent in Hong Kong was Johnny's brother, Alfred Hsieh, and he said, "I'll get a hold of Alfred and arrange for the shifting, and we'll try and get you a quay but if not we'll get barges for these containers." So we took the 40 containers. They never forgot it.

Paul Stillwell: In my brief time in Taiwan the thing that struck me was there's so much vegetation. It was such a green place.

Captain Shellenbarger: It is, and my understanding is that they'll get three crops a year on a single plot of land for things like the mushrooms and the soy and this stuff that they raise and they ship out as canned goods. As soon as one is harvested, they're ready to plant another one in its rotation. Because of the climate, the latitude and everything, and of course with proper fertilization and everything, on that same plot of land they get three crops a year out of it, and they certainly know how to do it.

Of course, as you come out of Kaohsiung you know as you're walking when the shift changes you're going to get run over by a million bicycles. I love the country and Taiwan.

Paul Stillwell: What ship and what year was it when you hauled the 40 containers?

Captain Shellenbarger: That was the Export Ambassador, and it had to be in 1969.

Paul Stillwell: So that was after Exiria.

Captain Shellenbarger: That was after the Exiria. After the Exiria I'd been on a ship to the Far East, the Export Champion. That was in 1968, and that was pretty much a routine trip, which was my first experience on one of what they called the C-class ships, engine aft, and all the quarters except the mates and the radio operator. Had a real narrow house roughly amidships. Actually, it was about a third of the way back behind number-three hatch, and it was very narrow. Just wide enough for a passageway and your room, and the bridge by the same token was just above you. But they were nice ships, and they handled beautifully. Had a lot of power.

And they, of course, like all the MarAd-built ships, were built with what they called certain Navy standards. In other words they were built so you could mount deck guns on them and all kinds of things. Plus the fact that you had certain features in the steam turbines which the Navy could utilize if they ever took over the ships. I think they called it a Navy bypass. They bypassed certain nozzles and you'd get additional nozzles in your turbines. I can't quite recall it.

But I had occasion to use it on the C ships a couple of times. Once I had to go into Midway with a mate that had had a heart attack, and the chief called up, and, of course, you have to log the fact that they were using the bypass—something to do with insurance and fuel consumption. Anytime you had to make a diversion, you have to start keeping a record on how much extra fuel because these things are all covered by insurance. Actually, I had to go into Honolulu for fuel after that because I'd used so much fuel. I was running at top speed for three days, and I did better than 21 knots to get to Midway.

I had a purser-pharmacist who had the hospital training; he was called HMA or something like that. They had to spend two years in the marine hospitals training for this, and they all had very good training and at that time the Coast Guard had the weather ships. They still had one in the Pacific. They had a doctor aboard, and as soon as we told them that we had this kind of a heart attack, they started giving us medical instructions for the purser-pharmacist, and, of course, we had the drugs aboard. And we had oxygen, various things.

They told me to divert immediately to Midway, and you have to get permission from the Navy to go in there. But the Coast Guard arranged it, because they came back with a message that said, "You have permission to enter this area." As a matter of fact, the Navy met me outside the harbor at Midway with a tug, and we transferred the fellow to the tug. And they told me they'd sent a doctor aboard to look at him. We had stabilized him. The doctor took a look at him and said, "We can take him. We've got a plane waiting that'll take him right to Hawaii." And they did. I proceeded on my way after the transfer. I got a message by radiotelephone within six hours saying that he was in the hospital. Can't remember the name of it, but you probably would know it, in Hawaii.

Paul Stillwell: Tripler Army Hospital?

Captain Shellenbarger: Tripler. That's right. They took him in to Tripler, and they said that he stabilized. The prognosis was good. Six months later he came back on the ship.

Paul Stillwell: That's a lot better outcome than the man who died in 20 minutes.

Captain Shellenbarger: Oh, yes. Much better.

Paul Stillwell: Well, how much latitude does a master have in controlling the speed of a ship?

Captain Shellenbarger: The master of a merchant ship has a lot of control over the speed, providing he stays within certain guidelines which the company sets up. You can vary the speed any way you want to to avoid threatening weather—heave to, stop if necessary. If you have a distress message or anything like that, you are required by law to go to their assistance. If you have a patient which you need to divert, then you have authority to go maximum speed, consume whatever fuel is necessary, only just make sure you don't run out of fuel and have to be towed in. That's the only guideline that they say, "No, you don't do things like that." Well, that's common sense, because if you do that you're endangering the ship and the rest of the crew. But you have a lot of latitude in that.

However, for normal passages, this particular bypass, the additional nozzles, to get this extra speed, because we could do 19 knots without it anyway, with our normal nozzle setup on those ships. I presume you've got enough engineering background to know what I'm talking about. Nozzles for the steam turbines?

Paul Stillwell: Right.

Captain Shellenbarger: They're in blocks, you know. They added three more, four more, whatever, and that each ship has a different setup with GE or whatever turbines.[*] And our normal operating was 19 nozzles, but if needed to go a little bit faster to make a schedule to arrive in port, we could go to 21 nozzles. And 21 nozzles would give us 19 knots, fully loaded, on those ships. However, once we went to the additional, we'd have 25 nozzles as I recall and you'd do 21-22 knots with the ships.

Paul Stillwell: Well, I would think that the two main considerations would be to be as economical as possible in fuel use and meet the schedule.

Captain Shellenbarger: That's right, but remember, fuel in those days was a lot cheaper. The principle with American Export Lines and I think from what I've talked to other people was in those days was to meet your schedule, because this is liner service. The freight rates they were charging were dependent on whether or not you get the cargo to a certain place at a certain time. Particularly in the Far East where you're running, say, Christmas goods to the States for the Christmas season, and they want in them there by, what?

Paul Stillwell: Thanksgiving.

Captain Shellenbarger: Yes, certainly by Thanksgiving. But we had a lot more latitude, I think, than they do today, because now I've talked to these people that we work with on these foreign-flag ships. Of course, I'm quite friendly with some of them because I've been

---

[*] GE—General Electric.

on the ships eight, ten times like this Captain Francisco Siveria Russo on the <u>Lady Maria Laura</u>. Here three or four years ago he left Birkenhead was his last port in England loaded with chemicals and stuff, and he had a lot of chemicals which required heat. Of course, this is diesel and they used the diesel fuel in their auxiliary boilers for the steam for heating. The company allotted him so much fuel based on these things, and they did not consider that heating requirement. He said that he suddenly realized halfway across the Atlantic that he was going to run short of fuel, plus the fact that he ran into some extraordinarily bad weather, so he wasn't making any speed.

I don't think I ever saw anything quite like it on any of the ships. They had two diesel engines, geared to a single controllable-pitch propeller. And he said what he did was he had to cut his speed. Of course, he was not making any speed anyway. He said he shut down one of his diesels, and he had to go into Bermuda for fuel he was so far south. He was headed for New York, mind you, and he had to go into Bermuda. Then he said the worst thing was that after he left Bermuda he ran into another gale. He got to New York, and he had to anchor in Gravesend Bay and get a fuel barge out there before he could even get to the dock.

And, of course, because of many years of experience and being a good friend he asked me to review all of his reports. He had pages and pages of weather reports, faxes, and what he had done in detail, because you have to go to a note of protest for insurance purposes. In his case he was going to the Italian consul with the equivalent of what we call a note of protest saying that, "Due to extraordinary circumstances this is what happened, why I had to do this and that." Because he said that he was afraid of being dismissed and he sent a couple of faxes. Since then I've talked to him on the phone and I have a standing invitation to visit him at his place in Sorrento in Italy.

Paul Stillwell: So you're taken care of in Taiwan and Italy at least.

Captain Shellenbarger: Yes. [Laughter]

Paul Stillwell: How was your family life during those long around-the-world cruises?

Captain Shellenbarger: I've been very fortunate. I don't know, I think I discussed earlier the fact that Mary is my second wife. We will have our 45th anniversary on January 15th, only a couple months away. I'm fortunate for the fact that she came from a British Army family, where the husbands are away for long periods of time. Her sister's husband was a Jap prisoner for over three and a half years, and her father died when she was very young. But being for most of her early life in Aldershot very familiar with Army. In the British Army, their men are gone from their families for long periods of time. Far more I think than ours. She accepted the fact and she knew that I was going to sea when we met.

Paul Stillwell: So she learned to manage on her own obviously.

Captain Shellenbarger: Obviously. Yes. And she did a wonderful job of it. Yeah, 45 years coming up.

Paul Stillwell: Well, what do you remember of your seagoing career in the early '70s then, after these ships you've just described.

Captain Shellenbarger: Well, Export Ambassador, that same trip where I picked up the 40 containers I did a rescue. I don't know whether I mentioned that or not. We were in Pusan headed around to Inchon, past the island of Cheju-Do, then around the Yellow Sea and south of Korea, a nice high island. Gale blowing out of the northeast. Somewhere in the records I have the dates and everything, but, funny, I can't remember it now. But the third mate called me. I'd gone in behind the island. I had passengers. It was one the A-Class ships. Those were the ships that we had the container business on. I had gone in behind the island, and I hove to. The Yellow Sea is shallow. You might be aware of it. When you get gale force winds there, you get a horrendous chop plus the fact there's a lot of little shallow spots around through the Yellow Sea.

And there was nothing really urgent on our schedule because of this longshore strike in the States. We had a little bit of leeway and so I said, "Well, to hell with it. I'm not going to go out there and pound the ship to pieces in the Yellow Sea." I went down and I got ahold of the mates and I said, "We're going to heave to behind Cheju-Do here," which we did. Got in fairly close. It's good water right up to the shore and, of course, with that ship by that time we had good radars and everything. So I said, "We'll stay about a mile offshore and lay here until the weather moderates," which it did.

The next morning it started moderating, and I guess it was about 8:00 o'clock in the morning we started out around. And, oh, I guess it couldn't have been but about 8:30 the mate on watch, the third mate, called me. He said, "Hey, Captain, there's a boat over here that looks like it's in distress." The wind was still blowing, maybe force seven. Quite a chop. It wasn't good weather, though it wasn't really horrible. I got up there and I got the binoculars and I looked across there and I could see this thing bobbing up and down. It looked like maybe three or four men on the bow, and they were waving their shirts or something like that. They saw us and I said, "Well, obviously it looks like they want something."

So we went over there, and the engine was on standby. Of course, they'd been on standby earlier due to the weather. You know, when you're in close at night the chief and the engineers were standing by the throttle. So we went over, and we could see about four or five guys on a fishing boat. It was a Korean fishing boat, and the whole aft end of it, was submerged. They motioned that they wanted to come aboard, so we put a net over. Being a cargo ship we had cargo nets, because we still were carrying bulk cargo in addition to a lot of containers on deck. In certain hatches we had only containers. We dropped the nets over the side, and we put a couple of pilot ladders over.

This was the first time in my life I'd ever attempted anything like this and, of course, you read all kinds of descriptions how to do this, how to do that. Turns out most of the descriptions they have in books aren't worth a damn. I'd read somewhere that in a case you can't get alongside of this boat in distress, you should try to float a raft down to them. I don't know what they were thinking about. I didn't know what I was thinking about either, but, anyway, we had these floatable rafts, inflatable rafts. Well, we popped one open and dropped it over the side. Whoosh! Gone with the wind. They're designed to release themselves from the ship. We forgot to put any kind of a rope or line on the thing when it inflated. [Laughter]

Paul Stillwell: Live and learn, as they say.

Captain Shellenbarger: Live and learn. There was about an $8,000 life raft gone with the wind. The chief mate I had was a very good man. He came up on the bridge, and I told him to keep the second mate down there to watch around the ladders and the whole thing. And I said, "You got any suggestions?"

He said, "Fine. After that fiasco with the raft?"

"Well, in the meantime," I said, "We'd better get these guys aboard. What do you think we should do?"

He came up with the idea, "Why don't we just drift down on them."

I said, "Yeah, but suppose we come down on top of them and go right over the top of them?" That's something I was thinking about. Because we were rolling fairly good. With the containers on deck we had quite a bit of sail area. That was the same reason I hove to the night before. But we drifted down alongside of them, and we drifted by and five guys came climbing up the net. You know, the Koreans are very athletic and agile and so they came up.

As I was looking over from the bridge wing and I looked down at it I said, "All these guys look like hunchbacks." I couldn't believe it.

The second mate came up, and he told me, "There's two more on board."

"Two more on board?" I said, "I didn't see anymore there."

He said, "Well, for some reason they're down back in there in that submerged deckhouse." So as we circled around and came out and drifted by again, two guys come out and again they looked like hunchbacks. I told this at a couple of places. I've told a lot of these stories at Rotary Clubs and stuff like that. We picked the other two guys up, and I went down below. By that time they were in the crew mess room, and I looked in there. Here were seven men and a pile of wheels. Anything that was brass, electronic gear, they had unbolted.

When we got to Inchon, we found out this was a brand-new fishing vessel with all new gear on board. And the seams had opened up in the seas in this storm the night before, and it was sinking. Because they told me according to this Korean newspaper which I couldn't read but I've had it translated because it was in the Inchon papers about the awards. They came down and give me some kind of award from the Korean Coast

Guard, and they said that it was a brand-new vessel and this was a lot of new equipment and these guys when they came aboard had this stuff lashed to their backs, then with their oilskin over the top. If they'd ever fallen off the thing they'd have gone right to the bottom. It was like tying an anchor around your neck.

But this was their idea. They had to salvage what they could when they could, and they came aboard. And, believe me, when they went off on the pilot boat, every bit of that gear had to go with them. So I don't know whether they got a medal or they took it off and sold it. I haven't the vaguest idea, but it's just one of those things you encounter. [Laughter]

Paul Stillwell: When did that happen?

Captain Shellenbarger: That probably happened either in March or April 1969, because I guess about a year later they came up from Washington from the American Institute of Merchant Shipping, which no longer exists. They gave the ship an award plus a certificate for myself. Of course, I got a fancy certificate from the Koreans for saving lives of these seven fisherman.

Paul Stillwell: Very satisfying feeling, I'm sure.

Captain Shellenbarger: It was but when I tell about these guys salvaging everything off that fishing boat—when I went down there and looked and saw all that gear I was speechless. [Laughter] And only one of the guys could speak a few words of English. It turned out that he had at some time had worked for the U.S. Army in Korea, and that's where he learned what English he had. But he couldn't make it clear to me as to why there was all this gear. I imagine the thing they did as soon as they got ashore was to wash it all in fresh water because it had salt, and some of the pieces of electronic equipment, you can't tell me it was worth anything. It was damaged beyond repair, but they had unbolted and unscrewed it. The wheel. The compass was there. You know, the compass was a small binnacle.

So, anyway, the chief mate and I got a big dinner in Inchon. The head of the Korean Coast Guard was there and gave us an award. In my office at home I've still got a certificate that they gave me. It's one of the little incidents that happened through the years.

That was the same trip that I had the incident where we went from Korea down to Keelung. That's where the incident where they loaded the containers in Keelung. We went around to Kaoshiung, a few more, and then went to Hong Kong and then from Hong Kong direct to the Panama Canal.

Paul Stillwell: Well, if that happened in spring it must not have been Christmas merchandise.

Captain Shellenbarger: It couldn't have been. That's what I'm thinking. It couldn't have been Christmas merchandise, but for some reason it had gone through customs and couldn't be returned to the shippers. I can't remember what it was, but it was some reason that they had called and they couldn't get a hold of--so I got hold of Frank Jung and he said, "No, go ahead and load it," and we did and like I said they never forgot it. They never forgot it.

I've often wished that sometime later on I'd get a chance to get back there, because I made a lot of friends there. I made a lot of friends with the Chinese, where I didn't with the Japanese. I don't know whether it's because of the fact that I'd been in the Pacific during the war or what. I don't know.

Paul Stillwell: Who knows?

Captain Shellenbarger: You don't know. It must be something in your mind that sort of stays there, and yet the Japanese are good people to deal with as far as agencies or officials or things like that. They have some weird rules about not working on Sunday, but I enjoyed that because if I got in on Saturday I knew I was going to have an extra day in port. They had a lot of safety rules which today they're observing all over the world. Believe me, I have a lot of respect for the Japanese, but to make friends and be friendly with them, personally I didn't. Boy, I can make friends with the Chinese, though, because I love the Chinese. Not to mention their food. [Laughter]

Paul Stillwell: Well, you're right. There may be something in your psychological makeup that still goes back to World War II.

What came after the Export Ambassador?

Captain Shellenbarger: I was assigned to a couple of ships, and I've got some crude words for them. This was 1969, about the time that Isbrandtsen had taken over control of the company, and they were moving into the container business. They had purchased two ships built in Sparrows Point, Baltimore. They were built for Bethlehem Steel, which owned the yard there. They were ore carriers, and they had been experimental high-pressure jobs. As I recall, the boiler pressure on it was something like 1,250 pounds per square inch, whereas our standard boilers were 850. They named these two vessels the Container Dispatcher and the Container Forwarder. They completely converted them. They put cell guides in and regular container hatches, and they put two traveling cranes on the deck because they were self-sustained.*

This was the early days of containerization—nearly 30 years ago. Today all you see are container vessels. We started off by going to North Europe. I made, I think, one trip on the Container Dispatcher and one trip on the Container Forwarder. The Dispatcher we ran from New York to North Europe, and other than the fact that once again I was going up the Elbe and the Weser, taking aboard the pilots. I think I told you earlier about the incident where they wanted me to dip the flag to a beer garden.

Paul Stillwell: Yes.

Captain Shellenbarger: My biggest problem with Dispatcher and the Forwarder came from the way they were converted. As ore carriers they had huge ballast pumps, and when they converted them I don't know what they did with the ballast pumps. I think they ditched the

---

* A self-sustained containership carries its own cranes, so it can load or unload in any port, whereas many containerships require specialized gantry cranes installed ashore for the purpose.

ballast pumps and took the motors from the ballast pumps and put it on the anchor windlass, something to that effect. Because whenever I had to go into Bremen or Bremerhaven with the ships, I'd have to lay out at the pilot station by the Lotse for maybe eight to ten hours pumping out ballast before I could get in to go up in the locks to Bremerhaven.

It used to cause me a lot of annoyance and grief because you're drifting around out there, and there's a tremendous amount of traffic going in and out of there. If it was bad weather or anything like that, it was not a good place to be. It was just one of these things that I blamed on my friend McLaughlin. He was still the marine superintendent.

Then the Forwarder was the first time that we took a container vessel into the Mediterranean, which was an experience to go into these ports where they were just starting to work with containers. Of course, we had to use our own derricks, because this crane that ran up and down the tracks on the deck to fill the hatches, and the same crane had to life the hatch covers off, move them over on top of another hatch. You never had any place to put them on the shore, because you had to keep a place on the shore clear for the trucks coming in with the containers. So it was like playing checkers, moving hatch covers around.

Paul Stillwell: Did you have any trouble with those 1,250-pound plants?

Captain Shellenbarger: A couple of times—I'm trying to remember. My problem was that on a merchant vessel I've only got two boilers. The Export Line had one ship called the Export Examiner, which they had had 1,250-pound boilers on, and the plant was operated. It was experimental, and it was financed by the Navy apparently, because I know it was a government subsidy which paid for all the extra expense due to the fact they'd installed that on that ship.

But the chief engineer that had been on there was on the Export Dispatcher with me, the first time that I was on of these two ships. He said, "Cap, if I have any kind of a leak in the engine room, you better be looking for a place to drop the anchor or get clear, because I won't be able to give you any power on the engine. Once the leak is discovered, you'll only have about two minutes. Because I've got to shut down immediately because of that pressure because the water's going to be gone from the boilers almost instantaneously." He said, "Just as fast as I can get the firemen to yank the fires out from under the boilers, I've got to shut down. And not only that, when I shut down, you're going to have clouds and clouds of black smoke because the blowers have to be shut down, so you've got no air whatsoever in them."

It happened to me twice. Fortunately, in both cases it happened where I was not in a critical situation and, boy, it's something because normally with a breakdown down below, you've got a little bit of warning to maneuver, but there you had none. And that was the thing you always had to keep in mind with those high-pressure boilers.

Paul Stillwell: You talked about the sail area from containers. Did that prove a problem in any instance?

Captain Shellenbarger: Not that I recall. As a matter of fact, in heavy weather if I had a lot of containers, say, four high on deck, I found that the ship rode fairly well due to that sail area. I don't whether it was true or not and wondered if I had ever would have liked to have had at some time or another a chance to talk to a sailing ship man. Because I would notice that the ship would lay over with the wind. As long as this winds remained fairly constant, you wouldn't roll back into the wind because it would keep you over and you'd stay fairly stable, even though you're running with maybe eight, ten degrees list. You know that you're not having shifting cargo or anything like that, and you just lay over and you'd ride much better. And, of course, when you're sleeping, why, you adjust your bunk and your mattress accordingly and go to sleep, whereas if you're bouncing back and forth at sea you don't get any rest.

Paul Stillwell: I had not heard of that phenomenon.

Captain Shellenbarger: It's true. It would actually happen. Of course, as soon as the wind shifted, you'd flop the other way, or if you had to change course. But it happened a number of times. It was an interesting thing for me to experience.

With the Export Courier, I used to carry a big deck load of containers, but there I always had a lot of cargo in the hold so the wind and the sail area didn't really affect me that much. But they were two interesting ships. I was glad to get off of them, though.

Paul Stillwell: Why do you say that?

Captain Shellenbarger: They were short trips, and, there again, we'd come into port, and they'd move the containers on and off. By the time I was on the Forwarder, it was later on in the year, and they were making amazing progress because I couldn't believe it. They put shore cranes up at our pier in Staten Island in a period of about three months. We still had to move our cranes out of the way, but the shore cranes would take our hatch covers out. They could go way across and drop our hatch covers all clear. The area alongside the dock was all clear for the trailers and chasses.

I was moving up in the company then. As a matter of fact, looking here now at my records, I went back on the Flying Fish in October '69 and was there until the end of January in '70. That was another round-the-world trip, only this time I didn't go through the Suez Canal.

Paul Stillwell: Because it was still closed.

Captain Shellenbarger: Yes, so I had to head from New York to Durban, where I'd be bunkers. On the way the chief came up and told me, "I've got problems with my fresh water supply."

We didn't have the equipment to manufacture fresh water like our sister ships did, so I told him, "Okay, we'll have to go in to Cape Town. Can you hold it together until we get in there?"

He said, "Yes." So we did.

We went in to Cape Town and called the agent and told him, I said, "Well, as long as we're here we'll take bunkers here instead of Durban."

He said, "Well, it will cost you 50-60 cents a barrel more."

I said, "Well, we're here. It will cost a hell of a lot more to go into Durban. Call New York and let them know." I don't know whether he ever got ahold of New York, because I never heard from New York until after I left Karachi. But I went in. We took bunkers in Cape Town, and that was the first time and the only time in my life I ever went into Cape Town.

Paul Stillwell: Any memories of apartheid there?

Captain Shellenbarger: Not particularly, because I was taken ashore by the agent, myself and the chief. We went to a place which there were no blacks or anything like that. And the agent was very fascinated with the fact that he had served this ship when it was with Robin Line, and he said, "I recognized the ship as soon as you came in the breakwater. That's the old Robin Wentley."

I said, "That's right. It was the Robin Wentley." I said, "That was its previous name."

So when we left, like in a lot of ports, photographers will take pictures of ships coming in out. Then they'll send proofs to the ship and ask you pass it around to the crew and see if the crew wants any pictures. We must have ordered about 40-50 pictures from him, and, of course, I didn't pay for mine naturally. I got a couple of pictures of the Flying Fish coming out of Cape Town with Table Mountain in the background. And we were loaded, so it's a nice-looking picture of the Flying Fish coming out, headed for Karachi, up the Mozambique Channel and bucking the Aughulas Current.

And, of course, we get close inshore, you had a slight counter current. If you haven't been into those waters, I wouldn't recommend it, because you've got to run in within half a mile of shore. And when you're sailing along a strange coast, you don't want to be half a mile off. But, of course, if you're coming from the other direction, why, you've got those tremendous swells down there. Ships have been sunk there. But it was interesting.

Paul Stillwell: Well, speaking of blacks in another context, what proportion, if any, did you have black crew members during the time you sailed, and did it increase over the years?

Captain Shellenbarger: Yes. That's definitely something that changed. At the end of the war and when I first started sailing as chief mate on these Export ships, I would say that we would have maybe one or two blacks in the deck crew. Seldom ever saw them in the engine room. You'd see a lot of Panamanians and black types in the engine room. You'd see maybe two or three in the steward's department. You might have two or three in the deck department, and I would say by late 1960s you ran close to 50% black in the deck department.

The majority of them were natives of Jamaica, Cayman Islands, Caribbean. Very few Puerto Ricans, which are sometimes black, sometimes are not. But they were all damn good sailors. Now, when I was chief officer on the Excalibur I had--not the boatswain, who was Italian, but a black boatswain's mate on the passenger ship. His name was Pannell, and he was one of the best sailors I've ever seen. He was a hell of a lot better sailor than the boatswain was, a fellow named Cecchini. And primarily because of this union--it was the National Maritime Union for the unlicensed men—and I think they had support for more African-Americans, as they say today, than the others. I've had very good stewards that were, you know, African-American, blacks.

I had one third cook who was one of the best I've ever had. We'd lay up occasionally in Norfolk in the shipyard, and he lived in Portsmouth. The company knew that he'd been with me and this was the Export Courier, my last ship, because I was on there six years, and he was on there all that time. He was an old-timer, grey-haired fellow. But he was one of the best men. He wouldn't sail anything above third cook though. Whenever they got ready to re-crew, put a regular crew aboard the ship, they'd tell me to call this guy in Portsmouth to get over there, and we'd get everything ready for the first meal. And then, of course, as soon as they got the full crew aboard, from the hiring hall, the steward and the chief cook and the others would come down to the ship. He and I would have everything laid out ready to go.

Paul Stillwell: Why didn't he want to advance?

Captain Shellenbarger: I don't know. It was just one of those things. Some of those people are like that. They don't want the responsibility. Apparently, he wasn't too good a baker. The second cook has to be a good baker because on those ships in those days they still did actual cooking. Today everything's pre-prepared. It's all frozen. You pull it out and put it in a microwave. [Laughter] But in those days the second cook had to be second cook and baker. That was his rating, and this fellow didn't want to be anything other than the third cook. He was good. Nice people.

Paul Stillwell: He found his niche.

Captain Shellenbarger: He did. Even today, where I'm working today, with the work I have now--it's contract work with the Sea River Exxon—one of my associates is African-American, Danny Preston, and he's been married 40 years to his wife, Jess. They were childhood sweethearts in Mobile, Alabama. You couldn't ask for a nicer guy. And I used to sit and talk to him. When I first started that work back in the '80s, he was a dispatcher for Exxon. He knows all the tugboats, tugboat companies, and everything. I talked to him yesterday.

I've always had a very good relationship with them—with some of them it was—just like any other human beings, you know. There's some of them that were foul balls, and the rest of them are nice people. I've always had no problem.

That's another thing. A sailor who's been around the world has dealt with Africans, Egyptians, Greeks, Arabs, all nationalities, the Russians. You meet all kinds, and you think nothing of it. When I'm with a guy today, unless he does something blatant, I'll never even realize whether he's black or white. I've had so many Mohammedan friends. You know, Karachi, Pakistan and East Pakistan and Chittagong and things like that. It's one of those things. It doesn't enter into it anymore. Never did, really.

Paul Stillwell: Well, it sounds like the maritime union must have had a fairly liberal membership policy.

Captain Shellenbarger: They did, yes, particularly the National Maritime Union. And to my knowledge it was never any problem. They had other problems. They had crooks running it. Three of them are in jail right now, because they spent all the pension funds. Oh, well.

So, anyway, that was the Flying Fish. Went back on the Export Champion, and then we moved up to the Export Courier in 1970. Made another trip to the Far East on the Export Courier and relieved Captain John Cain, one of the naval merchant marine reserves. He became a commander in the Navy and he got the Silver Star. One of the few that got a medal for his service. Most of them ended up on LCTs and landing ships and stuff like that in World War II, but I don't know how John ended up as skipper of a DE. He's a member of the Marine Society, and, of course, he's the guy I relieved on the Courier in 1970, because John spent eight years on the ship and I spent six. That's almost the whole life of the ship before it was sold to Farrell Lines. He was a good friend of mine. He lives in Dallas now. John was in the invasion of Sicily. He was skipper of some kind of a small patrol boat, and that's when John got the Silver Star. I've read his commendation about that. Later on he was in the Pacific and he ended up skipper of a DE, which was rather unusual for a merchant marine reserve.[*]

Paul Stillwell: Well, please tell me about the Export Courier.

Captain Shellenbarger: Well, the Export Courier, that trip I relieved John Cain, and it was very uneventful, really. It was a nice trip. Had good weather. Didn't have bad weather. When I came back in 1971, I had sort of fallen in love with the ship, and here was John waiting on the dock and couldn't wait to get back on the ship. Couldn't wait for me to get off. Then I went to the Mediterranean on a couple of A-Class ships: 12 passengers, amidship house. They were the Export Aid and Export Agent, and they were routine trips in and out of the Mediterranean.

---

[*] During World War II, Lieutenant Commander John R. Cain, USNR, commanded the high-speed transport Dickerson (APD-9), which had originally been a four-stack destroyer, commissioned in 1919.

I made three trips on the Export Agent. The only unusual thing about that is that these were ships about 595 feet long, and to my knowledge they were the largest ships that had ever gone up the Guadalquivir River to the port of Seville, through the locks, because we would just barely fit into the locks. My understanding now is that today this small shipyard which was there when I was running in there has now been enlarged and made larger locks.

Now, I don't know what they've done about the draft. I don't see how they could possibly dredge that river, because the bottom of the river is roughly 10 to 12 feet of mud. You would always go up the river until the tide would leave you in the mud, and being steam-turbine ships, you'd have to go to high suction then because the bottom suctions were in the mud. You know, for your cooling water in your condensers. But I understand now that ships continually go up and down that river. With us going up and down there, it was an adventure, to say the least. But the passengers loved it, because Seville, we were always there for at least four to five days, and we would load a lot of olives and almonds, sherry. In those days it was all bulk cargo. The olives were loaded in huge puncheons, and they weighed roughly one ton each. They were maybe six-seven feet in diameter, and they had to be as least that long.

Paul Stillwell: That's a lot of olives.

Captain Shellenbarger: When one of them broke, you realized there was a lot of olives in there. And because of their size and their weight they required very special stowage. You could stow them not more than three high in your lower holds, and that meant you had to put them in and you had to chock them carefully. The way you load barrels you make a tier like this, and the next tier has to be halfway out, so it that this puncheon will rest on four down below. And if one of them ever collapsed, you had olives all over. And the worst part about the olives was that they would go into the strainers of your bilges and plug up your strainers, so you couldn't pump anything out with them. But apparently at the time it was very profitable for us and, of course, we did this for a long time. Later on we started getting the olives that were pre-packaged in Spain in glass jars and cartons, and we'd load maybe 800-900 tons of olives in cartons rather than the big puncheons.

The sherry continued being shipped in the smaller barrel called a pipe. They were long. They would be seven feet long and maybe three foot in diameter, and sherry was shipped in those. And later on I think we started carrying that only in bottles and cases, but it was interesting while it lasted. Then we'd go to Portugal on these ships, load maybe at least 400 or 500 tons of skinless and boneless sardines. Of course, the port at the mouth of the Guadalquivir is the famous Huelva, where Columbus sailed from on his first voyage to the continent, the Indies as he called it.

But, anyway, when we left there it was only about four or five hours to the southern coast of Portugal. Cape Saint Vincent is on the corner there. Just inside there there's a small port called Portimao, and we'd anchor out there and they'd bring the skinless and boneless sardines out to us. I've loaded as high as 600 tons of sardines there in cases. They're small cases, about two feet long maybe, possibly ten inches wide and maybe six or eight inches thick. And I've forgotten how many tins of sardines were in them, but it was always a mystery to me—I've eaten so many of them—how do they get the skins and bones out of them? We would ask these guys there and they would give you a blank look. You know, it was a silly question and wasn't worth an answer.

But the thing I remember vividly there more than anything else was the barges that came out. This would have to be in the '70s was the last time I was there with the <u>Export Agent</u>, and they had these barges. They had diesels, and I had never seen anything like this. It must have been something designed and built by Rudolf Diesel, because they had a huge bulb atop of the cylinder, and they had a blowtorch to heat the diesel.[*] You'd see these things down there with this blowtorch blowing on this bulb at the top of this cylinder, because it was just a single cylinder, you know. All of a sudden the thing would go, "Boop-boop," and it would start turning.

I've asked other people about it, because I never had a chance to go down and look at one of them. I would have loved to know more about those things, because they said they were diesels. Well, you could smell they were diesels, but I never heard of anything being ignited with a blowtorch. I know some diesels start with compressed air, but I never heard of a blowtorch.

---

[*] In 1892 German mechanical engineer Rudolf Diesel invented a type of internal combustion engine that involves auto-ignition of fuel. The engine bears his name to this day.

Then we'd go on around to Lisbon and cross the bar there. Of course, in a gale it could be kind of a hairy thing, because you had to go across the bar before you got a pilot. There was no way a pilot could get out there. You'd go around into Cascais, but normally we picked up a pilot there. But when you got ready to leave, the pilot would leave up by the statue of Prince Henry the Navigator. And from there on out it was easy, straight shot, but when you went out over the bar, why, you better make sure everything was battened down. I wouldn't say it compared to the Columbia River bar, but certainly I've seen it as bad as on the San Francisco bar.

Paul Stillwell: Let me ask you a question prompted by your mention of the sherry. There is allegedly or supposedly a prohibition against alcoholic consumption on board Navy ships. What is the practice in merchant ships?

Captain Shellenbarger: The same. Today you will not find alcoholic beverages served aboard a merchant vessel. You won't find it in the stores. I won't say you wouldn't find maybe a bottle somewhere if you had to search the ship, in one of the officer's quarters. Certainly wouldn't see it in the crew's quarters because it would mean instant dismissal. Particularly on ships that I'm on today. Any kind of a petroleum carrier.

This Captain Russo that I mentioned earlier, that was one of his saddest things. He said that when the ship was delivered, the Lady Maria Laura, that was the first ship and the Bice the second one. He was lead skipper on both of them, because I worked with him on both the ships. He said when they first came out they had Italian flags. Well, under the Italian flag and Italian rules the Italian crews must be served wine with their meals. I think it's a government regulation, that if they so desire they must have, be given at least one liter of wine per day, and that's a hell of a lot of wine.

Paul Stillwell: Yes, it is.

Captain Shellenbarger: He said that in Italian ports it would be no problem, but he said every other port in the world, wherever he went, particularly the United States, U.K., and anyplace like that, even France, same thing. He said that you can't have it aboard, can't serve it to the crew. He said, "Not even my Italian crew."

Paul Stillwell: So this second mate you had in your first master's command was really way over the line.

Captain Shellenbarger: Oh, yes. Way over. When we undocked at midnight, I was talking to him on our CB radios. He sounded perfectly all right at midnight, because he was aft undocking. That's the normal procedure on most ships. You change around occasionally to get the guys different experience, but normally on most merchant ships you'll find the chief officer on the bow, second officer on the stern, third on the bridge.

However, quite frequently—and the company encouraged it—you'd put the second officer on the bow, third officer on the stern, and have the chief officer on the bridge so he could get some experience docking and undocking the ship, because if anything happens to you he's the guy that's going to relieve you. So we did that quite frequently actually. But in this case the second mate was on the stern, and he sounded all right undocking. But he must have gone right to his room with a bottle of vino or whatever, because when he went on watch at 4:00 o'clock he was blotto because it was shortly after he'd gone on watch.

I asked the third mate, "When Ed came up to relieve you, did he seem to be under the influence?"

He said, "I couldn't tell you. Actually, he seemed all right, but from what happened, obviously he wasn't." The third mate was a young fellow, right out of the school. He'd only been with us one trip and he was very conscientious. He said, "If I thought he was drunk, I wouldn't have let him relieve me. I'd have called you." And he said, "I didn't think so. I made a mistake maybe but—"

This was one of the things that I was always very conscious of. I did not permit drinking on the ship. You always had to entertain the passengers, and if you had passengers you had to serve wine and liquor. You had this small bar in the passengers' lounge. If you didn't have that you didn't have passengers. That's what it amounts to.

And, of course, the same way with the passenger ships, the Excalibur and those ships. They had a big bar there. They had a regular rating of bartender. Had 90 to 96 in the crew. Two-thirds of them were service personnel, stewards and waiters and cooks and bakers. After all, if you've got 120 passengers, they're all first-class passengers and they have to be taken care of. And, needless to say, the bar was a big thing. As a matter of fact, in those days as chief officer for the trip of six weeks I had a bar allowance of $75.00, and the skipper had a bar allowance of $150.00, plus his entertainment expenses which was separate, that the steward took care of the captain's party, the sailing party get-together, the captain's dinner, as they call it. They have different names aboard different ships.

And you'd have different parties during the trip. You know, for a six weeks' trip you had to entertain the passengers with parties and what have you. And, of course, the senior officers, the chief engineer, the captain, first officer and the first engineer were expected to mingle with the passengers. You know, act as hosts. When you're in a bar and they offer you a drink, you can nurse it for a long time, but you had to be reciprocate occasionally. That's why they gave you an allowance. These customs are gone now, of course. I don't know what the cruise ships do. I presume they leave it all up to their cruise personnel. I'm sure that the operating officers are not involved anymore like they were then.

Paul Stillwell: Well, I think they've got a staff captain who really oversees the entertainment.

Captain Shellenbarger: Yes, who oversees this thing. And, of course, certainly with the people standing watch with the world situation what it is today, it just couldn't be like it was in those days. In my case it didn't do me any good, because in four years on the Excalibur I gained 45 pounds. For the last 10 or 15 years I've stayed right around between 205 and 210, which is still more than I should weigh, but at one time I was up to 260 pounds. When I got off the passenger ships, I had to lose it in a hurry. Of course, it got worked off.

Paul Stillwell: Well, back to the Export Courier.

Captain Shellenbarger: Okay, well, that was the trip. I went back on the Ambassador again for another trip, but that was to the Mediterranean. I bounced around a lot in those ships, but then I finally went on the Export Courier, in June '73, and I sailed on it with the exception of vacation time until March 1979.

Paul Stillwell: Any highlights to mention from those six years?

Captain Shellenbarger: Well, most of the time was running to the Far East. Like I said, I had sort of fallen in love with the ship and I did. John Cain retired. Kurt Carlsen went on there for one trip, and I had seniority with the company more than Kurt, because he'd been with Isbrandtsen. He was very unhappy about it, but when Tom Collins called me and said that, he said, "The Courier's coming in. You're waiting for a job. Kurt's on the ship now. He's coming back from Japan. I'm offering the job to you, and Captain Blackledge says it's time that you should get a permanent job."

Well, actually some of the other jobs had been semi-permanent, but they weren't. In other words, a captain at a certain stage of his career in a company goes on a ship and it becomes his ship, which is a ridiculous sounding name. Nevertheless for years, when somebody said, "The Courier," the response would be, "Oh, the Courier—John Cain." And then it became, "Courier, well, that's Shelly." So, anyway, Kurt Carlsen came in, and he recognized the fact it was seniority. Of course, he'd exercised the same thing previously with other ships. I helped him off with his ham gear, and he helped me with mine.

Paul Stillwell: So I take it the change was amicable.

Captain Shellenbarger: It was, yes. So I started on the Courier, and nothing really remarkable in that time that I'm thinking of. There were no more rescues.

Paul Stillwell: Was she strictly a containership?

Captain Shellenbarger: It was a combination container-cargo. We carried general cargo, because most of this time was running to the Far East. When we went out, we carried a lot of general cargo in the lower holds and we carried maybe containers four high on deck on all the decks. I can't remember exactly what stage, but there was some stage in there that they were trying to carry more containers and less general cargo, and they needed ballast. They took some of our double bottoms and put in heavy ballast. It was bentonite, driller's mud, which has got a specific gravity about 3.1. In other words, you know, three times heavier than water. What it did was reduce our fuel capacity.

So we'd sail from the East Coast to the Far East, but because of this reduced fuel capacity when we went through the Panama Canal we'd have to go right up past Acapulco and into the outer harbor at Los Angeles for fuel. We must have made 15-18 round trips to the Far East, but I think there was only once that we went alongside of a dock. We bunkered always at anchor, and normally this quantity of fuel we were taking from barges, so invariably we were there for about 24 hours.

Which was always good, because I'd radio ahead to my brother, who is up in Lancaster. He'd come down and visit, and several times he came right aboard the ship. This is the brother who died just a year ago November. I'd always considered him not exactly a physical type. I can remember a couple of times looking down there, and Johnny was coming up the pilot ladder before we even had a chance to rig the accommodation ladder. He'd come aboard and visit, and then we'd go ashore and we'd go to Port of Call or one of the restaurants and have dinner. Then he'd take off back to Lancaster and I'd go back to the ship.

So it was a nice period, but there was one incident during this thing. There was one case where I had a guy going nuts on me coming into the Santa Barbara Channel, coming in on a modified great circle from Yokohama. I never went a full great circle, because that puts you up around the Aleutians. That's where Kurt Carlsen lost 15 containers, the trip that I relieved him, and I think maybe that's why they offered me the job.

Paul Stillwell: So this is on top of his earlier experience with Flying Enterprise.

Captain Shellenbarger: That's right. I've heard him make the comment, "I love rough weather. I love rough weather." You know, in that Danish accent. And thinking to myself, "Yeah, but does the ship love it?" He lost 15 containers that previous trip that were carried away by heavy seas.

On one trip I lost four containers coming down from Los Angeles to the Panama Canal. I got caught in one of those classic Tehuantepecers. Boy, they come up fast they're just like the storms up in the Gulf of Lyons. That heavy air coming over the mountaintops, they come swooping down, you know, and Whoom, it's got you. It was my fault. I didn't turn around fast enough. That thing caught me on the stern, and I started rolling heavily and a couple of lashings came loose and, Boom, next thing I know, the containers are floating past the ship. And, of course, there's no way you can pick them up or anything. You don't send a Mayday. You just send a notice to mariners for people to stay alert, that there are containers adrift such latitude and longitude. But these things happen.

Paul Stillwell: One of the interesting things you told me before we started the tape is that you've been giving a deposition in the case of a ship that was abandoned in the Atlantic and later salvaged.[*] That you had made 85 round-trip crossings of the North Atlantic, and the master of that ship hesitated at going out in a gale, force 12 weather, and—well, let me let you tell the story.

Captain Shellenbarger: Okay. I won't mention any names other than the fact that I will say it was a Greek ship. It had loaded a full cargo of steel products, plate, coils and various sheets, in Antwerp and Germany. Sailed from Germany, across the North Atlantic, bound for the East Coast of the United States. And they ran into very heavy weather. The ship had been originally designed as a bulk carrier and converted to, I think, a container or a car carrier, then converted back to a bulker. That's what they called it, a bulker. Yet as far as I was concerned, it was carrying general cargo, because it had five hatches carrying this steel. When they ran into this very heavy weather the ship's master slowed down. He had received messages saying that there were two more very bad storms ahead of him, and what they call bad I haven't the vaguest idea because I didn't have access to the logbooks.

---

[*] After his seagoing career ended, Captain Shellenbarger began testifying in maritime court cases as an expert witness.

All I had to go on was what they wanted me to testify as to normal heavy weather conditions found in the North Atlantic.

Paul Stillwell: So you were an expert witness.

Captain Shellenbarger: So I was there as an expert witness—strictly concerning weather, not as a oceanographer or anything of that sort, other than the fact I had been on the North Atlantic and could reasonably expect what kind of weather. These were the questions that they were concerned with.

But they got into a lot of detail about how many crossings I'd made and what latitudes, and when I did the research I was amazed to find out I'd made so many round-trip crossings. I came up with 85 and that's 170 crossings. I said, "I couldn't believe it," so I had to go back and recheck my records. And that didn't count round-the-world trips. Didn't count trips that were to the south, even to Cape Town, because I didn't go into the North Atlantic. They were all periods in which I'd been at least north of, say, 42 north latitude. So they went into a lot of detail on it. But it sort of fascinated me, because I'd done this sort of work when I first retired.

In this case I'm talking about, the weather moderated a little bit, and the master took off with his crew. They were picked up by the Canadian Coast Guard. The ship didn't sink. I saw a video that the U.S. Coast Guard had made of the vessel adrift in this storm, and from the aircraft it didn't look that bad. The thing was bouncing around a bit, but this is what you expect and this was my testimony: the fact that when you sailed from port you batten down everything and you expect the worst and be prepared for it, whether you get it or not. Hey, if you don't get it that's your good luck. But if it happens, it happens.

There was also an expert witness for the other side, and he made an interesting statement. He said he'd sailed as a master with one of the containerships. He had a British license issued in Hong Kong. He's a British national. He made the statement in his deposition to the fact that if he expected to encounter force 12 winds, 65 knots or over, he would flatly refuse to sail. The attorneys questioned him and he repeated it in his deposition. Well, fortunately, he did his deposition before I did so I had access to his deposition. And I looked at it and I could hardly believe my eyes.

I made some remark to Doug Burnett about it, and he said, "Maybe that's the reason why he's working ashore now."*

I said, "Well, no shipping company would ever hire him, for a guy that has that kind of an attitude." Because when you go to sea, you know the sea's going to be there. It's going to treat you good or it's going to treat you bad. You've got to be prepared for it, and that's what it amounts to. So this was why they went into a lot of detail about my crossings, how many times I'd encountered weather, you know, force 12 or over that I could remember, and I could remember about seven of them. There were probably more and a hell of a lot of them that were slightly less than that. But this is part of going to sea. I spent 42 years at sea.

Paul Stillwell: Did you feel in that sense a disappointment coming ashore in 1979 from your Export Courier?

Captain Shellenbarger: Yes. Well, actually, the circumstance of my leaving was peculiar. Jake Isbrandtsen had taken over American Export Lines.† He was later indicted for unethical practices, and it turned out that's what the courts had ruled. The courts said that what he did was unethical but it was not illegal, and that's what it ended up being, but actually he broke American Export Lines. It turned out that the stockholders booted him out. I don't know whether they paid him off or not, but they certainly booted him out, and they brought a fellow in from the banks, fellow by the name of Jim Horn. The name suddenly changed from American Export-Isbrandtsen back to American Export Lines, and our house flag changed once again. Didn't come back to the old E that I'd sailed under for so many years. Then it became the red, white and blue horizontal stripes with a blue E on a diamond high in the center of the flag. But it was too far gone by then.

The company had planned that about every two or three years they would get four new ships. Of course, the A-class, the B-class, the C-class, they were all lined up but the

---

* Douglas Burnett is a Naval Reserve officer who works as an admiralty lawyer. It was he who suggested Captain Shellenbarger for this oral history.
† Jakob Isbrandtsen had been head of Isbrandtsen Lines.

C-class. They'd had to get rid of the Independence and the Constitution, those two big liners, because the passenger traffic had gone to aircraft so they were no longer economical to operate, so they were laid up for a long period of time, and eventually they were sold to C. Y. Tung, to Orient Overseas Lines.

The Constitution and Independence were both rebuilt. After they'd been laid up, they'd been sold to him. I learned just a few weeks ago the Constitution now is being scrapped, but I would say for the last 10 or 12 years the two of them have been running out of Honolulu as American-Hawaii Cruises. Both of them had been rebuilt, because they were built in the '50s. The Independence was rebuilt, I think, in Japan. The Constitution was rebuilt in Taiwan, China Shipbuilding in Kaohsiung. That's when American-Hawaii Cruises began running them, and they apparently were doing fairly well because, but, of course, they were getting old. You know, long in the tooth.

They sent the Independence over to Newport News.* I think that there was an estimate something like, I don't know, they estimated that the refurbishing of the ship would cost something like $12 million. It turned out to be about triple that because as they went to work on it they found that this had to be done, that had to be done, to bring it up to Coast Guard regulations. Doubler plates, plating replaced, this and that. So I know there was a long legal battle over the settlement of the bill that Newport News had for refurbishing the ship, but apparently from what I hear it's in very good condition now, because the hulls when they were built were built very strong, far above normal specs, of what you'd have today. So the Independence is still running.

As a matter of fact, it was one of the maritime magazines just recently, and it said the Constitution is being scrapped, and this company is looking for a replacement for it. Because the way they work it is the two ships sail out of Honolulu and they have a route where one goes one way and the other one goes the other way and they cross mid-week. And then they both come back in the following week.

Paul Stillwell: They make a one-week circuit of the Hawaiian Islands. I've made that cruise and it's very pleasant.

---

* Newport News Shipbuilding and Dry Dock Company.

Captain Shellenbarger: Which one?

Paul Stillwell: It was the Independence in 1995. It was the 50th anniversary of V-J Day, and so we had a lot of veterans on board.

Captain Shellenbarger: That's great. Well, then you know the ship.

Paul Stillwell: Yes.

Captain Shellenbarger: Oh, I worked cargo on them. I was port captain doing cargo work. I'd work with an outfit called Banks Engineering. They'd come in, be in an extra day, because of the things we'd have to do for boom tests, stuff like that. I got to know the ships very well. Never sailed on them, but I got to know them because I did an awful lot of work on them in port. Yes, they were nice ships. And, of course they had that distinctive old-fashioned stern on them which was sort of a trademark of American Export Lines. But really was fascinating.

Paul Stillwell: Mai-tais on the fantail were very popular.

Captain Shellenbarger: [Laughter] Yes. I can imagine. I was aboard the Independence many times while it was laid up in Sparrows Point in Baltimore. My friend, Walter Johansen, was the ship keeper on there. Then when we got the word it was going to be sold to Tung, they were stripping everything off the ship that said Export in any way. They had mountains of things down by the baggage room—silverware, glassware—and it was going out and it was going into dumpsters. At that time I was on one of the A-ships, and I hired a pickup truck, come over and got a lot of stuff. Games. Things that had never been opened. Shuffleboard. You name it. Golf putters and stuff like that.

There was all kinds of stuff on there, and we went up to them and they said, "Take it over if you want it. It's all yours." So I'd take it over back to those other ships and, of course, a few little pieces here and there got home as souvenirs. After all, I spent over 30 years with them. I think that was Walter's last job with the company before he retired.

But he was ship keeper on there, and they went for refurbishment right then. That was their first rebuild.

We're getting kind of late here, aren't we?

Paul Stillwell: Yes, Mary's been waiting outside a long time.

Interview No. 5 with Captain Franklin F. Shellenbarger, U.S. Maritime Service (Retired)
Place: U.S. Naval Institute, Annapolis, Maryland
Date: Wednesday, 19 November 1997
Interviewer: Paul Stillwell

Paul Stillwell: Well, Captain, when we encountered each other this morning it was quite foggy outside, and we agreed it was not a good morning to take a ship out, but instead we are here inside, warm, and have a chance to recount some more of your career. Yesterday, as we finished up, you were talking about some of your final experiences in the Export Courier. If you could resume at that point please.

Captain Shellenbarger: All right. I think I recounted that we had made numerous trips to and from the Far East, and then they pulled us off of the Far East run to make a special trip to Saudi Arabia, port of Jidda, which I hadn't been in for quite a few years since I'd gotten off the India run. And it had been several years since I'd been back into the Mediterranean. We stopped at Alexandria and then Port Said for the convoy, which the convoy procedure they have going through the Suez Canal.

In the meantime, the vessel had not been cleared by the authorities to go to an Arabian port, and it's some sort of an agreement they have between the Muslim countries. When I got into Jidda the chief pilot came aboard. He saw the Export insignia and the name Export Courier. He was an old friend Ali, chief pilot of Jidda port. He claimed he remembered me, but I don't think he really did, just the fact that it was an Export ship.

I can recall going in and out of Jidda many years ago, when there was just one little dock. If you were in there loading or discharging cargo, you would always have to leave the dock in case of a Haji ship coming in with the pilgrims going to Mecca. But I couldn't believe how they had built and expanded this huge port. It was just incredible. The port was tenfold in size from what I'd remembered it 20 years before.

Paul Stillwell: Now, what year was it when you went in?

Captain Shellenbarger: This would have had to have been about 1978. It was about the year before everything folded up on us. So the weird part about it to me was the fact that we had a lot of cargo for what they call their militia or something to that effect. For instance, their Navy is called their Coast Guard. That is their Navy.

But, anyway, we were just tying up. The authorities came up the accommodation ladder, asked for some books and things. We were still doubling up the lines when Ali came back on the bridge, and he said, "Cap, I'm so sorry, you have to leave."

"What do you mean leave?"

He said, "You don't have the clearance." Well, the minute he said "the clearance," I knew what he was talking about. Normally if you were coming from the Suez Canal and Port Said, the authorities would come aboard, go through your logbooks, and check back to see whether you have called at an Israeli port. Then when they do that, they write in Arabic on the log page; they put it right into your deck log. They write in there the fact that you have been cleared. I didn't have the clearance.

Paul Stillwell: Had you been into an Israeli port?

Captain Shellenbarger: We had not been, because we'd been on the Far East run and I think that's the reason why they sent us there. But somebody slipped up in New York and didn't remind me of it. I should have remembered but I didn't. Anyway, crew back to the stations, unmoor, go back out to anchor. After we got anchored, our agent came aboard and said, "Well, so sorry for this problem." Our cargo was ambulance and military vehicles. It was all military for the Saudi government, but it didn't make any difference. Fortunately, we had a lot of our logbooks aboard. And so for the next three days I had to go into what they called the port commander's office and drink gallons of tea. I produced the logs and everything was being gone through. They're talking about that and everything all through interpreters with this gentleman over in the corner there with the headdress on.

Paul Stillwell: Burnoose?

Captain Shellenbarger: I don't know what they call it. After about three days, why, the interpreter said, "All right, Captain. You're cleared now. We are satisfied that you have not been involved in the trading with the Israelis." At which time the gentleman over the corner, who I thought he was, you know, just an official there, an Arab, spoke in very good English. He said, "By the way, Captain, when was the last time you were in Sunny Point?" That was an ammunition depot, over by Wilmington, North Carolina.

I said, "Pardon me, sir. You speak English?"

"Well, I'm a graduate of your Naval Academy. [Laughter] We were there another two days, and he took me out to dinner.

Paul Stillwell: He was an Arab, I take it.

Captain Shellenbarger: An Arab and probably one of the many distant relatives of the royal family, because that's where most of your officials are. He explained to me that this was protocol. He said, "There's no way you can get around it. In a way, it's sort of embarrassing, but you didn't have the clearance, and there was nothing we could do about it. As he put it, "You know, I can't get myself in trouble. That's the way it is."

Paul Stillwell: So your company should have made the arrangements.

Captain Shellenbarger: Yes, American Export should have made the arrangements. But, anyway, it gave us a couple of extra days there and I enjoyed it. It's something different all the time. You know, when I think back, I really enjoyed the life I had, even for the long periods away from home and everything.

Paul Stillwell: Well, I envy you the cosmopolitan experiences. You've seen so much of the world.

Captain Shellenbarger: And met so many people, and when I was looking over these records last night one of the incidents I neglected on one of those trips to the Mediterranean—on the Export Agent I had the opportunity to meet someone who was really fascinating, and his name was Melville Bell Grosvenor.* He's the grandson of Alexander Graham Bell, and he owned a yacht called the White Mist. It was based here in Annapolis, and they took it up to Baltimore, brought it alongside. He had one of his people who apparently sailed with him all the time, and I think actually it was one of the photographers for the National Geographic, and his wife came up with him, Anne. This was one of the A-ships, where we had nice accommodations for passengers, a nice dining room and a lounge and everything.

My wife was with me on the coastwise, so we had dinner together. They brought the White Mist alongside, and we started to lift it aboard. My chief officer who was a fellow name of Gus Svokos, whom I mentioned in another interview. He was of Greek descent, spoke Greek. Anyway, Dr. Grosvenor and I were having lunch and visiting after lunch and Gus came up and said they were ready to make the lift. It was about 60 tons, theoretically. He got ready to lift and the derrick and sling started groaning and everything. I turned to Dr. Grosvenor, and I said, "Are you sure that's what this is, 60 tons?" He had provided the slings and everything and the cradle on deck, because we were taking it to Piraeus, Greece. He stopped for a minute, and he said, "You know, I didn't add on the provisions and the water that I've got in there." So that was another five tons of provisions and water.

Well, we had to drain the water, but the provisions, of course, we left on board. It was touch and go to set the thing up on deck in the cradle. And, of course, we were going to have to discharge it with our gear in Piraeus, which we did. I guess he flew over. I met his wife a couple of times after that because he invited me to dinner at his house in Bethesda, Maryland. And, of course, have met people all over the world, but he was one of the most fascinating people to talk to.

Paul Stillwell: In what ways? What was it about him?

Captain Shellenbarger: He had been everywhere and done everything, I think, and no matter what the subject was, he could enhance it and then talk. He was a fascinating

---

* Melville Bell Grosvenor graduated from the Naval Academy in 1923 and resigned from the service in 1924. He had a long career with the National Geographic Society, including service as editor of National Geographic magazine from 1957 to 1967 and editor-in-chief from 1967 to 1977.

person to visit with. When we got to Piraeus, he came to the ship and watched while we put the yacht in the water. Then he told me that they were going to be cruising around the Mediterranean. Actually, they been up around a lot of places, and I think they crossed the Atlantic a couple of times with the boat.

Then he said, "Your next vacation, how about coming to crew with me on the White Mist?"

I said, "I've never sailed on a sailing vessel of any sort." So I thanked him and thinking to myself, and then I learned later that his crew were people who were on vacation, like airline pilots and things like that. He used to take maybe eight or ten people on this yacht, and eight or ten people on that would be kind of crowded. I don't recall exactly the size of it, but I remember seeing pictures and articles in the National Geographic of White Mist. It was fascinating. These are the sort of things that you think back on and say, "Oh, that was a little incident in my career." I wouldn't trade it for anything.

Paul Stillwell: About what year was that?

Captain Shellenbarger: That had to be sometime in the '70s.

Of course, back to the Export Courier, after we got cleared we went alongside the dock in Jidda, and it only took us about ten hours to discharge our cargo. But actually we were stuck there for about four days.

Paul Stillwell: You mentioned the logs. What became of those?

Captain Shellenbarger: When a merchant vessel is finally scrapped, my understanding from talking to people ashore, is that they save the logbooks because of possible lawsuits concerning cargo or this or that where they need to refer back to weather. They have to be retained for seven years.

Now, American Export, of course, folded up in 1979. Actually, in '78 it became part of Farrell Lines. I have often wondered what ever happened to the logbooks for those vessels, because through the years American Export operated some 80 ships. As a matter of fact, they were actually running 80 ships when I went with them in 1945. So I suppose somewhere the logs are turning to mildew if they haven't already been disposed of. Because after all these years, of course, the odds would be very much there'd be no lawsuits.

Paul Stillwell: Yesterday you alluded to the demise of Isbrandtsen and so forth. Could you please discuss how the fold-up came about and the impact on you personally?

Captain Shellenbarger: Well, it's documented. It's well known that Isbrandtsen bled American Export dry. They didn't have the money to proceed with the building of their D-class ships. It was rather peculiar. I've still got the clippings from The New York Times about them. Jakob "Jake" Isbrandtsen was the son of Hans Isbrandtsen, who founded the company at the beginning of World War II from some of the Danish ships that were not seized by the Germans. So there were a number of them in American ports. So Hans formed this Isbrandtsen Steamship Company, operated these ships for the Government, WSA, like everything was, War Shipping Administration.

But, anyway, when they started turning ships back, Isbrandtsen got these Victory ships which they called "Flying This," "Flying That." It was part of their names.

But, anyway, you have to go back to the history of Export Lines. It was formed by a man by the name Coverdale in the '20s with War Shipping Board ships. At that time it was known as Export Steamship Corporation. That was the name of it. Export. That's where they get the E on the flag. And they were based in Brooklyn. I can't recall. I've heard so many things. I'd like to see somebody sometime do a history of the American Export Lines. Coverdale had a lot of money, and he was involved with railroads. But the steamship was sort of tied in with that, so he operated these ships and he built, he built ships and it was expanding.

Apparently a going concern till the outbreak of World War II. They had the so-called Four Aces, which had been built in Philadelphia, Cramp's Shipyard. As soon as the war broke out, four of them became transports. Three of them were lost during the war. One survived, but it was in such bad condition they sold it to the Turks, and I've forgotten what they called it. I remember seeing it a few times over in Turkish ports.

Then it finally burned as a result of that tanker collision in the Bosporus here, oh, back in the early '60s.

Anyway, when Coverdale died, the stock was purchased by a man named Charles Ulrich Bay who also owned the majority interest in Kidder-Peabody. And when Coverdale died Bay purchased the stock and took control of American Export Lines. Somewhere in that period, the name had been changed from Export Steamship to American Export Lines. The stock was spread out through so many different people that if any one stockholder had, as I recall, something like 28%, he had control.

When Mr. Bay died it all went to his widow, Mrs. Bay, and she wasn't really interested in running steamships. So she sold her stock to Isbrandtsen, and Isbrandtsen took control for a period of about eight years. Well, instead of being one large corporation running ships, Jakob formed each ship into a separate corporation, which is the practice today, and the port engineers were a separate corporation. Port captains were a separate corporation. Each agency on the East Coast was a separate corporation.

So a ship would come in, maybe make a profit of a million dollars. But then they'd divide this up, out to all these different little corporations, and somehow or other he'd get a piece of the action for each one of these corporations. And they'd end up and say, "Well, your ship came in, and you didn't make any money that trip."

They'd say, "How could that be?"

"Well, you're not being efficient enough. You got to cut your overtime. You got to cut your costs." And they cut maintenance plus the cash. I don't know how a lot of the money that had been set aside, because the ships had all been built by government subsidy, and under the law you have to set aside a certain amount for replacement of your other ships. And this was where the government got involved, and they were very unhappy with this. Like I say, he was indicted, but it was dropped because the lawyers came up and said what he did was unethical but not illegal.

So what happened then was the banks apparently had a lot of stockholders. I guess they got together and they evicted him from the control of the company, because I know the first order we got was to paint out that Isbrandtsen name on the side of the ship. It used to say American Export-Isbrandtsen. It would start almost at the bow and go almost to the stern. [Laughter] And frankly that was a tremendous cost.

Paul Stillwell: All that paint.

Captain Shellenbarger: All that white paint on the black hulls. So after that, why, the name reverted back to American Export Lines, but it was just too far gone. It kept going until the stockholders put in a fellow as president by the name of Jim Horn, a banker. I met him several times. But they just couldn't make a go of it, so they put it up for sale, and Farrell Lines borrowed the money to buy our ships.

By that time we were down to about 14 ships, and then Farrell had about maybe 10 or 12, but they were newer ships than ours, and we'd already started replacing our ships. We'd started buying container vessels that were built from scratch as container vessels. They'd started building in Bath, Maine, the Resolute and the Argonaut. I've forgotten what the names of the others were. And, actually, some of them are still sailing today for Farrell Lines.

For us, because we were a company union called the Brotherhood of Marine Officers, in 1979 I was vaguely aware of it. I should have been much more aware of what was going on, but Farrell Lines had their deck officers contracted with the Masters, Mates and Pilots. We were BMO. When we were taken over by Farrell Lines, they considered us as a subsidiary, the Export ships, and we operated as a subsidiary. Therefore, we had a contract for our officers. MMP went to court, went to arbitration, and they decided in March 1979 that we would either have to join the MMP or lose our jobs.

Well, by 1979 I'd been with American Export Lines since April 1945, and I was 59 years old. I had some friends in the MMP. I went to the president and asked him what would happen. He said, "Well, as long as Farrell runs the ships," he says, "you have a job as master."

But I said, "The ships are getting old. What's going to happen then?"

He said, "Well, you go back on the open board as a third mate. You have to start over."

I said, "After the years as master, no way." So then I thought, "Well, it's going to be easy. I'll take early retirement," which I had to do anyway, because it was either that or sign up with them. I would say roughly 10% of our fellows also took early retirement.

But what had happened during this interim period when it was in the courts, our company union, the BMO, Brotherhood of Marine Officers, had borrowed money from District One, MEBA, Marine Engineers Beneficial Association, so when the BMO lost, I took early retirement.

Actually, my mate, Mike Blanton, had been with me for about four years on the Export Courier. He'd been second mate and then a long time as chief mate. The ship was lying in the shipyard in Baltimore, Key Highway Yard, and I'd gone home for about four or five days. Mike had relieved me as master. I guess I'd been home about two, three days when the phone rang in the middle of the afternoon, and Mike said, "Cap, we haven't got a job anymore. The court decision has gone against us, BMO, and we have to be off the ship, bag and baggage, by 8:00 o'clock tomorrow morning." So I had to take off to Baltimore, did it in an hour, Mary went with me.

Paul Stillwell: From where?

Captain Shellenbarger: From Point Pleasant, New Jersey, and went down to the ship. Of course, I had all my gear. I'd been there for six years. I had microwave, television. I mean it was my home, second home. The crew was staying, of course. It was actually just the deck officers that had to go: masters, mates and pilots. The engineers, even though they were BMO, they could stay on because they were backed by the engineers' union, MEBA, so it was only the mates and the master that had to get off the ship.

So we spent most of the night carting stuff from the ship and stuffed it in my Olds to get it out of there, and I asked Mike, I said, "What the hell you gonna do?"

Well, he lived in California, Grass Valley, and he said, "Well, they told me to stay here until the new master comes aboard to relieve me and turn the funds over and everything. Then I'm just going to grab a bag and fly back to California." Then he went with another company. He bounced around a little bit and ended up with Energy Transport, which operates the LNG ships, the eight Aquarius class, and he's been with them now for over 15 years.[*] So I never got my gold watch or anything like that. We used to joke about it. What we got was the finger. [Laughter]

---

[*] LNG—liquefied natural gas.

Paul Stillwell: It's not the scenario you would have written for your retirement.

Captain Shellenbarger: No, not at all. Not after 34 years, I guess it was, with Export.

Paul Stillwell: Well, you mentioned that the union had borrowed some money from MEBA. How did that figure into it?

Captain Shellenbarger: Well, that was a very critical matter, because the BMO had over three million dollars, because we were self-funded for our pension. If I had been able to stay with it until I was 62, instead of 59, I would have gotten a pension of about $1,200 a month from the union. As it was, I had to take early out on it, and I got a pension of about $840 from the union. But our funds were transferred to the MEBA, and actually for a period of a few months I was a member of the MEBA. I'm getting my pension from the MEBA because our funds were taken over by the MEBA.

Paul Stillwell: I see.

Captain Shellenbarger: They were our saving grace. Otherwise, we would have lost everything. And in that respect it could have been a lot worse. It would have been a lot worse because a lot of the big corporations merged, and people really lost out. So we were fortunate in that respect, and actually, I could have had a slightly larger pension. I probably could have had a pension of $1,000 a month, except that I'd been living in an apartment all my life. I cashed out about $50,000 to buy the house that I'm living in today, and I've been there for 17 years. Because I knew that I couldn't continue paying rent because everything was in a state of flux. It's one of those things.

Paul Stillwell: That was not a good era to buy a house, what with the mortgage rates the way they were.

Captain Shellenbarger: Actually I was fortunate. I had lived the last ten years in an apartment in Brielle, New Jersey, and I was able to buy this what they call a retirement or starter, two-bedroom one-story house. It's a small lot, 75 by maybe 98 or something like that. It's on a cul-de-sac. Well, you've seen it. That's right, you were there.

Paul Stillwell: Yes.

Captain Shellenbarger: And I bought it for $52,000, and today the houses all around it similar to it are going for a hundred and eighteen.

Paul Stillwell: Great.

Captain Shellenbarger: So if I get ready to leave in a few years, why, I think I'll come out ahead. Like I say, things could have been a lot worse.

Paul Stillwell: Yes.

Captain Shellenbarger: A lot worse. Of course, there was this sort of a state of flux. We didn't know what was going to happen, but I knew that I couldn't go back to sea. Right then I was still having some aftereffects from this heart incident in Karachi; I think a lot of it was stress at the time. I was not feeling too well. I ended up with all kinds of little medical problems.

That was when I had the time on my hands, and I started going and helping out at the Marine Society. And due to my ham radio operations I spent eight years as county radio officer. In the state of New Jersey the county radio officer is a division of the state police, your civilian component of the state police. So I got the chance to meet a lot of state cops. The major is in charge of the R.A.C.E.S., as they call it, the civil emergency services.* But that was a very interesting period.

But, of course, in the meantime I'm working very actively with the Marine Society, helping out in the office in New York. The presidents at that time were busy with their

---

* R.A.C.E.S.—Radio Amateur Civil Emergency Service.

companies, their work, and what have you, so I had the free time to assist the lady who was our full-time secretary. And maybe I shouldn't be patting myself on the back, but I think that I brought them out of the 17th century up to the 18th or 19th anyway.

Paul Stillwell: Well, please tell me an overview. What does the Marine Society of New York do? What's its mission?

Captain Shellenbarger: The Marine Society of the City of New York was founded, first organized in 1769, and was chartered in 1770 by George III through the instances of his governor. Actually, the name on there is the lieutenant governor of the Colony of New York. There were many marine societies; they had a Marine Society of Boston, Portland, Maine, New Haven, Salem, Baltimore, Philadelphia had a marine society. All these ports had them because of the ships that sailed out of those ports.

In the 1700s there was no such thing as social security, insurance, or anything else. The ship masters formed their little society in each port, and each time they had a successful voyage they'd take a certain percentage of their profits, because invariably the shipmaster was part owner in those days. And that's how profited under the letters of marque. So what they would do, if they had a successful voyage there'd be a certain amount of money set aside into a kitty, funds—they had various names for it. Boston always called it the trunk and others called it the box and what have. But it would be money and invested, so that if at any time the ship was lost and the master was lost, this was to take care of the man's widow and children.

However, each of the organizations, including ours, in their charter said their purpose is not only to take care of widows and orphans and destitute seamen belonging to this group but also for the advancement of maritime knowledge, and they have been active in a lot of things. For instance, the New York Society was active getting the lighthouse on Sandy Hook, which was not there. There's a number of things in our history that we can go back to and say that this was the things that we did as part of this advancement of maritime knowledge.

However, due to the recent sad state of the American merchant marine, there's not that many shipmasters that hold U.S. licenses. Our charter up until I took over here a few years ago said that to be a member of the Marine Society you must have been a ship master who sailed on an American-flag ship as a ship master and had made a foreign voyage. Well, due to the decrease our membership got below 300 now of regular members. We do have honorary members and associate members, but regular members are the ones that vote.

This was one of the things that I did only about three years ago. I got together with two of the previous presidents, and we decided we'd have to change our rules and by-laws and we did. We now accept any man who is a licensed officer, a chief officer and above, and we also will accept pilots who are comparable. In other words, full pilots in ports. As a matter of fact, I have three ladies as members now. They have been ship masters. Allison Ross. She's a pilot on the Chesapeake. She's a member of the Marine Society and I have Cynthia Smith. She sailed master with Exxon and then went ashore with the Galveston group, Texas A&M. I think they have a school ship down there. And now she's a professor at Kings Point. That's Captain Smith.

One of them made the newspapers here some years ago, Debby Dempsey. She was with Lykes, and she was the one that was lowered down with a couple of other people on this ship, the Lykes ship, the Lyra, off of Cape Hatteras when it broke loose from its tow. They lowered her down on deck along with a couple of others. They got the emergency generator going, and they dropped the anchors before the ship went ashore. It was one of their containerships that was being laid up. Made the newspapers anyway.

But Debby had been sailing with Lykes. She married one of the captains, Jack Dempsey, who died recently. But, anyway, she's now a pilot, Columbia River pilot, out of Portland, Oregon. So we've got three members of the Marine Society that are lady members. Allison gets up to our luncheons usually, because she's based here on the East Coast. They're nice people, and that's one of the things that happened to the Marine Society.

Paul Stillwell: How is your organization funded?

Captain Shellenbarger: Well, we have one fund-raising affair each year, and we been probably lucky the last few years. We have an annual dinner, which is in April each year.

It takes a lot of solicitation, but in recent years we've been getting about 200-225 people to attend. And the last few years we been clearing about $15,000 each year, but mostly it's from our investments. I keep my fingers crossed and knock on wood because with the market today, right today, we got a portfolio of roughly two and a half million, and we operate on the income from it. We've been fortunate. Now, and tied into the Marine Society is the fact that Thomas Randall, one of our founders, had a son, Captain Robert Richard Randall--now, I don't know how familiar you are with the name Sailor's Snug Harbor?

Paul Stillwell: No.

Captain Shellenbarger: Sailor's Snug Harbor was an organization founded about 1805 by Captain Randall. That's Robert Richard Randall, who was the son of Thomas. And Robert Randall did not have a wife or children. He had a sister who fought his will, but the Randalls owned 21 acres, farmland, on the island of Manhattan in what is today Greenwich Village and right up, oh, I been a trustee for what, since 1988. But, anyway, to get back why I'm a trustee is the fact that when Robert Randall died and his financial advisor was Alexander Hamilton. Hamilton and Burr both were members of the Marine Society. When you look at our listing of members from those days, there were a lot of familiar names.

Paul Stillwell: Well, how does Sailor's Snug Harbor work?

Captain Shellenbarger: There's no documentation to this, but he was a member of the Marine Society, and Hamilton suggested to Captain Randall, "Well, your wealth came from the sea. You have no one to leave it to. Why don't you leave it to somebody from the sea?" So they drew up the will, which I have seen many copies and I have a copy saying that his fortune would be used to establish a hospital for aged and decrepit seamen. Now, this is in the early 1800s, around 1805 I think is when he died, and of course, his father had made considerable money.

See, this is a formation of the U.S. Navy. These people were the captains of these ships and they were operating under letters of marque, but when they'd seize a British ship the goods were seized and sold, and so that's how a lot of these people made money, and they set up their fortunes from this. So Captain Randall said, "Well, I want to establish this hospital for aged and decrepit seamen and for the advance of maritime knowledge," which is how it comes out in our charter.

He said that he wanted seven trustees to administer this, to build this hospital: the mayor of the City of New York, the president of the chamber of commerce of the City of New York, the President of the Marine Society, the first vice president of the Marine Society, the rector of Trinity Church, and the first minister of the Presbyterian Church, plus at that time they had another one, official. I think they called him the chancellor of the state of New York. Or maybe it was the chancellor of the city. I'm not really sure. It was something that was abolished in the early 1800s, shortly after this, so they ended up with six trustees instead of seven.

Well, today--to sort of digress a little bit--today the mayor and the president of the chamber of commerce never come to a trustees' meeting. There's no votes there. They're politicians. So we'd sort of joke about it. These two politicians, two ministers, and two sea captains. [Laughter] So the ministers and the sea captains run the trustees.

Paul Stillwell: Why ministers?

Captain Shellenbarger: Because in those days that was part of charity. The churches were involved in the charity, because there was no social security, there were no pensions. There was nothing for these people except what people gave them, and so there was a need for it. At one time Sailor's Snug Harbor which was supposed to have been on the 21 acres on Manhattan Island, was where it was supposed to have been built.

However, Randall had a sister. Said, "Hey, he's giving this money away to charity. I want it." And it was fought in the courts for, oh, maybe 10, 15 years before it was settled that the money would go to build Sailor's Snug Harbor. Well, during this period Manhattan was expanding. Everything is moving from the south to the north so fast that this land here, this 21 acres, which is today Greenwich Village, was too valuable to do anything like that. I got some of the old charts which shows the platting and the laying out of the land, you know, the blocks that it covers. As a matter of fact, we've still got one property there. Don't ask me why, but the owner is still paying a 10% interest on it and a lot of our early properties, a lot of leases, are 1% for a long period of time.

But, anyway, so they decided and the way the thing was written they had to get everything approved by the New York State Legislature, the way this charter was set up, because it was an old charter from, you know, George III's time. And then it had to be changed, that due to the success of the late Revolution it will now be known as the, you know, charter of the state. But, anyway, they said, "We can't put it on Manhattan. We'll put it over there on Staten Island, where there's a lot of farmland and everything else."

And so they bought about several hundred acres, and they built Sailor's Snug Harbor, which is on the Kill Van Kull, the north side of Staten Island. And they stayed there up until 1976, at which time the City of New York said, "Your buildings are getting old." You know, there has to be a hospital with this thing. A nursing home. Because once the seamen are taken in to Sailor's Snug Harbor they're there, if they choose, for the rest of their lives. So as they get older you have to have a nursing home, and you have to have a hospital.

Of course, these buildings were built in the 1800s. They had 16-foot ceilings, 12-foot windows. The walls, stone walls, 18 inches thick, and they had to be upgraded, you know, for the hospital and the modern standards. And the cost would have bankrupted the trustees, but they said that's all right. Now, of course, there's a lot of discussion I've had with people at the time was maybe the city just wanted the property. Seemed they wanted to take the property, which I think by that time was down to, I don't know, a little over 100 acres. But they were going to sell it to developers.

But then I guess a lot of people on Staten Island got up in arms and eventually they turned it into a cultural institute. And the city did buy the property from the trustees, because the trustees said, "Hey, we've got to go somewhere and build a modern facility," which they did. And the reason for that was a gentlemen by the name of Captain Wilbur Dow. Turned out to be a good friend of mine, because I had just joined the Marine Society. And, of course, there's only about four years later that I became more active because I lost my job basically, so I became quite active and I became a good friend of Wilbur's.

He was president of the trustees. He was president of the Marine Society at the time in 1976 when they sold this property to the city for around $5 or $6 million, and the reason they went to North Carolina, a place called Sealevel, out near the Outer Banks, was because Wilbur Dow was an admiralty lawyer. He'd been to sea, a shipmaster, and went ashore and got his legal papers. He was a lawyer with another man by the name of Stonebridge.

When Wilbur started looking for a place to move the harbor, he was looking all the way from Maine to the Carolinas. I don't think he ever considered Florida because I talked to him about it a number of times. Wilbur passed away about five years ago, Wilbur did. But anyway, he had some clients, the Taylors, who told him that if he would establish this in Sealevel, North Carolina, which was where they were from, they would donate something like 100 acres of land plus one million dollars for bringing it down there. So it was an offer they couldn't refuse. Built the place. Beautiful little place there but it's a backwater. It's 35 miles from Beaufort. That is the large town near Morehead City.

Over the years, I moved up in the various offices in the Marine Society and became much more active. I was treasurer, second vice president, first vice president. Well, as soon as I became first vice president, in 1988, that automatically made me a trustee of Sailor's Snug Harbor. Well, then I got more and more involved with Snug Harbor. I'm vice president of the trustees of Snug Harbor, and Dr. Mathews, the rector of Trinity is the president. And I probably spend more time in Snug Harbor than any of the other trustees, other than the other ship captain, Captain Leo Kraszeski.

Leo had been master with Moore-McCormick Lines. Went ashore long time ago, right after the war. He'd been a surveyor for a while. He had been second vice president of the Marine Society, but from there he became the executive director of Sailor's Snug Harbor on Staten Island. And he was executive director there at the time of the move, 1976, so he's been very involved with Snug Harbor. Executive director for what, 19 years?

But I can't remember the exact time. It was shortly after I became first vice president, because I became a trustee and Wilbur came to me and at this time Leo, that's Captain Kraszeski, had retired as director and he's on a stipend for the rest of his life, you know, in lieu of a retirement because they don't have any retirement fund. Something we are working right on now for the present director. But it was a question of moving and staying up with the times.

As a residency it's not feasible to keep the Sailor's Snug Harbor running the way it is. To start with, there's not that many seamen who want to come to a residency, even though it's like a high-class hotel for them, because in 1805 the American seamen, to start with, very few of them were citizens. They were not married. They didn't have families. They might have a girlfriend in every port, but they didn't have families, that's for sure. And by the time that they were 40, 45 years old, they were old and decrepit seamen, so there was a need for a residency at that time.

Today the sailors have got pensions from the unions. They got social security. They've got all kinds of aid programs. So we're not getting that many applicants. I mean, we could handle 120 people down there, and we right now have got maybe 82 or 83. So what this present board, which basically was formed roughly ten years and, of course, this is why we trying to get it done while we there before our successors moved in. Because I know that Dr. Barrie Shepherd, the Presbyterian minister, is planning on leaving in a couple of years. Dan Mathews will be leaving in a couple of years. I'll probably be leaving in a couple of years so we want to get everything up and running before we leave.

Paul Stillwell: What is your vision for the place?

Captain Shellenbarger: My vision for the place is to turn it over to an organization which will continue operating it as what it is or extended care, senior care, and we are already in the process because we got approval from the courts. Everything used to have to be with the legislature. Then the legislature in New York said, "The hell with it. We've got enough problems." They passed an act that turned all the operations of Sailor's Snug Harbor over to the probate courts in New York, and that's where it belongs actually. Well, basically we're executors of Captain Randall's estate. Well, through the years this estate has grown and today with the present market the Sailor's Snug Harbor has a fund of something like $42 million. But, even so, this place is expensive to run, and we want to close it down because we can use the money to much more advantage by helping the seamen in their hometowns, their place of retirement or their residency, and do it by paying their rent or nursing care or whatever it is where they are living.

Because we've had a number of instances where seamen have come to us and said, "Hey, I don't want to leave my hometown and my friends, but I do need assistance." And we got about, oh, I guess we got over 50 seamen who get various amounts. And, of course, at that time we're only going to need an administrative staff, maybe 15, 20 people-- that's what we have right now--to take care of this, because we are working through a lot of various social agencies. But this is all things that I'm still involved with, plus the running of the Marine Society. Believe me, it keeps me busy.

Paul Stillwell: Plus consulting work.

Captain Shellenbarger: Well, occasional consulting work. Occasional expert witness work.

Paul Stillwell: You told me about one of those cases yesterday.

Captain Shellenbarger: Yes, that's right. I keep busy.

Paul Stillwell: Yes, you do. Just the difficulty of scheduling these interviews has been a demonstration of that. I appreciate your graciousness in coming here yesterday and today for these.

Well, I'm certainly grateful to Doug Burnett for recommending you for this program and to you for your generosity in participating. Because, as you know, we've got a lot of naval memoirs in the collection and this really enhances it by getting one that's both naval and merchant marine, and I make a point to label you as a merchant mariner rather than as a merchant marine.

Captain Shellenbarger: [Laughter] Yes. I appreciate that.

Paul Stillwell: You have a rich history in the field, and we're delighted to get it on tape and make it available for future study.

Captain Shellenbarger: Well, let's hope that it's of use to someone.

Paul Stillwell: I'm sure it will be.

[Interruption with tape recorder off]

Paul Stillwell: We are here with a little postscript. We just got to talking afterward about the long delay it took for merchant marine veterans to be accorded status of war veterans. If you could discuss that from your perspective, please.

Captain Shellenbarger: Well, strangely enough, it didn't really affect me personally, and I didn't realize it because right at the end of the war I got from the Veterans Administration what they called a C number. And my first wife and I purchased a house on Long Island with a VA loan.[*] Because theoretically and due to my Neutrality Patrol service in 1941 they considered me a veteran at that time. And then somewhere along the way that got lost, primarily because I had gone into the merchant marine and had ended the war as a ship captain. And, of course, a lot of the others hadn't had that naval service that I'd had.

However, while we were operating during the war under the War Shipping Administration, we were under military orders. We were trained. I was trained on a 20 millimeter myself, to fire an Oerlikon, because with your naval gun crew, they had the gun on the fantail, which in most cases was an old 4-inch, and they had sometimes a 3-inch on the bow. Or like when I was on the Reverdy Johnson, which was a trooper, a Liberty trooper, we had Oerlikons on the bridge wings. We had little gun tubs on each side of the ship, and the armed guard crew, which might have been 17-18 men, they didn't have enough men to man all these guns, so the merchant crew was trained to fire them. And they put a lot of 5-inch open mounts on merchant ships aft. The Navy gun crew, pointer,

---

[*] Veterans Administration.

trainer, and the loaders were up on top. Who do you think was passing the ammunition from the ammunition magazine?

Paul Stillwell: Merchant mariners.

Captain Shellenbarger: The ship's crew, and they were listed on the station bill as loaders, so therefore we were literally part of the crew.

Paul Stillwell: Why were you not accorded veteran status?

Captain Shellenbarger: Nobody knows why. Roosevelt, Truman, MacArthur always sent these glowing testimonials, which in some cases were certificates issued to us, saying that we should be treated as though we were part of the armed forces, which we were literally. Believe me, when a ship blew up with 8,000 tons of ammunition, it didn't distinguish whether you were armed guard or merchant crew. You all went up. And it's just one of those things that was my feeling was an injustice, and many others felt the same way. But a lot of people in Congress didn't feel that way, and they frankly didn't give a damn. It wasn't going to affect them anyway.

Paul Stillwell: How did it finally get turned around?

Captain Shellenbarger: It finally got turned around through various organizations that recognized this. In the late 1980s Congress passed a law saying that those who had served between such and such a date and such a date were eligible, but they made the cutoff date August 15 in 1945. There were ships blown up after that. All the other services went to, I think, the end of the next year which they declared as the date of end of hostilities. But so again there's still a small segment that got left out of the merchant mariners. They got left out, but it's just one of those things that happened, shouldn't have happened. And one of the organizations was the armed guard. They fought for us because, hey, they were right with us.

Paul Stillwell: They knew.

Captain Shellenbarger: They knew and we got along. Oh, there were exceptions like any exceptions where there was a little bit of friction maybe between them. But in my case, boy, did I get along great.

Paul Stillwell: What has been the practical effect then for the merchant mariners who got this status?

Captain Shellenbarger: Well, basically all of us by the time we got it were too old to take any advantage of any educational benefits. That's the thing I regret more than anything else, even though I probably wouldn't have taken advantage of it because by the end of the war I was sailing chief officer with a master's license, and I knew it would only be a short time I'd have a master's job. I'd been working for Glenn Martin when I went into the war, and I wasn't about to go back to work for them. We knew that those places all were going to be closing down very shortly which they did, of course.

Basically, all we got is recognition, the fact that we had been there and done that. That's what it amounted to. And the only other benefit we got from it is for funerals. In my case it wouldn't matter because I get it anyway, but at my burial service I'll have a flag on the coffin. And basically that's all that we gained, because there's only a couple of hundred thousand left now. They're not interested in educational benefits.

Paul Stillwell: Yes, but there is a psychological value.

Captain Shellenbarger: There's a psychological value of the fact that, hey, we are veterans. That's the thing. And we did our part because I can remember going aboard ship. Now, I was a youngster, really. But I can remember going aboard a Liberty ship where the master was 75 years old, but he happened to be in good health and he was there. You'd have other people there that were 4-Fs.[*] They couldn't do anything else. They couldn't get in the

---

[*] 4-F was a classification that kept a man from being drafted into military service because of a medical problem.

services, but they could go in the merchant marine. And there was many, many cases like that, I would say. It would be inevitable, just like during the Vietnam War. There were certain guys that went in the merchant marine and figured, "Boy, this is a safer place to be than in the Army."

Paul Stillwell: In that case it probably was.

Captain Shellenbarger: In that case it wasn't.

Paul Stillwell: Oh, really.

Captain Shellenbarger: And this is a matter of record. That on a percentage basis the merchant marine was second to the Marine Corps in World War II by one tenth of one percent in the number of people killed by enemy action.

And now we find from research of the merchant marine veterans organizations that at the beginning of the war there were many, many merchant mariners who were on foreign-flag ships, Panamanian, what have you. They were not recognized as being part of the U.S. merchant marine, and yet they were lost on these ships. So probably on a percentage basis the merchant marine lost even more men than the Marine Corps, in spite of their horrendous losses in Tarawa and places like that, because there were a lot of ships, especially in the early part of the war.

There again, I was fortunate. The fact that I was in that first class at Fort Trumbull, and maybe it's due to the fact that I'd been a Navy man. I came out of that class I think number ten out of a class of about 400, and they asked the first 25 of us if we would stay on as instructors. And the pitch that they made they said, "Hey, we need you here."

So we figured, "Well, if they need us that's where we should go." And, of course, I'd been waiting to go to that class and continued to work at Glenn Martin. That's why I continued on at Glenn Martin because I'd already signed up to go to this class and somehow or other it was delayed. I don't know why because we'd heard that originally it was supposed to be formed by the Coast Guard, this class up there. And then it was some kind of a business that is was turned over to the War Shipping Administration, and they didn't have any bureau or whatever in order to set the place up. Because actually when we came in, there were still a lot of the merchant marine naval reservists as our instructors.

I remember one of them that I knew very well was a seamanship instructor, Jack Cooney. He was a jaygee and he left there to become skipper of a LCT or something or other. We got word that something had happened to him later, and he was killed very soon after he left. I stayed on there until June 1944. At the time of the Normandy invasion was the time I was leaving Fort Trumbull.* I was under attack a number of times after that, later on in '44, because I started running to North Europe, but I missed the worst time at sea. Probably that's the reason why I'm here today. Because in 1942 your odds were not good.

Anyway, I have a baseball cap that says, "I'm an American merchant marine veteran." The State of New Jersey recognizes us. Now we have a license plate says, "Merchant Marine Veteran" on it. So it's recognition, and that's all we really wanted. That's all we really wanted was recognition of the fact that we were there and we were getting shot at. I can remember being strafed by a German plane. He came down between the columns of the convoy, and, so help me, there was more damage done by the ships shooting at this plane because this ship's on the other side. And we had strict orders not to shoot at them if they came below a certain height. Nevertheless, you always got these gung ho people that shoot when they can. [Laughter]

Paul Stillwell: Well, thank you for that postscript.

---

* D-Day for the Allied invasion of France at Normandy was 6 June 1944.

Index to the Oral History of
Captain Franklin F. Shellenbarger
U.S. Maritime Service (Retired)

Achilles, HMS
British light cruiser in the operation against the German cruiser Admiral Graf Spee in 1939, later part of the Indian Navy as RIN Delhi, 49

Admiral Graf Spee (German Cruiser)
In December 1939 the ship's crew scuttled her at Montevideo, where the hulk was later visited by crewmen from the U.S. light cruiser Helena (CL-50), 47-48, 51-55; the crews of the two ships met soon afterward in Buenos Aires, Argentina, 48-49

Alcohol
In 1964 the cargo ship Extavia had a collision in the Mediterranean because the mate on watch was drunk, 192-193, 196-197, 244; in Italian merchant ships the crews must be served wine with their meals, 243-244; commercial passenger ships carried well-stocked bars over the years, 244-245

American Export-Isbrandtsen Lines
Background on the history of the two companies, 258-260; for many years operated its own company union, the Brotherhood of Marine Officers, 118, 130, 141, 208, 211, 261-263; operated a number of ships in the 1940s and 1950s, 118, 130, 134; shortly after World War II resumed its service between the United States and the Mediterranean, 137-138; flexible personnel policies, 139-140, 211; rundown on inventory of ships in the late 1940s, 140; support of ships through agents, 158-160; in the 1960s operated the nuclear-powered cargo ship Savannah, 164-181; in the 1960s was slow to follow the trend toward containerization of cargo, 212-213; in the mid-1960s the chief mate of the cargo ship Extavia had a heart attack and died, leading to legal action against the company, 194-196, 199-201; in the 1960s the company chartered Victory ships to the government to deliver cargo to Vietnam, 216; emphasis on meeting the posted schedules, 226; economic conditions and the actions of Jakob Isbrandtsen led to the downfall of the company in the late 1970s, 250-251, 259-260; in 1978 the company became part of Farrell Lines, 258-259, 261

See also: Names of individual ships

Antiair Warfare
In December 1944 guns at Saipan fired at Japanese aircraft in the area, 109; during World War II crews were trained on light antiaircraft guns by means of simulators, 128

Argentina
In early 1940, in Buenos Aires, crewmen of the light cruiser <u>Helena</u> (CL-50) met with former crewmen of the German cruiser <u>Admiral Graf Spee</u>, which had recently been scuttled in Uruguay, 48-49

<u>Arkansas</u>, USS (BB-33)
In early 1941 served briefly as flagship for Commander Battleships Atlantic Fleet, 69-70

Armed Guards
In World War II many U.S. merchant ships carried armed guard detachments made up of Navy men, 96-97, 105, 273-274

Army, U.S.
In 1945 the Liberty ship <u>Reverdy Johnson</u> transported soldiers between the United States and Europe, 120-125; during World War II Shellenbarger's sister served in Australia, 136

Army Air Forces, U.S.
In 1941-42 Shellenbarger worked for the Glenn L. Martin Company, which was producing B-26 bombers, 74-78

B-26 Marauder
In 1941-42 Shellenbarger worked for the Glenn L. Martin Company, which was producing B-26 bombers for the Army Air Forces, 74-78

Babcock & Wilcox Company
In the 1950s built the nuclear reactor for the cargo ship <u>Savannah</u> and later provided operators during labor problems, 169, 181

Battleships Atlantic Fleet
Command that in 1940-41 took part in Neutrality Patrol operations, 59-73

<u>Bismarck</u> (German Battleship)
Her sortie into the Atlantic in May 1941 caused concern for the U.S. battleship <u>New York</u> (BB-34), which was at sea at the same time, 61

Black Sea
In the mid-1960s the cargo ship <u>Extavia</u> delivered goods to Russian ports on the Black Sea, 188-191

Bombs/Bombing
In 1941-42 the Norden bombsight was installed in B-26 Marauder bombers produced by the Glenn L. Martin Company, 74-76; in 1944 the damage inflicted by German bombs was evident in English cities, 99

Boston, Massachusetts
    The old wooden frigate <u>Constitution</u> has long been berthed in Boston as a symbol of the U.S. Navy's history, 72-73

Bown, Lieutenant Commander Thomas H., USMS
    During World War II taught at the Maritime Officers Training School in New London, Connecticut, and then became an officer on board the Liberty ship <u>John R. McQuigg</u>, 87-88, 99, 102

Brazil
    In early 1940 crew members of the light cruiser <u>Helena</u> (CL-50) enjoyed liberty in Santos, 50

Buenos Aires, Argentina
    In early 1940, in Buenos Aires, crewmen of the light cruiser <u>Helena</u> (CL-50) met with former crewmen of the German cruiser <u>Admiral Graf Spee</u>, which had recently been scuttled in Uruguay, 48-49

Cain, Captain John R., USMS
    In World War II commanded a Navy destroyer escort, later became a merchant ship master, 240, 246

Carlsen, Captain Kurt
    Was master of the cargo ship <u>Flying Enterprise</u>, which was lost in early 1952 after suffering storm damage, 207-209; later was in other ships, 207-209; was perceived as a captain who took risks in heavy weather, 208-209, 247-248; in the early 1970s was briefly master of the cargo ship <u>Export Courier</u>, 246

Casablanca, Morocco
    In the 1960s and 1970s tugboat companies in the port paid kickbacks to merchant ship personnel that used tugs, 179-181

Cashman, Commander David M., USN
    As commanding officer of the frigate <u>Constitution</u>, 1987-91, considered his job ideal for networking in the Boston area, 72

<u>**Catawba Victory**</u>**, SS**
    Victory ship that in 1947 had a former prisoner of war, Elmar Saar, as master, 142

Ceylon
    In the late 1940s received shipments through the American Export Lines, 145-146

<u>**Coaldale Victory**</u>**, SS**
    Victory ship equipped during World War II to carry troops to and from the United States, 135-136

Coast Guard, U.S.
Early in World War II operated the Maritime Officers Training School at New London, Connecticut, 77, 81; in 1945 made periodic checks on commercial ships in San Francisco, 114-115; after the end of World War II, took in a number of former merchant marine officers, 123; Coast Guard inspection service was in charge of checking qualifications for merchant marine officer licenses, 129-130

Collisions
In the 1950s, the passenger ship Constitution, had a collision with a tanker, 146-147; in 1964 the American cargo ship Extavia collided with the Italian cargo ship Luigi Martini in the Mediterranean, 192-193, 196-197, 244

Colorado, USS (BB-45)
Messing and berthing arrangements on board in the late 1930s, 19, 26; operation of the radio shack, 19-21, 23; participated in fleet maneuvers in the Caribbean in early 1939, including gunnery practice at Culebra, 21-25; repairs to guns at the Norfolk Navy Yard, 22; signal bridge watches in 1939, 26-27; crew's liberty in Long Beach and the Caribbean, 28-30; operation of SOC biplanes, 28-29

Commercial Ships
Operation of U.S. Liberty ships during and shortly after World War II, 87-88, 90-135; seizure of German ships by the United States during World War II, 128-129; heavy losses of merchant marine personnel during the war, 129; operation of U.S. Victory ships in the late 1940s, 135-144; operation of ships by American Export-Isbrandtsen Lines from the late 1940s to the late 1970s, 135-258; the SL-7 class operated by Sea-Land in the 1970s could run at 33 knots, 46-47

Communications
Training for prospective radiomen in 1938 at the San Diego Naval Training Station, 13-15; operation of the radio shack in 1938-39 on board the battleship Colorado (BB-45), 19-21, 23; visual communications in 1939 from the signal bridge of the Colorado, 26-27; radio link between the ship and her SOC biplanes, 28-29; visual signaling in 1940 when a boat crew from the light cruiser Helena (CL-50) visited the scuttled German cruiser Admiral Graf Spee, 51-52; in 1940-41 by the flag allowance of Commander Battleships Atlantic Fleet during Neutrality Patrol operations, 59-60, 65-66; radio communication in 1945 by the Liberty ship Reverdy Johnson, 122; ham radio operations in different periods, 207

Constellation, USS (IX-20)
Old sailing ship to which Shellenbarger was assigned temporarily in 1938 when the ship was berthed at Newport, 15-19, 73; in the early 1940s, at Newport, was used as relief flagship for Commander in Chief Atlantic Fleet, 71-72

Constitution, SS
In the 1950s, this passenger ship had a collision with a tanker, 146-147; in the 1970s and 1980s operated out of Hawaii before being scrapped, 251

Constitution, USS (IX-21)
Old wooden frigate that has long been in commission, berthed in Boston, as a symbol of the U.S. Navy's history, 72-73

Container Dispatcher, SS
American Export-Isbrandtsen Lines ship used in 1969 to transport containers after being converted from an ore carrier, 233-236

Container Forwarder, SS
American Export-Isbrandtsen Lines ship used in 1969 to transport containers after being converted from an ore carrier, 233-236

Convoys
In September 1944 a German U-boat sank the British merchant ship Empire Heritage while she was part of Convoy HX305, 90-92; a number of Allied ships were in a transatlantic convoy in May 1945 when the war in Europe ended, 123, 125-126; many of the convoy commodores were senior or retired naval officers, 126-127; convoying in the Atlantic essentially ended with V-E Day in May 1945, 127

Cuba
In the summer of 1939 the old destroyer Herbert (DD-160) visited Havana, during a midshipman training cruise, 56-57; later in 1939, the new cruiser St. Louis (CL-49) ran speed trials near Guantanamo Bay in company with her sister ship, the Helena (CL-50), 45-47

Disciplinary Problems
As a teenager, Shellenbarger got involved in some juvenile delinquency in the state of New York, 7; in the mid-1950s, when the merchant ship Exminster was in Bombay, an Indian policeman was arrested for trying to steal cargo and sentenced to prison, 150-152

Dunham, Quartermaster First Class Alonzo, USN
In the summer of 1939 taught Shellenbarger a great deal when they were serving together on board the destroyer Herbert (DD-160), 32-34, 37, 39-40

Empire Heritage, SS
Former Norwegian whaling ship that was sunk in September 1944 while under British operation, 90-92

Enlisted Personnel
Boot camp in early 1938 at the Naval Training Station in Newport, Rhode Island, 9-13; training for prospective radiomen in 1938 at the San Diego Naval Training Station, 13-15; in the summer of 1939 there was a gulf between the executive officer and the enlisted crew of the destroyer Herbert (DD-160) in 1939, 33, 35

Equator Crossing
   Hijinks in 1939 on board the light cruiser Helena (CL-50) when she was en route South America, 51, 205-206

Erlich, Joe
   In 1944-45 served as master of the Liberty ship John R. McQuigg, 102-103, 105, 108-109, 113-116

Excalibur, SS
   American Export Lines cargo ship that installed yardarms to facilitate visual signaling, 141-142

Exhibitor, SS
   American Export Lines cargo ship that was run quite formally in the late 1940s and early 1950s, 144-145; long trips to India and Ceylon, 145-146, 150, 157-158; the master, Jimmy La Belle, was a skilled navigator, 146-149

Exiria, SS
   Used as a troop transport in World War II, 217-218; operations in the 1950s, 149; description of, 217; operations in the late 1960s, 217; in 1968 was scrapped at Valencia, Spain after her final voyage, 218-220

Exminster, SS
   American Export Lines cargo ship that ran to India in the mid-1950s, 150-151

Export Agent, SS
   American Export-Isbrandtsen Lines cargo ship that made runs to Europe in the early 1970s, 241-243, 256-258; hauled Melville Bell Grosvenor's yacht White Mist from the United States to Greece, 256-258

Export Ambassador, SS
   American Export-Isbrandtsen Lines cargo ship that in 1969 carried goods from the Far East to the United States and did a rescue at sea en route, 222-223, 228-232

Export Champion, SS
   American Export-Isbrandtsen Lines cargo ship in operation in the late 1960s, 224

Export Courier, SS
   American Export Lines that ran to various ports in the 1970s, 179-180, 184, 246-248, 254-256, 258; had a top-notch cook with many years of service, 238-239; in the early 1970s the master was Captain John Cain, who had been a Naval Reserve officer in World War II, 240, 246; the ship was used in the Gulf War in the early 1990s, 219; wound up in a reserve fleet at Beaumont, Texas, 218

Extavia, SS
    American Export Lines cargo ship that was used briefly by the British in World War II with the name Empire Widgeon, 158; in the mid-1960s carried cargoes to a number of different ports, 158-159, 187-194; in 1964 collided with the Italian cargo ship Luigi Martini in the Mediterranean, 192-193; Lane Wilkins, the chief mate, had a heart attack and died, leading to legal action against the company, 194-196, 199-201

Exton, SS
    Victory ship used in the late 1940s to carry a variety of cargos between the United States and the Mediterranean, 136-139; renamed Exton after purchase by American Export Lines, 138

Fire
    On board the German cruiser Admiral Graf Spee after her crew scuttled her in December 1939 and set explosive charges, 52-53

Flying Enterprise, SS
    Isbrandtsen Lines cargo ship that was lost in early 1952 after receiving storm damage, 207-208

Flying Fish, SS
    American Export/Isbrandtsen Lines passenger/cargo ship that made around-the-world cruises in the late 1960s, 153, 201-205, 214-216, 221, 236-237

Flying Spray, SS
    American Export/Isbrandtsen Lines cargo ship that operated in the mid-1960s to a number of ports, 197-199; had a history of mishaps, 198

Food
    In the late 1940s a converted Victory ship used as a troop transport fed its passengers well, 121-122, 136; in the 1970s the cargo ship Export Courier had a top-notch cook with many years of service, 238-239

Ford, Commander A. G., USMS
    During World War II commanded the Maritime Officers Training School, Fort Trumbull, New London, Connecticut, 87

Fort Trumbull
    See: Maritime Officers Training School, Fort Trumbull, New London, Connecticut

France
    Shortly after World War II, the Liberty ship Linn Boyd carried cargo to French ports, 132

Germany
In the 1960s a beer garden in Hamburg saluted ships that went by on the Elbe, 199

German Navy
In December 1939 the crew of the German cruiser Admiral Graf Spee scuttled the ship at Montevideo, Uruguay, where the hulk was later visited by crewmen from the U.S. light cruiser Helena (CL-50), 47-48, 51-55; the crews of the two ships later met up in Buenos Aires, Argentina, 48-49; in 1940-41 the Royal Navy intercepted plain-language U.S. reports of German submarine positions in the Atlantic, 59-60, 65-66; the battleship Bismarck's sortie into the Atlantic in May 1941 caused concern for the U.S. battleship New York (BB-34), which was at sea at the same time, 61; in September 1944 the submarine U-482 sank the British cargo ship Empire Heritage in an Atlantic convoy, 90-92

Glenn L. Martin Company, Middle River, Maryland
In 1941 produced bombers for the Army Air Forces, 74-78

Graf Spee (German Cruiser)
See: Admiral Graf Spee (German Cruiser)

Great Britain
In 1944-45 the Liberty ships John R. McQuigg and Reverdy Johnson stopped in England, Scotland, and Wales between transatlantic runs, 92, 95-100, 122, 126; English cities received a lot of damage from German bombing, 99; in 1946, even after World War II ended, there were still minefields in the English Channel, 133-135

Greece
In the early 1970s the cargo ship Export Agent hauled Melville Bell Grosvenor's yacht White Mist from the United States to Greece, 256-258

Grosvenor, Melville Bell
In the early 1970s the cargo ship Export Agent hauled Grosvenor's yacht White Mist from the United States to Greece, 256-258

Guam, Mariana Islands
In late 1944 the Liberty ship John R. McQuigg delivered cargo to Guam, 109-110

Gunnery—Naval
In early 1938, during recruit training at Newport, the recruits practiced gunnery with a 3-inch cannon, 11; small-arms practice during recruit training, 12; in early 1939 the battleship Colorado (BB-45) fired target practice at Culebra in the Caribbean, 21-25; in 1939 the destroyer Herbert (DD-160) sometimes fired her 4-inch guns, 40; arrangement of the gun batteries on board the light cruiser Helena (CL-50) in 1939, when she was commissioned, 44-45; in World War II the Navy put gun crews on

board merchant ships for protection against aircraft and submarines, 96-97, 105, 273-274; in December 1944 guns at Saipan fired at Japanese aircraft in the area, 109

Guns
In 1941-42 the Glenn L. Martin Company installed .50-caliber machine guns in new B-26 Marauder bombers, 75-76; during World War II crews were trained on light antiaircraft guns by means of simulators, 128

Habitability
Messing and berthing arrangements in 1939 for the crew of the destroyer Herbert (DD-160), 38-40

Haiti
In 1939 crew members from the battleship Colorado (BB-45) encountered miserable conditions while on liberty in Gonaives, 30; tents were sent up for prevention of venereal disease, 31

Harry Lee, USS (AP-17)
Former commercial passenger ship used as a Navy troop transport in a 1941 amphibious warfare exercise, 140

Havana, Cuba
In the summer of 1939 the old destroyer Herbert (DD-160) visited Havana, during a midshipman training cruise, 56-57

Helena, USS (CL-50)
In 1939, while the ship was still under construction, prospective crew members lived on board the old receiving ship Seattle, 41-43; fitting out in 1939 at the New York Navy Yard, 43; commissioning in September 1939 and subsequent shakedown cruise to South America, 43-58, 205-206; arrangement of the gun batteries, 44; speed trials over off Rockland, Maine, and Guantanamo, Cuba, 45-47; in 1940 transferred to the West coast for operations, 58

Herbert, USS (DD-160)
Veteran destroyer that in the summer of 1939 provided underway training for midshipmen and for crewmen such as Shellenbarger, 31-37, 56-57; had old-fashioned anchors, 30; visit to Boston for Bunker Hill Day, 32; steering mechanism, 34-35; gulf between the executive officer and the enlisted crew, 33, 35; camaraderie among the crew, 38; messing and berthing arrangements, 38-40; firing of the ship's 4-inch gun, 40; visited Havana, Cuba, and Santiago, Chile, 56-57

Honduras Victory, SS
Victory ship used in the late 1940s to carry a variety of cargos between the United States and the Mediterranean, 136-139; renamed Exton after purchase by American Export Lines, 138

Hunter, William
In the 1960s was a mate on board the nuclear-powered cargo ship Savannah, 175, 177, 180, 187; in the 1970s was chief mate of the cargo ship Export Courier, 179-180

Independence, SS
Passenger ship that was laid up for many years at Baltimore, then was refurbished and in the 1970s and 1980s operated out of Hawaii, 251-253

India
In the late 1940s, when American Export Lines cargo ships made runs to Indian ports, Mother Teresa came aboard to seek alms, 154-155; in the mid-1950s, when the merchant ship Exminster was in Bombay, an Indian policeman was arrested for trying to steal cargo and sentenced to prison, 150-152

Isbrandtsen, Jakob
His actions led to the downfall of American Export-Isbrandtsen Lines in the late 1970s, 250-251

See also: American Export-Isbrandtsen Lines

Israel
In the 1970s ships going from the Suez Canal to Saudi Arabia had to have logbooks checked to make sure they hadn't been to Israel, 255-256

Italy
In 1945, shortly after World War II ended, the Liberty ship Reverdy Johnson visited Italian ports, 124-125

Japan
During World War II some merchant marine officers were held in prisoner-of-war camps in Japan, 142-143

Jidda, Saudi Arabia
In the late 1970s the commercial ship Export Courier visited the port to deliver cargo but had to wait to get cargo clearance, 254-256, 258

John R. McQuigg, SS
Liberty ship that operated in the Atlantic in 1944, 87-88, 90-95; in September 1944 suffered hurricane damage, 90, 95-97; description of the ship, 93-94, 99-100, 110; in England the ship received repairs for damage, 95-96; in World War II the ship carried an armed guard made up of Navy men, 96-97; loaded equipment at Davisville, Rhode Island in late 1944 and delivered it to the Pacific, 101-110; in early 1945 returned to the United States, 110-116

King, Admiral Ernest J., USN (USNA, 1901)
　　In early 1941, as Commander in Chief Atlantic Fleet, inspected the battleship Texas (BB-35) and her crew, 66-70

Korea
　　In 1969 the cargo ship Export Ambassador rescued the crew of a Korean fishing boat that got into distress in heavy seas, 229-232

Korean War
　　Marine Private First Class Robert Shellenbarger was badly injured when his tank hit a mine, and he was disabled from then on, 143

Kwajalein, Marshall Islands
　　In late 1944 the Liberty ship John R. McQuigg stopped at the atoll, 103-105

La Belle, Captain James
　　In the late 1940s was strict and formal while serving as master of the American Export Lines cargo ship Exhibitor, 144-146; in the 1950s, as master of the passenger ship Constitution, had a collision with a tanker, 146-147; navigation practices while in command, 147-149

Leave and Liberty
　　In 1938 San Diego offered a number of attractions, 14-15; liberty for the crew of the battleship Colorado (BB-45) in 1939 in Long Beach, 28-29; miserable liberties in early 1939 in Haiti, 30; in Cuba in the summer of 1939, 56-57; for crewmen of the light cruiser Helena (CL-50) in South America in 1939-40, 48-50; in late 1944 at Kwajalein, 104-105; policies for vacation time in American Export Line in the late 1940s, 139-140

LeBreton, Rear Admiral David McDougal USN (USNA, 1904)
　　In 1940-41 served as Commander Battleships Atlantic Fleet during Neutrality Patrol operations, 59, 62-63, 68; during World War II, was a convoy commodore, 126-127

Linn Boyd, SS
　　Liberty ship that carried cargo to Europe shortly after World War II, 130-131; the ship carried Norwegian aviators to the United States to pick up planes for a new airline, SAS, 132-135; in June 1946 the ship was turned over to Lykes Brothers at Galveston, Texas, 133, 135

Luigi Martini
　　Italian cargo ship that in 1964 collided with the American cargo ship Extavia in the Mediterranean, 192-193

Mariana Islands
　　In late 1944 the Liberty ship John R. McQuigg delivered cargo to Tinian, Saipan, and Guam, 106-110

Marine Corps, U.S.
During the Korean War, Private First Class Robert Shellenbarger was badly injured when his tank hit a mine, and he was disabled from then on, 143

Marine Society of New York
Role in a number of areas in the 1980s and 1990s, including the retirement home Sailor's Snug Harbor, 264-272; history of the organization, 265, 268-269

Maritime Officers Training School, Fort Trumbull, New London, Connecticut
Operated during World War II to train officers for merchant marine service, 77, 81-89, 276-277; some of the graduates wound up serving on board Navy ships, 81-82

Maritime Unions
In World War II and afterward the Masters, Mates and Pilots had a role in providing deck officers to merchant ships, 114, 118, 130, 260-261; in the 1940s American Export Lines had its own company union, the Brotherhood of Marine Officers, 118, 130, 141, 208, 211, 261-263; the National Maritime Union has been liberal in hiring minority personnel for ships' crews, 238-240; role of the MEBA engineers' union in the 1970s, 262-263

Marshall Islands
In late 1944 the Liberty ship John R. McQuigg stopped at Kwajalein Atoll, 103-105

Martin, Glenn
See: Glenn L. Martin Company, Middle River, Maryland

McLaughlin, Captain C. H.
In the 1960s was marine superintendent for American Export/Isbrandtsen Lines, 194, 196-197

McMichael, Captain David
In the 1960s was master of the nuclear-powered cargo ship Savannah, 165-166, 168-169, 176, 186

Medical Problems
In 1939, when crew members from the battleship Colorado (BB-45) were on liberty in Gonaives, Haiti, tents were sent up for prevention of venereal disease, 31; in early 1945 the first mate of the Liberty ship John R. McQuigg had to be removed because of mental illness, 113; during the Korean War, Marine Private First Class Robert Shellenbarger was badly injured when his tank hit a mine, and he was disabled from then on, 143; in the mid-1960s the chief mate of the cargo ship Extavia had a heart attack and died, 194-196, 199-201; in the late 1960s Shellenbarger suffered from irregular heartbeat, 203; diversion of a cargo ship to Midway Island after a crew member had a heart attack, 224-225

Mediterranean Sea
Shortly after World War II, American Export Lines resumed its service between the United States and the Mediterranean, 137-138; in 1964 the American cargo ship Extavia collided with the Italian cargo ship Luigi Martini in the Mediterranean, 192-193

See also: Greece, Italy

Mine Warfare
In 1946, even after World War II ended, there were still minefields in the English Channel, 133-135

Moldestad, Captain Gustav
Shortly after World War II served as master of the Liberty ship Linn Boyd, 130-131, 134

Montevideo, Uruguay
In December 1939 the crew of the German cruiser Admiral Graf Spee scuttled her at Montevideo, where the hulk was later visited by crewmen from the U.S. light cruiser Helena (CL-50), 47-48, 51-55

Morocco
In the 1960s and 1970s tugboat companies at Casablanca paid kickbacks to merchant ship personnel that used tugs, 179-181

Naval Reserve, U.S.
During World War II, graduates of the Maritime Officers Training School received Naval Reserve commissions, 81-82

Navigation
As done in the summer of 1939 on board the destroyer Herbert (DD-160), 35, 37; taught during World War II at the Maritime Officers Training School, 83; in World War II by the crew of the Liberty ship John R. McQuigg, 103-104; in the late 1940s the master of the American Export Lines ship Exhibitor was an excellent navigator, 147-149

Neutrality Patrol
Operations by U.S. warships in the Atlantic in 1940-41, before the United States was officially at war, 59-61, 64-65, 70

Newport, Rhode Island, Naval Training Station
Site of recruit training in early 1938, 9-13

New York, USS (BB-34)
   Operations of the ship in 1940-41 as flagship for Commander Battleships Atlantic Fleet, 59-61, 70; concern in May 1941 about being attacked by the German battleship Bismarck, 61

New York Navy Yard, Brooklyn, New York
   In 1939, while the light cruiser Helena (CL-50) was under construction, prospective crew members lived on board the old receiving ship Seattle, 41-43

New York Shipbuilding Corporation, Camden, New Jersey
   In the late 1950s built the nuclear-powered cargo ship Savannah, 165-166

Nimitz, Fleet Admiral Chester W., USN (USNA, 1905)
   In early 1945 moved the Pacific Fleet headquarters from Pearl Harbor to Guam, 107-108

Norden Bombsight
   Installed in 1941-42 in B-26 Marauder bombers produced by the Glenn L. Martin Company, 74-76

Norfolk Navy Yard, Portsmouth, Virginia
   In early 1939 replaced damaged gun barrels in the battleship Colorado (BB-45), 22

Norway
   Soon after World War II, the Liberty ship Linn Boyd carried cargo to Norwegian ports, 130-131; the ship carried Norwegian aviators to the United States to pick up planes for a new airline, SAS, 132-134

Nuclear Power
   In the late 1950s and early 1960s, the cargo ship Savannah was powered by a nuclear reactor, 165-178, 181-183, 185, 187; shore-based reactors, 184

Pakistan
   In the 1940s and 1950s Shellenbarger went in Pakistani ports on board merchant ships, 152-154

Prisoners of War
   Elmar Saar, a merchant marine officer, became a POW in World War II when his ship was sunk by a German raider, 142-143

Propulsion Plants
   In 1939 the new light cruiser Helena (CL-50) ran trials over measured miles and achieved a speed of 37 knots, 45-47; in 1941 the old battleship Texas (BB-35) was run by triple-expansion, reciprocating steam engines, 61, 70-71; Victory ships built during World War II had two basic types of steam turbine power plants, 135-136; in the late 1950s and early 1960s, the cargo ship Savannah was powered by a nuclear

reactor, 165-178, 181-183, 185, 187; use of extra nozzles in the steam turbine plants of commercial ships to get additional speed, 224, 226; in 1969 the cargo ships Container Forwarder and Container Dispatcher operated with high-pressure boilers, 233-235; in the early 1970s Portuguese barges were run by diesel engines started by blowtorches, 242

Racial Issues
Over the years, from World War II onward, the proportion of blacks increased in the crews of U.S.-flag merchant ships, 238; the National Maritime Union has been liberal in hiring minority personnel for ships' crews, 238-240

Radar
Was installed on board the German cruiser Admiral Graf Spee when the crew scuttled her in December 1939 at Montevideo, 47-48

Radio
Training for prospective radiomen in 1938 at the San Diego Naval Training Station, 13-15; operation of the radio shack in 1938-39 on board the battleship Colorado (BB-45), 19-21, 23; radio link between the ship and her SOC biplanes, 28-29; transmission of messages in 1940-41 by the Commander Battleships Atlantic Fleet flag allowance during Neutrality Patrol operations, 59-60, 65-66; in early 1941 Shellenbarger's personal radio was confiscated while he was on board the battleship Texas (BB-35), 63-64; communication in 1945 by the Liberty ship Reverdy Johnson, 122; ham radio operations in different periods, 207

Ranger, USS (CV-4)
In early 1945, while operating near San Francisco, took green water over the flight deck, 112-113

Recruit Training
Conducted in early 1938 at the Naval Training Station in Newport, Rhode Island, 9-13

Recruiting/Retention
In the spring of 1941 officers on the staff of Commander Battleships Atlantic Fleet tried hard to get Shellenbarger to reenlist, 61-62; in 1941 a Navy recruiter urged Shellenbarger to join the Maritime Service rather than returning to the Navy, 77

Red Cross, American
During World War II Shellenbarger developed a disdain for the organization because it did not give merchant mariners the benefits it provided to servicemen, 95, 97-98

Reuben James, USS (DD-245)
Veteran destroyer that was torpedoed and sunk in October 1941 while on convoy duty in the Atlantic, 41-42, 65-66

Rescue at Sea
　　In 1969 the cargo ship Export Ambassador rescued the crew of a Korean fishing boat, 229-232

Reverdy Johnson, SS
　　Liberty ship that was rigged for carrying troops in World War II, 119-121; voyages to Europe and back during the latter part of the war and shortly afterward, 122-129, 273-274

Royal Navy
　　Operations in 1939 in the Battle of the River Plate against the German cruiser Admiral Graf Spee, 49; in 1940-41 intercepted plain-language U.S. reports of German submarine positions in the Atlantic, 59-60, 65-66; visual communications with U.S. warships in on Neutrality Patrol in 1940-41, 65

Russia
　　In the mid-1960s the cargo ship Extavia delivered goods to Russian ports on the Black Sea, 188-191

SOC Seagull
　　Biplane operated in the late 1930s by the battleship Colorado (BB-45), 28-29

Saar, Elmar
　　Merchant marine officer whose ship was sunk in World War II, later became a ship master after his release, 142-143

Sacramento, USS (PG-19)
　　In 1939 this old gunboat returned to the United States from the Philippines and needed coal passers for her engineering plant, 42

St. Louis, USS (CL-49)
　　In 1939, when this cruiser was brand new, she ran speed trials in company with her sister ship, the Helena (CL-50), 45-47

Saipan, Mariana Islands
　　In late 1944 the Liberty ship John R. McQuigg stopped at Saipan, where Fleet Admiral Chester Nimitz visited, 107-109

San Diego Naval Training Station
　　In 1938 provided training to prospective radiomen, 13-14

Saudi Arabia
　　In the late 1970s the commercial ship Export Courier visited the port of Jidda to deliver cargo but had to wait to get clearance, 254-256, 258

Savannah, NS
Design of in the 1950s, 165, 171; launching in 1959 produced an unexpected sag that had to be fixed, 165-166; in 1963-64 was based in Galveston, Texas, which had a special pier for the ship, 164-169, 174-178, 185-186; nuclear reactor issues, 165-178, 181-183, 185, 187; trial runs in early 1964 in the Gulf of Mexico, 174-175, 178; handling characteristics, 178-179; operations in the 1960s, 175, 179, 184; in mothballs in James River, Virginia, after retirement, 170

Sawokla, SS
Merchant ship sunk in World War II by a German raider, 142

Seabees
In late 1944 the Liberty ship John R. McQuigg loaded heavy equipment at Davisville, Rhode Island, and delivered it to Seabees in the Pacific, 101-102, 106-107

Seattle, USS (CA-11)
Old cruiser that served in 1939 as a receiving ship in New York and housed the future crew members of the new light cruiser Helena (CL-50), 41-43

Shellenbarger, Captain Franklin F., USMS (Ret.)
Boyhood and youth in the 1920s and 1930s in Ohio, Pennsylvania, and New York, 1-9; parents of, 1-2, 9, 11; siblings, 1-2, 5, 7, 12, 136, 143-144; first wife Mona, 115, 117, 129, 145, 161-162, 247, 273; second wife Mary, 159, 161-165, 186, 199-200, 228; children of, 116-117, 145, 161, 163, 188, 257, 262; education of, 1-5; enlisted in the Navy at Buffalo, New York, in January 1938, 8-9; in early 1938 received recruit training at Newport, Rhode Island, 9-13; spent a month in the summer of 1938 assigned to the old sailing ship Constellation in Newport, 15-19; later in 1938 received radioman training at San Diego, 13-15; in 1938-39 was a radioman and signalman in the crew of the battleship Colorado (BB-45), 19-30; service in the summer of 1939 in the crew of the destroyer Herbert (DD-160), 22, 25, 30-41, 82; in 1939 was temporarily housed on board the receiving ship Seattle (CA-11), a former cruiser, 41-43; in 1939-40 served in the commissioning crew of the new light cruiser Helena (CL-50), 43-58, 205-206; in 1940-41 was attached to the flag allowance for Commander Battleships Atlantic Fleet, at various times on board the Texas (BB-35), New York (BB-34), and Arkansas (BB-33), 58-71; worked in 1941-42 for the Glenn L. Martin Company in Middle River, Maryland, 74-78, 81; in 1942-44 was first a student and then an instructor at the Maritime Officers Training School, Fort Trumbull, New London, Connecticut, 77, 83-88, 276-277; in 1944-45 was a mate on board the Liberty ship John R. McQuigg, 88, 90-117; for several months in 1945 was second mate of the Liberty ship Reverdy Johnson, 119-129, 273-274; in 1945-46 was chief mate in the Liberty ship Linn Boyd, 130-135; in 1946-48 served in a series of Victory ships: Coaldale Victory, Honduras Victory, Catawba Victory, and Drake Victory, 135-142; from 1948 to 1951 served on board the Exhibitor, 144-150, 157-158; in 1963-64 was chief mate, acting master, and ship superintendent of the nuclear-powered cargo ship Savannah, 164-187; in 1964-65 was master of the cargo

ship Extavia, 187-197, 199-201; in 1965 was master of the Flying Spray, 197-198; in 1967-68 was the last master of the Exiria, 217-220; in 1968 was master of the Export Champion, 224; in 1969 was master of the cargo ship Export Ambassador, 222-223, 228-232; in 1969 was master of the cargo ships Container Forwarder and Container Dispatcher, 233-236; in 1969-1970 was master of the cargo ship Flying Fish, 153, 201-205, 214-216, 220, 236-237; in the early 1970s was master of the cargo ship Export Agent, 241-243, 256-258; during much of the 1970s was master of the cargo ship Export Courier, 179-180, 184, 238-240, 254-256, 258; after he stopped going to sea, Shellenbarger testified as an expert witness in legal cases, 248-249; role in the 1990s as president of the Marine Society of New York, 264-272

Sherman, Lieutenant Commander Earl V., USN (USNA, 1922)
In the summer of 1939 commanded the destroyer Herbert (DD-160) while she was training midshipmen, 33-34, 36-37, 41; later commanded the destroyer Reuben James (DD-245), 41-42

Ship Handling
Of the single-screw cargo ship Extavia in the mid-1960s, 187

South America
In December 1939 the crew of the German cruiser Admiral Graf Spee scuttled the ship at Montevideo, where the hulk was later visited by crewmen from the U.S. light cruiser Helena (CL-50), 47-48, 51-55; the crews of the two ships later met up in Buenos Aires, Argentina, 48-49; liberty for the crew of the Helena in various South American ports, 48-50

States Marine Company
In the early 1960s operated the nuclear-powered cargo ship Savannah, 166-167, 169

Stone, Lieutenant Martin R., USN (USNA, 1927)
When he was executive officer of the destroyer Herbert (DD-160) in 1939, there was a gulf between him and the enlisted crew, 33, 35, 41

Suez Canal
When merchant ships passed through the canal, bribes were useful to get priority, 160-161; in the late 1960s the merchant ship Flying Fish made a canal transit, 202; was closed in the wake of the 1967 Middle East War, 236; in the 1970s ships going from the canal to Saudi Arabia had to have logbooks checked to make sure they hadn't been to Israel, 255-256

Sylvester, Lieutenant Commander Malcolm D., USN (USNA, 1925)
In 1940-41 served on the staff of Commander Battleships Atlantic Fleet during Neutrality Patrol operations, 59, 61-62

Taiwan
Ship repair facilities in the 1960s, 221; shipment of goods to the United States in 1969, 222-223

Taylor, Lieutenant Ennis W., USN (USNA, 1932)
 In 1940-41 served on the staff of Commander Battleships Atlantic Fleet during Neutrality Patrol operations, 59, 61-63; in 1941 confiscated Shellenbarger's personal radio, 63

Texas, USS (BB-35)
 Operations of the ship in late 1940 while serving as flagship for Commander Battleships Atlantic Fleet, 58-59; powered by triple-expansion reciprocating engines, 61, 70-71; in early 1941 was inspected by Admiral Ernest J. King, Commander in Chief Atlantic Fleet, 66-70; accommodations for the admiral's staff and flag allowance personnel, 69

Tinian, Mariana Islands
 In late 1944 the Liberty ship John R. McQuigg delivered cargo to Tinian, 106-107

Training
 Boot camp in early 1938 at the Naval Training Station in Newport, Rhode Island, 9-13; training for prospective radiomen in 1938 at the San Diego Naval Training Station, 13-15; in the summer of 1939, the veteran destroyer Herbert (DD-160) provided underway training for midshipmen and crewmen such as Shellenbarger, 31-37; during World War II crews were trained on light antiaircraft guns by means of simulators, 128

Trumbull, Fort
 See: Maritime Officers Training School, Fort Trumbull, New London, Connecticut

Tunisia
 A crew member of one of Shellenbarger's ships died in Tunis and was buried in a cemetery for American veterans, 209-210

Turkey
 In the mid-1960s the cargo ship Extavia carried various items to Turkey and Black Sea ports, 158-159, 188-191

Uniforms—Naval
 In early 1939 Shellenbarger had to replace one of his uniforms because it was ruined by the blast of gunfire on board the battleship Colorado (BB-45), 24-25; as Commander in Chief Atlantic Fleet in early 1941, Admiral Ernest King prescribed some unusual uniforms for those on board his flagship, the battleship Texas (BB-35), 66-68

Uruguay
 In December 1939 the crew of the German cruiser Admiral Graf Spee scuttled her at Montevideo, where the hulk was later visited by crewmen from the U.S. light cruiser Helena (CL-50), 47-48, 51-55

Venereal Disease
    In 1939, when crew members from the battleship Colorado (BB-45) were on liberty in Gonaives, Haiti, tents were sent up for prevention of venereal disease, 31

Vietnam War
    In the 1960s the U.S. Government chartered Victory-type ships to deliver cargo to Vietnam, 216

Visual Signaling
    Use of flag hoists and flashing light in 1939 by signalmen on board the battleship Colorado (BB-45), 26-27; signaling in 1940 when a boat crew from the light cruiser Helena (CL-50) visited the scuttled German cruiser Admiral Graf Spee, 51-52; in 1940-41 by the flag allowance of Commander Battleships Atlantic Fleet during Neutrality Patrol operations, 59-60, 65; when he served in merchant ship crews after World War II, Shellenbarger liked to add Navy-style yardarms for signaling, 140-142

War Shipping Administration, U.S.
    In World War II operated the Maritime Officers Training School at New London, Connecticut, 77, 81-85; during the war, operated hiring offices to provide ships' crews, 114, 117-118, 128, 273

Weather
    In September 1944 the Liberty ship John R. McQuigg suffered hurricane damage, 90, 95-96; in early 1945 the same ship faced heavy seas en route the United States, 112-113; the cargo ship Flying Enterprise was lost in early 1952 after receiving storm damage, 207-208; in 1963 Galveston, Texas, was hit by a hurricane, 185-186; in the late 1960s the passenger/cargo ship Flying Fish ran into a typhoon in the Pacific, 204; in 1969 the cargo ship Export Ambassador rescued the crew of a Korean fishing boat that got into distress in heavy seas, 229-232; in 1970s the Export Courier ran into trouble in high seas, 248; in the 1980s Shellenbarger testified in a legal case concerning a Greek ship that was abandoned during stormy weather, 248-250

Wilkins, Lane
    Merchant marine officer who died of a heart attack in the mid-1960s while serving as chief mate of the cargo ship Extavia, 194-196, 199-201

www.ingramcontent.com/pod-product-compliance
Lightning Source LLC
Chambersburg PA
CBHW082200070526
44585CB00020B/2209